ties that bind

ties that bind

Economic and Political Dilemmas
of Urban Utility Networks, 1800–1990

Charles David Jacobson

University of Pittsburgh Press

Published by the University of Pittsburgh Press, Pittsburgh, Pa. 15261

Copyright © 2000, University of Pittsburgh Press

Manufactured in the United States of America

Printed on acid-free paper

10 9 8 7 6 5 4 3 2 1

Library of Congress Cataloging-in-Publication Data
Jacobson, Charles David.
   Ties that bind : economic and political dilemmas of urban utility
networks, 1800–1990 / Charles David Jacobson.
     p. cm.
Includes bibliographical references and index.
   ISBN 0-8229-4133-3 (alk. paper)
   1. Public utilities—United States—Case studies. 2. Public
utilities—deregulation—United States—Case studies. 3. Water
utilities—United States—Case studies. 4. Electric utilities—United
States—Case studies. 5. Telecommunication policy—United States—Case
studies. 6. Cable television—Government policy—United States—Case
studies. I. Title.
   HD2766 .J33 2000
   363.6'0973—dc21

                                          00-010610

To Tanjam

Contents

Preface

This book began life some years ago as a dissertation in the Applied History and Social Sciences program at Carnegie Mellon University. My interests in history, technology, and the environment, however, are of much longer standing. I still remember my fascination as a child with roads and bridges and the magic of maps. I also remember from that time a vividly held sense of technology's destructive and apocalyptic potentials. In my mind, I can still hear the sounds of dynamite in the night as engineers blasted Interstate 89 through the hills of New Hampshire. I can still see in my mind's eye the big machines building the Long Island Expressway and remember the sadness I felt watching suburban sprawl chewing up the landscape. As a child of the sixties I also remember duck-and-cover drills and wondering if I would one day see a mushroom cloud rising over New York City.

In the interim between college and graduate school, I came to the realization that my temperament inclined me more in the direction of scholarship than of activism. I continued to hope, however, that I could develop skills and knowledge that could help in engaging contemporary concerns and problems. Serving as a research assistant under economic historians Gerald Friedman and Robert Fogel at Harvard University also proved formative. I came away from this experience with a feel for the grunt work needed for original research, an admiring yet critical attitude toward the simplicity and rigor characteristic of economic modes of reasoning, and a belief in the value of explicit hypothesis testing in doing history. During my years as a graduate student at Carnegie Mellon and in my varied work as a professional historian since that time, I have continued to think about how one can do research and analysis that deepen our understanding of past events while serving as a source of insight for acting in the present.

I remain convinced that knowledge of what occurred in the past and a feel for processes of historical change and continuity can be of great value to those seeking to make good public policy in the present. Paying attention to contemporary public policy concerns without degenerating into presentism or into the propounding of sterile and one-dimensional "lessons of the past" can also inspire the writing of better history. In particular, attention to questions of what can be learned from historical experiences can prompt the historian to think more deeply and systematically about factors at work in shaping past conditions. In this study, I bring together insights from the history of technology, comparative case-study analysis, and economics to gain greater understanding of public policy issues associated with different kinds of fixed networks and of the factors that have consistently shaped outcomes. Along with whatever particular insights can be gleaned from what is presented here, I also hope that the study will inspire other historians to take up the challenges of comparative and interdisciplinary inquiry and to think explicitly about the policy implications of their work.

I have undertaken much of the work on this book away from a university environment. Perhaps paradoxically, this has heightened my awareness of the importance of the scholarly community and of the manifold ways in which one's own scholarly work builds upon and responds to that of others. I am grateful to more people than can possibly be mentioned here in this regard. When I came to Carnegie Mellon University in 1982, I found a fruitful environment for interdisciplinary and unpretentiously practical scholarship. From the time I arrived to the present day, Joel Tarr has been a generous and insightful mentor, collaborator, and friend. I have always known to give great weight to his judgment. For the original idea of comparing government involvement in different utility industries, I am indebted to economist Steven Klepper. When he made this suggestion, I remember scoffing inwardly at his comment that study of this area might become a major focus of my scholarship for years after completion of my dissertation. I was wrong.

For comments and advice along the way, I am indebted to numerous other scholars. These include John Modell, Harold Platt, Mark Rose, Edward Woodhouse, and an anonymous reader at the University of Pittsburgh Press. In undertaking research, I received assistance from many librarians and archivists in Boston, Pittsburgh, Seattle, and San Francisco. The courtesy and help I received from the Massachusetts Historical Society, the Pacific Northwest and Manuscript sections of the Suzillo Library at the University of Washington, the Seattle City Clerk's Office, the Pennsylvania Room at the Carnegie Institute in Pittsburgh, the Bancroft Library, and the San Francisco History and Archives section of the San Francisco Public Library were all outstanding.

Additional acknowledgments are due to David Sicilia, who shared with me insights and research materials compiled in pursuing his own research on the history of the Boston Edison Company, and to Peter Epstein and Thomas Cohan of the Boston Office of Cable Communication and Debra Lewis of the Seattle Office of Cable Communication for generously sharing with me their knowledge and perspectives on cable television franchising issues in their respective cities during the mid-1980s.

And finally, there are my families—the family into which I was born and the family I have helped to make along the way. To my parents I am indebted for learning what it means to be thoughtful, decent, and quietly confident; for conveying to me the courage to pursue my own paths; and for supporting me unstintingly (if occasionally bemusedly) as I have done so. At the other end of the generational continuum, my son Adam has been no help at all on this project, and for that he has my gratitude. Tanjam has lived with this book, and with me, for more than a decade. I have leaned on her far more than she knows. My gratitude is inestimable.

ties that bind

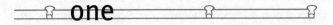

one

Introduction

FLICK A SWITCH, THE LIGHT COMES ON; TURN A FAUCET, water flows; touch a remote, a cable television program appears. These are mundane acts. Yet the construction and the elaboration of the fixed networks over which these kinds of services are delivered have been among the greatest—and one of the most problematical—human endeavors of the last 150 years. In ubiquitous ways easily taken for granted, networked systems of electric power and lighting, piped-in water, telecommunications, and media delivery are now woven into the very fabric of our day-to-day lives. Our growing use of these systems to carry out even the most intimate functions of our lives—to communicate and cooperate with one another, to exercise authority over one another, to produce and distribute a wide range of goods and services—constitutes one of the major ways in which our lives differ from those of our ancestors.

This book is about some of the political and regulatory tensions and dilemmas that have arisen from our growing reliance upon fixed networks for the provision of different goods and services. As shall be seen, there is a stubbornly protean quality about the issues. Resolve the tensions in one guise, they promptly appear in another—tied at the hip, most likely, to whatever solution has been chosen and leering gleefully. This is not, however, a counsel of despair. Conscious human choice and hard-fought human struggles have mattered in the past and continue to do so. Decisions about ownership and regulatory arrangements and choices

I

about the shapes of technologies themselves can and do affect outcomes.

I explore the issues as they have played out over time in three different networked systems in the United States—waterworks, electric utilities, and cable television. I selected these three for investigation not just because of their significance in and of themselves but also because of possibilities for fruitful comparison. The aim is to leave the reader with a richer understanding both of the character of the political and regulatory puzzles presented by these kinds of systems and of the strengths and weaknesses of different approaches to addressing the problems.

Patterns of similarity and variation are of central concern. Although waterworks, electric utility, and cable television systems are obviously far from identical with one another, they do have major characteristics in common. The three are akin in that they all consist, at least in part, of fixed networks of pipes or wires to which consumers are physically linked. Ways in which the three have historically been employed also bear something of a family resemblance to one another. As distinguished from telephone and computer networks designed to facilitate contact between users, they have thus far been developed primarily as instruments for the one-way delivery of services. That is, products such as water, electricity, or television programs flow one way through the networks from a relatively small number of producers to a relatively large number of consumers. Furthermore, waterworks, electric utilities, and cable television systems alike have all been viewed at times as playing important public roles in society.

Amid these and other commonalties, however, much variation can also be discerned. Technologically, for example, the pipes, pumps, and reservoirs that make up a municipal waterworks differ in obvious ways from the satellite down links, coaxial cable, and other electronic components that make up a modern urban cable television system. Products and services furnished over the networks have also varied. Specific public services demanded, for example, have ranged from fire protection and public health in the case of waterworks, to street lighting and cheap power for economic development in the case of electric utilities, to public access channels and diverse noncommercial programming in the case of cable television.

Patterns of system development, ownership, and regulation over time have also been characterized by variation amid common themes.

Early construction and elaboration of waterworks, electric utility, and cable television systems took place in very different historical settings. In the case of waterworks, private firms and municipal governments built systems throughout the nineteenth century as cities developed and grew in size. During this period, waterworks represented a critical element in a distinctively growth-oriented American style of city-building, elements of which have survived to the present day. The first small electric lighting systems, by contrast, began to be put in place in American cities only during the 1880s. The blossoming of such systems into full-fledged multipurpose urban and regional electric utility networks is really a phenomenon of the first decades of the twentieth century.

The historical setting for cable television is different yet again. Development of cable television in the United States began during the years following World War II, with construction of systems in major cities taking place largely during the 1970s and 1980s. Viewed broadly, however, cable television systems represent but one relatively new element in a fluid and shifting ensemble of over-the-air as well as wired technologies that have been used for delivery of media "products" over the past one hundred years. Hence the history of cable television can be properly understood only in the context of its closely related over-the-air counterpart and of broader trends in media and mass communications.

Although early waterworks, electric utility, and cable television development took place in very different historical settings, the initial forms of ownership and regulation bore remarkable resemblance to one another. At the outset, nongovernmental ownership predominated in all three industries. As of 1800, private firms owned fifteen of the sixteen waterworks then operating in the United States. Likewise, during the 1880s and 1890s, private firms also built and operated the vast majority of pioneering electric lighting systems in American cities under the terms of municipal franchising arrangements and street lighting contracts. In cable television during the 1950s and 1960s, the pattern was similar. Private firms developed the first systems under franchise arrangements eerily akin to those employed in both waterworks and electric utilities decades before.

As each industry developed, however, patterns of ownership and regulation increasingly diverged. In the case of waterworks, municipal governments in the largest and most rapidly growing of American cities consistently made the decision to invest the large sums of money needed to purchase and/or construct their own waterworks. By 1897, as a consequence, municipally owned waterworks served all but nine of the fifty largest cities in the United States. In electric utilities, too, municipalities or other governmental entities sometimes built or acquired their own systems. With important exceptions, however, government ownership campaigns went down to defeat in most major cities and private ownership has continued to predominate. In cable television, government ownership initiatives made even less headway. As a consequence, almost all cable television systems in the United States remain under private ownership.

If waterworks, electric utility, and cable television systems were either totally identical with one another or completely different, little would be gained by comparing them. Rather, it is the combination of both similarities and differences in technology, patterns of industry development, historical contexts, and public policy that affords analytical leverage otherwise unattainable. To further aid in understanding public policy issues presented by networked systems, I draw inspiration from a diverse array of scholarly traditions. The history of technology and related areas of urban history are of particular importance. Much recent scholarship in these domains is concerned with the roles played by ideas and ideology, social groupings, power relationships, and political and institutional arrangements in shaping or constructing different kinds of technological artifacts and in determining how they are employed in different social contexts. The emphasis is on technology as a cultural, social, or political product rather than its effects on society.

Historian Mark Rose, for example, identifies a number of contexts that shaped the development of gas and electric utility systems in American cities and that played roles in inspiring increased demands for service. Important contexts identified by Rose include municipal politics, urban and suburban growth, and the activities of a range of actors, including "educators, home builders, architects, and the executives and salespersons who worked for the great gas and electric corporations." Such "agents of technological diffusion," according to Rose, "defined gas and electricity as part of the effort of Americans to enhance comfort and convenience; and nearly as often, agents of technological diffusion defined appliances as appropriate for men or women, but never for both."[1]

Rose asserts, as do other historians including Thomas P. Hughes and David Nye, that the basis for subsequent patterns of electric utility development had been set by the end of the 1920s. By contrast, Ronald Tobey highlights the importance of political changes during the 1930s in determining roles played by electrical appliances in day-to-day life. He argues convincingly that New Deal initiatives in housing finance and in electric utility ownership and regulation played key roles in laying the groundwork for mass home electrification and modernization during the decades that followed. For all but the most affluent, Tobey declares, "electrical modernization resulted directly from the New Deal's transformation of the nation's homes."[2]

Such quarrels notwithstanding, historians of technology and urban historians generally agree that the shaping of any technological system cannot be understood without reference to a multitude of ideological, social, and political factors and contexts. Many scholars today also share a primary concern with the shaping of different technologies—and an implicit belief in the malleability of technological artifacts themselves. This emphasis has greatly enriched our understanding of why things (quite literally) are the way they are. It has also been a useful corrective to older and more deterministic views of technological change as a kind of inexorable force to which institutions and societies must and should somehow adapt themselves, or fall by the wayside.[3]

At the same time, focusing solely on the social and political construction of different technologies may leave important questions unanswered, even unasked. As philosopher of technology Langdon Winner has pointed out, technological artifacts may sometimes have political and institutional effects *irrespective* of the intentions of the actors involved. There may be ways "in which the intractable properties of certain kinds of technology are strongly, perhaps unavoidably, linked to particular institutionalized patterns of power and authority. Here the initial choice about whether or not to adopt something is decisive in regard to its consequences."[4]

Fortunately, some historians of technology and urban historians have remained committed to teasing out political and institutional consequences of particular technological choices. In the case of networks in particular, a number of historians have observed relationships between development of systems and dominance by centrally controlled and hierarchically structured organizations. Functional requirements of the technologies themselves are commonly cited as a cause.

In the case of New York City's Croton Aqueduct and Waterworks, for example, historian Joanne Abel Goldman states that "construction of the aqueduct itself mandated the creation of a centralized mechanism for its management, the Water Commission, which evolved as a well-defined managerial infrastructure with 'technical experts' in key decision-making positions."[5] Similarly, according to business historian Alfred Dupont Chandler, demands for coordination over broad geographic areas and "the requirements of high-volume, high-speed operations" resulted in a few large firms gaining control over nineteenth-century telegraph and telephone networks.[6]

Relatedly, the sheer physical durability of the artifacts that make up networks can have institutional and organizational consequences. Historian Thomas P. Hughes, for example, notes that large-scale technological systems such as electric utility networks are human creations, shaped by individual inventiveness and a wide range of political, social, economic, and geographical factors. Once such a system is in place, however, "durable physical artifacts project into the future the socially constructed characteristics acquired in the past when they were designed."[7] Over time, such momentum is likely to be reinforced by the interests and mind-sets of the increasingly large number of people and organizations committed to system development. Thus, "manufacturing corporations, public and private utilities, industrial and government research laboratories, investment and banking houses, sections of technical and scientific societies, departments in educational institutions, and regulatory bodies," according to Hughes, all "add greatly to the momentum of modern electric light and power systems."[8]

Values and mind-sets engendered through involvement in the development of such systems may even take on something of a life of their own. Reasoning along these lines, historian Joel Tarr has postulated that the developing technology of large-scale, capital-intensive sewerage systems in American cities "itself shaped and reinforced other values." According to Tarr, "a belief in the need for planning expertise, bureaucracy, and centralization in government, as well as for an expanded state regulatory role, were all supported by the technology."[9]

To summarize, the history of technology teaches us that forms taken by networked systems or other technological artifacts cannot be understood without reference to the societies in which they are embedded. And that technology does not predetermine many aspects of how such systems have been developed. It is people who make choices and struggle with one another over how systems are to be designed, built, and used. Yet these choices and struggles over technology matter in part because attributes of systems do have political and institutional consequences. For networks to function properly or even to be built at all, large-scale and centralized financing, management, and control may be required. Because of the physical durability of components themselves and aggregations of interests invested in system development, choices made at one moment in time concerning a given technology may powerfully constrain future options.

Additional insights into political and regulatory issues presented by networked systems can be gleaned from a discipline quite different from that of history—economics. Simple concepts derived from economic theory are used here to help in understanding such questions as: What is it that is so specifically "public" about some of the goods and services that are furnished over waterworks, electric utilities, and cable television systems alike? And why is it that issues of monopolistic and centralized economic and political power have arisen so stubbornly and consistently in association with the development of these systems? Economics also helps in understanding the workings of various public policies devised to address these issues in different historical settings.

Historians are often inclined to be wary of relying on the sort of reasoning from assumptions that is characteristic of much economic analysis.[10] History, after all, is primarily concerned with questions of "what actually happened" at different times and places in the past. Carefully and sensitively deployed, however, theoretical insights developed by economists and other social scientists can be used to increase our understanding of situations and problems faced by people in the past. Furthermore, the benefits of bringing the disciplines together are mutual. The very attributes of historical inquiry that distinguish it from economic theory making—its close attention to specific and contingent realities of local circumstance, human motivation, and processes of change over time—can aid the economist in developing, refining, and testing more general hypotheses.

From an economic perspective, public policy issues presented by networked systems can be viewed as problems of incentives gone awry and market failure. In the ideal world of freely and perfectly competitive markets posited by neoclassical economists, the pursuit of self-interest has benign consequences. Exchanges among numerous buyers and sellers set price and output levels and the "invisible hand" of the market suffices to ensure that the good of all is served. Neither altruism on the part of participants nor regulation from outside is needed. With networked systems that provide diffuse public benefits or raise property values over broad areas, by contrast, matters may be different. In this kind of situation, economic theory suggests, market forces may not suffice to ensure optimal levels of provision and some form of governmental intervention may be needed. A waterworks, for example, may afford a residence or business great benefits and higher property values in ways virtually unrelated to the actual quantity of water consumed. If dependent on user fees alone, a private firm may have little incentive to make the investments required to furnish proper provision even if the benefits to society as a whole far exceed the costs. With respect to public goods of this kind, even many of those who celebrate the wonders of a market economy acknowledge that some form of governmental subsidy or public provision may be justified.[11]

Furthermore, the ability of competition to protect consumers against inefficient limitations on output and high prices set by the owners of networked systems may also be restricted. In the language of economics, fixed and specialized networks of pipes and wires manifest "natural monopoly" attributes.[12] Constructing and operating a water main, electrical distribution line, or cable television feed that serves every house on a block is little (if at all) more expensive than building a facility that serves every other house. The result is a dilemma. Competing systems in a given area represent a wasteful duplication of expensive capital facilities that is unlikely to be sustained by profit-seeking enterprises for any length of time.[13] In the absence of competition or some form of regulation, however, the profit motive can be a powerful incentive for exploitation as well as for efficiency.

The technological attributes of networked systems also have consequences for ownership and regulatory approaches designed to provide for public goods and to protect against monopoly exploitation. I derive insights into the character of these relationships from a form of economic theory known as transaction cost analysis. Analysis of transaction costs suggests that shared characteristics of waterworks, electric utility, and cable television systems might be expected to affect the functioning of ownership and regulatory arrangements in consistent ways. Transaction cost analysis also can be used to help in understanding why it has been far more difficult for conflict between private firms and government regulators to be avoided in some situations than in others.

Economist R. H. Coase set forth the fundamental premises of transaction cost analysis in a well-known 1937 paper.[14] Coase asserted that there would be no efficiency justification for the existence of private firms in a market economy if the very act of buying and selling goods did not carry with it difficulties and costs—transaction costs. Types of transaction costs cited by Coase included the costs of determining relevant prices for a particular good or service and the costs of negotiating and concluding separate contracts for each exchange transaction. To render this more concrete if less precise, think about the difference in time and effort required to buy breakfast cereal at the supermarket versus that required to sell or buy a house. In the first case, transaction costs are relatively low—in the second, relatively high.

For business firms, transaction costs issues typically arise in the context of deciding whether it makes more sense to produce a good or service inside an organization or to purchase it from an outside supplier. By producing in-house, a firm may be able to economize on transaction costs. But there may be trade-offs. As anyone who has worked for a large corporation (or read the comic strip "Dilbert") is aware, costs and inefficiencies can also arise when goods and services are produced and exchanged within organizations. Coase hypothesized that the actual size of private firms in a market economy is determined by relationships between the transaction costs of using the price mechanism in different situations and the marginal costs of internal organization, such as coordination difficulties and poor management.

Subsequent inquiry by economists has focused on gaining a more refined understanding of transaction costs, particularly the relative merits of engaging in transactions in the market, within organizations, or through forms of complex contracting. Much of this inquiry has focused on questions of industrial organization in the private sector, but some of the insights are highly relevant to issues that arise in providing public goods and can help to address natural monopoly dilemmas presented by networked systems. Oliver Williamson's recent elaboration of a transaction cost approach is particularly useful. Williamson stresses the roles played by "transaction-specific assets" in rendering simple forms of market organization ineffective and increasing the relative advantages of complex contracting or vertical integration. Asset specificity can arise in a variety of ways. Transaction-specific assets can take the form of fixed physical facilities tailored to the specific needs of a single buyer by a single seller. More subtly, advantages gained through "learning by doing" and through the development of personal relationships between buyers and sellers also constitute forms of asset specificity.[15]

The networks of pipes and wires that make up waterworks, electric utility, and cable television systems represent archetypal examples of what Williamson means by a transaction-specific asset. The facilities are fixed, long-lived, and location-specific. Once put in place, it is generally not feasible at reasonable cost to move such assets as buried water mains or an electricity distribution system for use elsewhere. The result is to limit the effectiveness of contracting and franchising approaches, which are otherwise promising, in that they offer the advantages of competition without the costs and inefficiencies of duplicating physical networks of pipes and wires on the ground. The basic principle involved is simple and rather elegant. In its ideal form, contracting or franchising involves private firms bidding for the right to be the monopoly supplier of a good. The firm that offers the best price and service terms wins the bidding competition. By competing for the contract or franchise to supply the good rather than competing directly in the good's production, market discipline would seem to be preserved without wasteful and unsustainable duplication of capital investment.[16]

Williamson allows that such competition may be viable at the outset under some conditions. Once networks of pipes and wires or other transaction-specific assets are put in place, however, a "fundamental transformation" occurs and rival firms can no longer vie for contracts or franchises on an equal basis. Instead, winners of initial bidding contests enjoy advantages over nonwinners and "what was a large numbers bidding condition at the outset is effectively transformed into [a relationship] of bilateral supply thereafter."[17] To the extent that such a fundamental transformation takes place, government agencies can not rely upon new bidding contests to ensure that contractors and franchisees fulfill commitments made at the outset. Nor can market forces be easily brought to bear if initially agreed-upon arrangements need to be modified to accommodate changing conditions.

In addition, private firms and government agencies each may have points of vulnerability that can be exploited by the other for bargaining leverage. Private firms may face risks of exploitation and even outright expropriation once large investments are tied up in fixed facilities. Unlike the owner of a fleet of garbage trucks, for example, a private waterworks, electric utility, or cable television firm cannot easily "pick up" its network and install it elsewhere. Therefore, even if an oversight agency sets a price at a level less than that needed to cover both fixed and variable costs, a private firm may find that it has little alternative but to continue to provide service if it is to receive any revenues at all. Government agencies, for their part, face risks because private firms control network operations and future investment. A waterworks firm, for example, might refuse to extend service to a growing area of a city unless it receives a higher price for its product or franchise or contract concessions. Moreover, these areas of vulnerability and bargaining power do not necessarily balance one another in a stable or equitable fashion. Instead, efforts by one or both sides to defend against perceived opportunistic behavior on the part of the other may result in a stalemate that serves the interests of neither and prevents any needed investment. A private firm, for example, might refuse to invest in new facilities because it fears that government regulators may provide inadequate compensation in the future. At the same time, government regulators may be reluctant to make such guarantees because of fears that a private firm will reap monopoly profits.[18]

The picture, however, is not entirely grim. Concepts derived from economic theory and transaction cost approaches also suggest factors that can affect outcomes and ways in which public policy choices can make a difference. In this regard, the concept of natural monopoly needs to be used with care. Forms of market discipline may be present even in situations in which there is natural monopoly. Under some conditions, inter-product competition can serve as a check on the ability of network owners to exploit their position as sole service provider. In many of the markets served by electric utility firms, for example, manufactured and natural gas has repeatedly waxed and waned as a competitive factor over the years. Similarly, cable television systems today face direct competition from direct broadcast satellite systems of a kind not present twenty years ago.

The willingness of consumers to simply forego purchase of a good or service if prices are raised too high can also serve as a check on monopolistic exploitation by network owners. Should competition from satellites disappear, for example, a cable television system might find it profitable to raise prices of premium channels such as HBO from ten dollars per month to twenty-five dollars. Few consumers, however, would be willing to pay a thousand dollars per day for such a channel and a price increase of this magnitude would almost certainly not prove profitable no matter how secure the cable system's monopoly.

Transaction cost analysis suggests additional factors that can shape the efficacy of forms of government involvement irrespective of roles played by market discipline. Such analysis suggests that the quality of information available to decision makers can play a major role in determining how challenging it is to structure working relationships between government agencies and private network owners.[19] In regard to costs, expenses, and profits, private firms are likely to enjoy an informational advantage. Private network owners, unlike government regulators, can easily draw on knowledge of costs and expenses gained in the course of simply managing the business. Even if a government agency has the legal authority to audit claims made by a private firm, difficulties in gaining access to information and analyzing costs and profits may still arise because of perfunctory cooperation or outright obfuscation by the firm and because of the complexity of the accounting questions themselves.

However, the extent of the informational advantages enjoyed by private firms will vary in different situations, as will the knowledge and capabilities of government regulators. Indeed, a sophisticated regulatory agency may enjoy greater knowledge of costs and pricing than a relatively small or inexperienced firm. Ease in measuring outputs and monitoring quality is also crucial. Disputes over costs and price can still arise even if quantities of goods produced can be specified in simple terms and their quality unambiguously monitored. But problems in devising and enforcing workable contractual and regulatory arrangements are likely to be far easier to solve under these conditions than under circumstances in which it is difficult to specify how much of a product is really being furnished and there is room for disagreement as to quality.

Close attention is also needed to the extent to which conditions change over time and unexpected contingencies arise. Even in a static world, bargaining difficulties may arise as one or both parties seek to wriggle out from burdensome commitments. But there is less occasion for bargaining difficulties in a world in which conditions remain the same than in a more dynamic setting. A private firm, for example, will not be able to use control over new investment as a means of extracting concessions from government regulators if demand is steady and expanded facilities are not needed. Under conditions in which demand is rising and expanded facilities are desperately needed, by contrast, a private firm's control over investment may be a powerful source of bargaining leverage.

Relatedly, the degree to which change occurs also has implications for the viability of long-term contracting and franchising arrangements. Under static conditions, it is at least theoretically possible to devise equitable long-term arrangements under which firms enjoy protection for their investments in fixed facilities and agree to provide service at a given price. Indeed, assuming that no enforcement problems arise, a single episode of contract or franchise competition could arguably suffice to protect public and consumer interests forever. In a world that is not static, however, both the enforceability and the relevance of original contract or franchise terms may become increasingly problematical as time passes and conditions change. If contract terms need to be repeatedly renegotiated to cope with change, chances for the sorts of bargaining difficulties described above to arise are also greatly multiplied.

To recapitulate, economic theory suggests many similarities in the public policy challenges presented by the development of waterworks, electric utility, and cable television. The concept of public goods suggests that market forces cannot be relied upon to ensure that private waterworks, electric utility, and cable television firms furnish services over networks that may be valuable to society as a whole but that are not immediately profitable. Even for goods and services that are profitable, the concept of natural monopoly indicates that simply permitting private firms to build rival waterworks, electric utility, or cable television networks will not suffice to ensure either that real competition will occur or that such competition as does arise will efficiently and sustainably protect consumer interests. Transaction cost analysis tightens the screws further, suggesting that competition for contracts or franchises to furnish public or private consumer goods over waterworks, electric utility, and cable television networks will afford only a temporary respite from the dilemmas of natural monopoly. Regardless of the details of contracting or franchising arrangements, government agencies and private firms are likely to find themselves enmeshed in long-term relationships, in which private firms are likely to enjoy informational advantages but both parties may find themselves at risk of opportunistic behavior.

Economic theory and transaction cost analysis also point to factors that can affect the severity of these challenges and make for varied outcomes. Important variables include the extent to which network owners face inter-product competition or other forms of market discipline, the character and the perceived importance of the public goods furnished, and the ease or difficulty of measuring quantities and monitoring the quality of both public and private consumer goods. It is also worth paying close attention, transaction cost analysis suggests, to how different ownership and regulatory arrangements fare in the face of change and unexpected contingencies.

The limits as well as the strengths of these analytical tools also need to be appreciated. The history of public policy toward waterworks, electric utilities, and cable television cannot be entirely explained in terms of economics and transaction costs. A broader perspective is needed. Analysis of transaction costs, for example, can help us understand why government officials and managers of networks have often found themselves enmeshed in two-party bargaining relationships. In and of itself, however, such analysis cannot tell us why people chose to pursue a particular bargaining strategy in a particular case. Furthermore, as critics of economically derived forms of "public choice" analysis point out, people quite often do not see fit to pursue individual interests in the public realm as they would when buying and selling on the market.[20] It is not at all inconsistent, for example, for the same person both to bargain vigorously for the best possible price on a new car and to vote to raise taxes for the good of the country.

As shall be seen in the chapters that follow, people in American cities have at times sought to realize extremely ambitious social and political goals through development of different networked systems. With large-scale waterworks in place, for example, some nineteenth-century reformers believed that cities could be transformed from filthy to clean, unhealthy to healthy, and fire-prone to safe. At its most utopian, the vision encompassed not only gleaming cities but a society of temperate and morally as well as physically clean individuals. By the beginning of the twentieth century, electrification too, had become "inextricably bound up," according to historian David Nye, "with ideas of social progress and the transformation of human nature."[21] Electricity's very mystery, its ability to be somehow conveyed over thin strands of wire, its flexibility and ability to be drawn upon for heat, light, and power for a myriad of labor-saving, useful, and amusing devices all inspired visions of a better world amid the smoke, grit, and congestion of real life in late-nineteenth-century and early-twentieth-century American cities.[22] In the case of communications systems, utopian hopes have been if anything even more extravagant. Among the new forms of electronic communication excitedly hailed by enthusiasts as instruments of human amity and harbingers of world peace, for example, was the telegraph during the 1840s and 1850s, broadcast radio during the 1920s, and broadcast television during the 1950s. More modestly, cable enthusiasts during the late 1960s and early 1970s viewed development of advanced systems as a means of enriching culture and enhancing democratic decision making while at the same time breaking "the hold on the nation's television fare now exercised by a small commercial oligarchy."[23]

Although such hopes and aspirations have obviously not been completely realized, their historical significance should not be underestimated. As noted previously, ideological, social, and political contexts all play important roles in shaping technological systems. Only by reference to such contexts can many aspects of how waterworks, electric utilities, and cable television systems have come to be developed in the United States be understood. Municipal governments in nineteenth-century American cities, for example, typically built water supply and distribution systems on a far grander scale than did their European counterparts. Explaining this pattern requires examining both ideas concerning public health and morality and aspects of legal and institutional history. Similarly, many features of how cable television systems have come to be developed in the United States cannot be understood without reference to ideas concerning the role of the media in a democratic society and to features of communication law and regulation.

Moreover, the sort of monopoly associated with networked systems has a political as well as an economic dimension. A monopoly presents issues of power and accountability as well as pricing and market failure. Indeed, the very idea of leaving it to the discretion of a single entity to control availability of service in different locales as well as price and quality can be viewed as problematical in political as well as economic terms. Left unaccountable or in the wrong hands, such sole discretion can present risks to society arising not only from the unchecked pursuit of profit on the part of a rational monopolist but of a whole range of costs or harms arising from incompetent, arbitrary, or even capricious decision making. Allegations that overly concentrated power in the hands of those who control networked systems has resulted in the corruption or vitiation of democratic accountability have been common criticisms of many different ownership and regulatory arrangements in waterworks, electric utilities, and cable television alike. Aversion to monopoly has also had profound effects on the institutional settings in which decision making concerning these systems has taken place. Indeed, distrust of unchecked power of any sort is woven into the very warp and woof of the American polity.

Even before the American Revolution, many politically conscious people in the Thirteen Colonies were greatly influenced by the ideals of the English Commonwealthmen or "True Whigs." The Commonwealthmen emphasized the dangers of unchecked executive power both to individual freedom and to trade and the generation of wealth. They believed, in the words of historian Bernard Bailyn, that "if the vigilance of the people was ever thoroughly softened by negligence, sloth or corruption, the ever-watchful monopolists of power would soon act."[24] After the Revolution, denial by the Articles of Confederation of independent authority on the part of the national government to enforce its resolutions or levy taxes represented a continued manifestation of this fear of concentrated and centralized power. Although the Constitutional Convention assembled in 1787 put in place a framework for a far stronger national government than would have been possible to create under the Articles of Confederation, states continued to retain a high degree of autonomy and the authority of the central government was divided among the three branches.

To say the least, much has changed in the United States over the course of the last two hundred years. Amid the cataclysm of civil war during the 1860s, slavery was abolished and the principle that states could not secede from the Union established. During the years since the Civil War, the relative importance of the federal government has greatly increased and the size and administrative capabilities of government at all levels have grown. Nevertheless, complex divisions of governmental authority and decision making remain that have no real counterpart in France, Great Britain, or the other relatively unitary states of western Europe.

As shall be seen, these divisions of governmental authority have often worked to the advantage of private network owners in the United States. In many instances, firms have been able to gain relief from unfavorable actions by one level of government by appealing to another or by turning to the courts.[25] Competition among a multitude of local and state jurisdictions for the fruits of economic growth has also tended to spur local and state governments to implement policies designed to encourage or even subsidize the construction of networked systems and infrastructure while reducing their willingness and ability to impose restrictions on the private firms involved.[26] Nevertheless, private network owners have not always had things their own way. Allegations of abuses of power, beliefs that public ends were being inadequately served by private firms, and concerns with economic development have at times combined to inspire stringent regulatory initiatives and even turns to outright government ownership.

I bring these themes together in the chapters that follow.[27] I discuss political and institutional contexts in which the development of waterworks, electric utilities, and cable television systems took place in the United States. I also compare the character of public and private consumer goods demanded in different settings, problems and controversies that arose in arranging for provision of these goods, roles played by economic and transaction cost issues in engendering these problems, and how different factors ultimately came together to shape the choice of ownership and regulatory arrangements. For each network I both survey broad trends and present detailed historical case studies of events in individual cities. The case studies afford examples of more or less typical outcomes with respect to technology, ownership, and regulation as well as examples of outcomes that diverged from the norm in revealing ways.

In chapter 2, I turn my attention to urban water supply and distribution systems during the nineteenth and early twentieth centuries. As shall be seen, these systems came to be increasingly relied upon to serve a range of pressing consumer and public demands as major American cities swelled in size. Unfortunately, municipal governments faced severe difficulties in arranging to have private waterworks firms serve the demands. I describe the kinds of problems that arose and explore the roles played by lack of market discipline, informational issues, change, and contingencies in causing the difficulties. I also consider how people understood and responded to waterworks issues and why municipal ownership movements more frequently triumphed in rapidly growing cities than in their more stable counterparts.

I then look at the issues through detailed accounts of events in three very different cities— Boston, San Francisco, and Seattle. As shall be seen, attributes of technology made for similarities in public policy issues presented by the waterworks in all three cities. The commonalities stand out in particularly sharp relief because of the very distinctiveness of the historical and geographic contexts in which waterworks development and decision making took place. During the first years of the twentieth century, for example, San Francisco experienced some of the same kinds of difficulties in obtaining public services from its private waterworks firm as did Boston during the 1820s and 1830s. However, experiences in the three cities were not entirely homogeneous. For example, private waterworks ownership persisted far longer in San Francisco than in either Boston or Seattle. San Francisco's private waterworks firm also invested in far more elaborate supply and distribution facilities than did its counterparts in most other American cities. To place the roles played by technological and economic factors in broader context, I conclude the chapter with a brief comparison of experiences in American and western European cities. I explore some of the subtle yet powerful ways in which characteristics of political and institutional arrangements have shaped waterworks technology itself in different locales.

In chapter 3, I extend the analysis to electric utilities. The primary focus is on the development, ownership, and regulation of electric utilities in major American cities during the formative decades of that industry's development: from the 1880s through the 1920s. I compare the kinds of issues that arose in arranging for provision of public services and consumer goods by private electric utility and waterworks firms and consider the roles played by economic and transaction cost factors in determining why problems occurred in some settings but not in others. I also consider ways in which outcomes in both electric utilities and waterworks have been affected by aspirations for economic growth on the part of urban political leaders, suspicions of undue concentrations of economic and political power in the hands of either governmental or private entities, and the divisions of governmental authority built into American federalism.

As in waterworks, I both survey broad trends and present detailed accounts of events in Boston, San Francisco, and Seattle. In these and many other American cities during the late nineteenth and early twentieth centuries, complaints of monopolistic abuses and corrupt practices by private electric utility firms arose and large numbers of people called for municipal governments to build or acquire their own systems. In both Boston and San Francisco, however, campaigns for municipal electric utility ownership foundered. Instead, state governments asserted jurisdiction over private electric utility firms and restricted roles played by municipal authorities in either providing or regulating services. Municipal ownership campaigns fared similarly in most other major cities in the United States. In a significant minority of cases, however, advocates of municipal ownership realized their goals. During the first decades of the twentieth century, Seattle's municipal government developed and extended its own electric utility network throughout the city. Events in Seattle were also unusual in another respect. Despite the natural monopoly attributes of electric utility distributions systems, private and government-owned electric utilities directly competed with one another in many areas of the city for decades. I use analysis of this unusual case to gain insight into factors driving more typical outcomes in both waterworks and electric utilities.

In chapter 4 I turn to cable television and the communications and media complex of which it forms a part. As noted, cable television systems resemble waterworks and electric utilities in that they have been developed (at least thus far) primarily as instruments for the one-way delivery of services. But there are also major differences. Cable television systems are not really vital infrastructures in quite the same sense as are waterworks and electric utilities. Even a long-term disruption of cable television service in a major American city would be only a nuisance—not a disaster. At the same time, however, provision and control of media content is of central importance to social and political life in a way that is not true of either water or electricity. For this reason, concerns over undue concentration of political power have loomed even larger in cable television than in either of the other two networks.

I place these concerns in historical context with a broad overview of major themes and tensions in the politics of communications in the United States over the last two hundred years. I then discuss public policy issues that have arisen in association with the development of broadcasting and cable television during the twentieth century, exploring ways in which these issues have been influenced by basic attributes of broadcasting and cable television technology. I also consider the roles played by public policy in shaping how broadcasting and cable television systems were actually built and operated in the United States.

As compared to either waterworks or electric utilities during their formative years, a larger share of the policy making "action" in broadcasting and cable television has taken place at the federal level. Judicial decision making also has consistently been important. For this reason, the discussions of broadcasting and cable television largely focus on developments in these domains. In the case of cable television, however, municipal governments have also been significant actors. Particularly during the 1970s and 1980s, a number of cities in the United States engaged in elaborate exercises in which they arranged for private cable television firms to compete for the right to furnish service in a given locale based upon price and service terms offered. In examining developments in particular cities, my primary emphasis is on the achievements and vicissitudes of such franchise contracting.

I present detailed accounts of events in Pittsburgh, Boston, and Seattle. Pittsburgh and Boston represent exemplars of cities that engaged in relatively well-structured bidding contests for such cable television franchises. Seattle is of interest, by contrast, because of the diversity of regulatory approaches employed and the relatively limited role played by franchise bidding. In a rough kind of way, Seattle affords a kind of baseline against which the strengths and weaknesses of more elaborate bidding approaches can be discerned more clearly. As shall be seen, some of the same factors affected the functioning of regulatory and franchising arrangements in cable television as in waterworks and electric utility systems more than one hundred years before.

I conclude the book with a discussion of contemporary issues presented by networked systems in historical context. The emphasis is not on prediction (an enterprise fraught with risk of embarrassment to the author) but on delineating ways in which sense can be made of contemporary and future happenings in light of historical patterns of change and continuity.

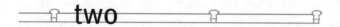

two

Waterworks

THE STORY OF URBAN WATER SUPPLY IN THE UNITED
States is intimately associated with that of the government and growth
of the country's cities themselves. Indeed, in at least a few cases, municipal government involvement in provision of water to city residents pre-
dates the founding of the United States itself. As early as the mid-1700s,
for example, the municipality of Philadelphia began to purchase and develop local wells and pumps in different neighborhoods of the city for use
by residents. Fifty years later, in 1799, the municipal government went
much further. Prompted by a deadly yellow fever epidemic mistakenly
believed to be caused by contamination of wells, the municipality began
development of a piped distribution system supplied with water pumped
from the Schuykill River. Completed in 1801, the system constituted one
of the largest and most technologically innovative waterworks developed
in the world up to that time.[1]

For the most part, however, municipal governments during the eighteenth and early nineteenth centuries did not play leading roles in financing and building infrastructures of any kind, including waterworks.
Urban places themselves during this period were few in number and
small in size. Philadelphia was the largest city in the United States as of
1790, yet had a total population of fewer than forty-three thousand. As
late as 1840, even such a major city as Boston still contained fewer than

one hundred thousand people. Financial resources too were limited. In raising money for either provision of services or for infrastructure development, municipal governments faced severe constraints. In many states, legislatures maintained tight control on a case-by-case basis of the borrowings undertaken by municipalities. In each case, legislatures specified the object and type of loan to be obtained.[2] Imposing taxes too usually required special enabling legislation.

Beginning about 1840, however, matters changed. About this time, the pace of urbanization itself began to pick up. Large numbers of small- and medium-sized cities sprang up in many regions of the country. In the relatively few locales that developed into really big cities, rates of growth were phenomenal. The population of Chicago, for example, exploded from hardly 30,000 in 1840 to over 2,740,000 in 1890. At least for short periods of time, other major American cities grew equally or even more rapidly.[3] In Seattle, for example, population increased from fewer than 4,000 in 1880 to almost 240,000 a mere thirty years later. In this context, large numbers of individuals and property-owners found their own fates and fortunes bound up in highly tangible ways with those of the particular urban places in which they lived and had invested. Far more than civic pride or mindless boosterism was at stake. Positively, living or owning property in a rapidly growing city could directly translate into enhanced individual fortunes. With urban growth came trade and jobs, new business opportunities, and the gains to be reaped from rising property values themselves. At the same time, problems and dangers impossible to address by individuals acting alone also arose as more and more people crowded into urban centers so as to seize these opportunities. In this nexus between individual and community interests municipal governments came to occupy a vital position.

Starting in about 1840, state legislatures and new state constitutions began to give municipal governments freedom to tax property within their jurisdictions and carte blanche to borrow moneys and issue bonds.[4] Obtaining their revenues primarily from property taxes and at least theoretically responsible to a local electorate, municipal governments could borrow against the value of the properties in a community to make investments or furnish facilities that would (they hoped) in turn attract growth, increase property values, and generate the tax revenues needed to pay back the loans. And in practice, nineteenth- and early-twentieth-century municipalities did play a wide variety of roles in developing, financing, and regulating infrastructures believed necessary both to attract and underwrite urban growth and to cope with some of its consequences.

Initially, a large share of municipal investment went to the development of railroads and other transportation linkages. So long as a community had good transportation connections, many people believed, urban growth and prosperity was virtually inevitable. In the absence of such connections, by contrast, specters of economic decay and stagnation loomed. Municipal governments donated land for railroad or terminal construction, endorsed and guaranteed railroad company securities, exchanged municipal bonds for railroad shares, or simply donated municipal bonds to railroad companies outright.[5] But despite the significant role played by municipal governments in financing intercity transportation linkages, outright government ownership was uncommon.

Municipal underwriting of railroad construction began to decline during the 1870s in the wake of widespread defaults and revelations of abuses. At this time, many states initiated bans on municipal borrowings for such purposes and also began to put in place laws limiting municipal taxation and debt to set proportions of the assessed value of real property inside a community.[6] With respect to municipal expenditures in general, however, the effects of such constraints were often surprisingly limited. Because the task of assessing property values generally continued to remain in the hands of municipal governments, local officials retained a degree of latitude in setting taxing and spending levels.[7] In any case municipal borrowings for waterworks, roads, streets, and a wide range of other purposes continued to increase during the late nineteenth and early twentieth centuries.

In waterworks, as in transportation, patterns of development and questions of ownership were closely bound up with the growth of cities. By the end of the nineteenth century, more than 3,100 waterworks served large, medium-sized, and even quite small urban places in the United States.[8] Waterworks development in turn represented an essential underpinning for the concomitant spread of indoor plumbing, flush toilets, and baths in hotels, public facilities, and residences in American cities. By century's end, waterworks had become so deeply enmeshed in day-to-day patterns of urban life as to be easily taken for granted.

Waterworks themselves were a distinctly urban technology. Few such systems existed outside of built-up urban areas during this period. Even in some cities, water supply and distribution networks did not reach outlying areas or serve poor neighborhoods. But for those to whom service was available, the resulting gains in the ease of day-to-day life, standards of living, and cleanliness were very great. Writing in 1897, waterworks authority Moses Baker rhapsodically (but realistically) described the advantages of access to piped-in water for day-to-day life as follows: "In place of the labor attendant upon lifting water by the old oaken bucket, the more prosaic hand pump, or of carrying water in pails from some spring or stream, only a turn of the faucet is now necessary in hundreds of communities to secure either hot or cold water on any floor of a dwelling."[9]

Ownership and regulatory arrangements varied. In many American cities, the earliest waterworks to be developed were constructed and operated by state chartered corporations financed and controlled by private investors. Particularly during the first decades of the nineteenth century, distinctions between corporations of this kind and municipal corporations entrusted with governmental responsibilities were much less clearly articulated than is the case today. Each corporation, whether a municipality enjoying political responsibilities or a more private association of limited liability shareholders, operated under a unique charter and enjoyed unique privileges and responsibilities. Corporations were, in the words of economic historian Stuart Bruchey, "bodies politic . . . accorded certain exclusive privileges to encourage the devotion of scarce private capital to public ends."[10]

Nevertheless, ownership mattered. Although large sums of money were required and difficult-to-surmount ideological, juridical, and political obstacles lay in the way, municipal governments in rapidly growing urban centers consistently made the efforts needed to acquire or build their own water supply and distribution systems. As of 1897, only nine of the fifty largest cities in the United States still relied upon nongovernmental enterprises for provision of piped-in water. By 1900, municipally owned systems served all but one of the eleven cities in the United States with a population of more than three hundred thousand. Growth in the number of municipally owned waterworks occurred both through new construction and by purchase. While shifts from private to government ownership took place in about two hundred cities over the course of the nineteenth century, there were only about twenty cases of government-owned systems reverting to private ownership.[11]

As shall be seen in the accounts that follow, the exact circumstances under which municipal governments in different cities came to build or acquire their own waterworks varied greatly. Depending on the city, selection processes for nongovernmental enterprises, details of the contractual or regulatory regimes under which firms operated, and the scale and duration of private waterworks development also differed. Nevertheless, certain consistent themes can be discerned in the development of private waterworks and in the sorts of difficulties that resulted in turns to municipal ownership.

Much of what occurred can be understood in terms of the analyses of economic and transaction cost issues presented in chapter 1. As would be expected given the natural monopoly attributes of water supply and distribution facilities, private waterworks firms in American cities generally did not face direct competition from rival enterprises. Just as is the case today, residents of American cities during the nineteenth and early twentieth centuries did not enjoy a choice of companies from which to obtain piped-in water.[12] Examination of the contracting and franchising of waterworks during the period also reveals Williamson's "fundamental transformation" in action. At first, in a few cities, a degree of competition for franchises to build and operate waterworks facilities did occur. Once facilities were actually put in place, however, rivalry ceased and municipal governments and private waterworks firms found themselves bound together for the long term.

Neither for people who lived in American cities nor for waterworks companies themselves were the consequences of such lack of competition necessarily disastrous. In small- and medium-sized communities in which population growth was modest, waterworks firms and municipal governments sometimes managed to forge quite workable long-term relationships; throughout the nineteenth century, privately owned waterworks continued to be developed and operated in many communities of this kind.[13] In larger and more rapidly expanding urban centers, however, disputes between private waterworks firms and issues of service quality proved far more difficult to either avoid or to resolve than in more static locales. Why did problems presented by urban growth for private waterworks development prove so intractable? To address this question, I turn a historian's eye to factors suggested by economic theory and transaction cost analysis.

As suggested by economic theory, I pay close attention to markets served by waterworks firms in larger as compared to smaller cities. As noted in chapter 1, forms of market discipline may arise in some settings even for networks, such as waterworks, with strong natural monopoly attributes. In small nineteenth-century American cities, for example, inter-product competition from local sources of water such as pumps and wells sometimes presented waterworks firms with at least a modicum of market discipline. No matter where one lived, of course, lack of piped-in running water could be highly unpleasant and inconvenient at times—on cold winter mornings, for example. But piped-in water from a waterworks was not absolutely essential: obtaining water by hand-pumping at a well and using an outdoor privy remained options in smaller communities. Whatever market discipline such alternatives presented in small cities, however, tended to weaken with urban growth. As cities expanded in size and became more built up, the attractiveness and viability of alternatives to piped-in supplies declined for most consumers. In rapidly growing cities, quantities of water available from wells and other local sources often proved insufficient to meet increased demands from industrial, commercial, and domestic customers. Indeed, as drafts on the water table increased, existing wells sometimes gave out altogether. Quality also suffered. Contamination of wells and other local water sources by the unsavory contents of privy vaults and cesspools became increasingly difficult to avoid as cities increased in size, greatly enhancing the risk of contagion and epidemics in big urban centers.

Property too faced danger as cities increased in size. In particular, the crowding together of large numbers of wooden buildings in rapidly growing American cities made for greatly increased fire risks. A technological innovation, the "balloon frame," exacerbated the problem. Invented by Chicago builder Augustine Taylor in 1833, balloon framing made it possible to erect buildings quickly and economically using light-weight lumber milled to standard widths and depths.[14] Unfortunately, fires spread through balloon frame buildings even more quickly than through wooden structures built using older methods.[15]

Thus people found themselves increasingly dependent on water supply and distributions systems for a wide variety of wants and needs as cities grew in size. Ongoing demands for modifications and additions to waterworks facilities also arose. With urban growth came calls for provision of larger quantities of water and for development of new sources of supply. As outlying neighborhoods became developed and central areas became more built up, calls also arose for extension and reconstruction of distribution networks. Public health and fire protection concerns increased the magnitude and heightened the urgency of demands for changes and improvements in existing water supply and distribution facilities.

In the case of public health, the role of specific bacteria in transmitting waterborne disease began to be understood by sanitary engineers and medical professionals only during the 1880s and 1890s. Even during the early and middle years of the nineteenth century, however, public health concerns lent impetus at times to calls for development and expansion of water supply and distribution networks in American cities and for protection of supplies against contamination. To prevent epidemics, abundant supplies of pure water were seen as necessary not only for drinking and bathing but for the flushing of filthy, excrement-covered city streets. Individual and community hygiene was also seen by some sanitary reformers as a matter not just of health but of morality. Writing in 1851 in the *North American Review*, sanitary reformer E. H. Clarke made the connection as follows: "The sanitary movement does not merely relate to the lives and health of the community; it is also a means of moral reform. . . . The ultimate connection between filth and vice has been noted by all writers upon this subject. Outward impurity goes hand in hand with inward pollution and the removal of one leads to the extirpation of the other. Cleansing the body is not more a symbol than it is a means and condition of inward purity."[16]

Over the course of the nineteenth century, American cities also came to rely heavily (if not always successfully) upon their fire departments and waterworks in order to quench the great numbers of fires that inevitably broke out and to protect themselves against large-scale conflagration. In order to successfully perform this role, waterworks had to be capable of supplying large and concentrated quantities of water at very short notice.[17] Even in cases in which day-to-day demands for water could be met without taxing existing facilities, provision of the quantities of water required to protect against fire in rapidly growing cities generally necessitated additional investment.[18] If fire protection demands were to be served at all adequately, larger distribution mains, higher pressures, more generous provisions for storing water in tanks and reservoirs, and (in cities without gravity-fed water supplies) higher capacity and more reliable pumping facilities all had to be put in place.[19]

Under these circumstances, protection of consumer interests and provision of public goods in rapidly growing cities depended almost entirely upon the efficacy of franchising, contracting, and regulatory arrangements and/or the public-spiritedness of the investor-owned water companies themselves. Neither inter-product competition nor other forms of market discipline could be relied upon to ensure that private waterworks firms invested in expansion and in the new facilities needed to provide for public health and fire protection demands. At the same time, demands for new investment associated with urban growth also made it harder for municipal governments and waterworks firms to devise workable long-term contracting and franchising arrangements. Examination of factors suggested by transaction cost analysis can help in understanding why this was so. Such analysis suggests that close attention should be given to the character of the information available to government officials and private managers in different settings, to difficulties encountered in measuring outputs and monitoring quality, and to the extent to which changing conditions required existing contracts and franchises to be modified and renegotiated. As shall be seen in the historical accounts of events in Boston, San Francisco, and Seattle, these factors came together in ways that made for severe difficulties in structuring workable relationships between municipal governments and private waterworks firms in rapidly growing American cities.

In major east coast cities such as Boston during the first decades of the nineteenth century, fundamental decisions concerning waterworks ownership and investment had to be made in a context of great uncertainty and expert disagreement concerning the kinds of facilities needed to furnish fire protection, guard against disease, and provide for future growth. Perhaps not surprisingly, limited understanding of the investments required to serve public needs resulted in poorly drafted contracts with private waterworks firms and severe service problems. As time went on, knowledge and expertise concerning waterworks design and the character of investments needed to protect against fire and disease did increase greatly. As shall be seen in the accounts of events in San Francisco and Seattle, however, such knowledge did not necessarily suffice to prevent problems from emerging in making and enforcing contracts for the provision of specifically public services as conditions changed and cities grew. Arranging for provision of water for fire protection presented particularly thorny transaction cost problems.

Accurately predicting how a waterworks would actually perform in the event of a major conflagration represented no easy task. Careful physical inspection and the exercise of considerable expertise and judgment by highly trained engineers were required.[20] Even when problems were identified, lack of an easily observed and objectively measured standard of performance made it difficult for a municipality to impose sanctions on an errant waterworks firm. Urban growth compounded the difficulties. In order for private waterworks firms to be compensated for investments in the improvements required to serve growing needs, parties with directly opposing interests had to repeatedly come to terms over issues of facility design and quality of service as well as price.

To compensate waterworks firms for furnishing fire protection, municipal governments in San Francisco, Seattle, and other American cities during the later years of the nineteenth century paid annual fees based on the number of fire hydrants installed. Unfortunately, this apparently sensible and straightforward approach to paying for the delivery of an important public service did not obviate the need for repeated case-by-case negotiation between municipal government and private water company as conditions changed and fire protection demands increased. The reason is that the number of fire hydrants contracted for by a city bore little more than a coincidental relationship to the amount and quality of the fire protection actually received. As a result, even if a municipality and a privately owned water company did manage to negotiate a mutually acceptable price per hydrant and both sides sought to behave honorably in living up to contract terms, conflicts could still easily arise. A municipality, for example, might complain of inadequate investment in new facilities as demand for water for fire protection increased, even as a privately owned water company expressed dissatisfaction at being inadequately compensated for those system improvements it did make. Worse yet, as shall be seen in the account of events in San Francisco, both of the parties involved in such a conflict could reasonably believe themselves to be in the right.

Under municipal ownership, by contrast, public officials could arrange for construction of facilities serving public and developmental needs without the sort of difficult head-to-head bargaining between parties with directly opposing interests required when waterworks were owned by private firms. In addition, financing could be drawn from property tax revenues as well as from user fees. This recourse made economic sense because of the ways in which improvements in water supply and distribution facilities contributed to increased property values and other public benefits—even for those who consumed relatively little water.

This is not to say that problems arising from ignorance, uncertainty, and other human frailties simply went away once waterworks came into the hands of municipal governments. Although effective water filtration technology already existed by the 1870s, for example, the value of filtration for protecting the public health went mostly unrecognized.[21] Nor, in many cases, was the danger arising from contamination of water supplies recognized. Running water purified itself, many experts believed, and any contamination of water stored in reservoirs would tend to diminish over time due to sedimentation.[22] As a consequence of these beliefs, few filtration plants were built in cities served by either municipally or privately owned waterworks and large numbers of people fell prey to typhoid and other waterborne diseases.

But although problems arose, the ability of municipally owned systems to invest in system modifications and improvements without having to confront contracting difficulties made it easier for them to correct mistakes and respond to new conditions. And in general, government-owned waterworks in rapidly growing cities in the United States during the nineteenth and early twentieth centuries did invest far more aggressively in water supply and distribution facilities than had their privately owned predecessors.

Private and Municipally Owned Waterworks in Boston

Those confronting waterworks ownership, investment, and regulatory decisions in Boston during the early and middle years of the nineteenth century had to face what must have seemed a truly bewildering array of uncertainties. These included the magnitude of future urban growth to be expected, relationships between the water supply and public health, and the nature of requirements for investments to furnish protection against fire. With respect to water and public health, for example, clean places were generally believed to be healthier than dirty ones but precisely formulated concepts did not yet exist of how filth caused disease, why some people did not get sick and others did under apparently similar conditions, and how such sickness could be prevented or cured. While some physicians and lay people believed that flushing streets with clean water could be a prophylactic against epidemic diseases such as cholera, many of those who believed in contagionist theories of disease did not place great store by this measure. Even more fundamentally, experts disagreed as to what exactly distinguished clean from unclean water supplies for drinking and bathing. In his 1833 inaugural speech, for example, Mayor Wells of Boston drew the connection (in retrospect valid) between sewage contamination and unsafe drinking water in his city as follows: "It is an undeniable fact that the well-water of the city has greatly deteriorated within a few years, from causes which are increasing daily. . . . A great portion of the water that supplies our wells, is merely the oozings of the ground, which must be highly impregnated with the deleterious contents of cesspools and drains; and although it may not be offensive to our senses, it is injurious to our health."[23] But, writing in 1845, pioneering epidemiologist and public health reformer Lemuel Shattuck described well water, at least in South Boston and in the western parts of the city, as of good quality in the present and likely to be adequate for many years to come despite the ongoing growth of these areas and the likelihood of increased contamination by cesspools.[24] Advocates of different sources of water from outside the city also disputed the relative cleanliness of each supply based upon such considerations as number of "animalcules" found in water samples and relative "peatiness."

Despite these uncertainties, advocates of private and government ownership alike came to agree that *something* needed to be done to improve Boston's water supply as the population of the city increased from about eighteen thousand in 1790 to over ninety thousand fifty years later. A conflagration on April 27, 1825 underlined the growing danger of fire caused by increased density and the crowding of wooden buildings. The blaze destroyed fifty-three houses and stores and caused losses of about five hundred thousand dollars.[25] At least by 1845, it was also clear that available ground water (whatever its quality) was being depleted in some of the more densely populated parts of the city. In 1845 hearings before the Massachusetts legislature, former mayor Martin Brimmer described the shortage of water for domestic uses as desperate. "On the easterly side of Beacon Hill there is constant complaint of the failure of wells from the effect of new ones which have been dug. There is constant war going on under ground and many wells have to be deepened from time to time. . . . On the lower level water is very scarce. On the Mill Pond, South Cove, and the Neck there is hardly any water to be obtained except by Artesian wells, and water is wanted as well for drinking as for washing and other domestic purposes."[26]

Backers of private and government ownership differed, however, in their judgments concerning both the importance to the public welfare of a generous water supply and likely future growth in demand. In general, waterworks entrepreneurs and those who backed private ownership defined piped-in water as primarily a consumer good and minimized the need for investment for specifically public purposes. Although they did permit the city to tap mains free of charge to obtain water for fire protection, the charters obtained by private waterworks firms in Boston consistently committed the firms to no investments beyond those needed to serve private consumers. At the same time, backers of private waterworks development and entrepreneurs thought it preferable to risk investing too little in supply and distribution facilities rather than too much in the face of uncertainties as to present and future demands.

From their perspective, this preference was quite rational. Under the conditions prevailing in Boston during the early and middle years of the nineteenth century, a privately owned waterworks could eventually make some money even if it furnished poor service or served only a small area of the city. In 1795, for example, the Boston Town Meeting approved a proposal by a group of private investors to pipe water into the city from Jamaica Pond four miles away in Roxbury. From the point of view of investors, the venture was not initially a success. There were no dividends for the first ten years and the market value of shares originally purchased for one thousand dollars fell to as low as three hundred dollars. In later years, however, matters improved. By 1810, the waterworks was generating a modest return, with shareholders receiving average yearly dividends of about fifty-two dollars on shares with a market value of five hundred to six hundred dollars. This amounted to an annual return of about 8 percent to 10 percent on the shares' market value and about half that on their original cost.

But however modestly the Aqueduct Company performed in generating returns for its investors, those who actually relied upon the system for provision of water fared far worse. From the beginning, the small size of the pond limited the area of the city that could be served. Even where the Aqueduct Company's pipes did run, pressures were insufficient to fight fires, reliability was poor, and many residents continued to rely on their own wells and cisterns for drinking water.[27] In 1845 testimony before the state legislature, Aqueduct Company manager Allan Hinckley himself described the system's performance in terms that suggest its inadequacies: "We have about 3,500 customers—3,000 well supplied and 500 not fully supplied. . . . In Franklin Place they get it pretty well. I know that recently it failed for a fortnight. There are always complaints. The bills read that there will be deduction when the water fails for over three weeks. . . . Last year the supply was cut off in some streets for a fortnight by the gates being shut down. I have known the water in the pond so low that it would not run into the pipes, and I have known it some nine feet above."[28]

Even when it became clear by the mid-1820s that markets for water existed in areas of the city not served by the Aqueduct Company, private investors still preferred to risk under-investing in a system that might prove to be too small than over-investing in one that might be too large. For the most part, backers of private waterworks development looked to Spot Pond, about eight miles north of the city, as a source of supply. Initially recommended by local engineer Daniel Treadwell in 1825, the pond had several desirable features. First, it lay at a high elevation and expensive pumping would not be needed to bring water into the city. Second, the pond lay closer to Boston than other proposed gravity-fed sources. Third, the quality of water in Spot Pond was universally conceded to be of good quality. Almost from the beginning, however, the limited capacity of the proposed Spot Pond supply attracted professional criticism. Writing in 1825, Frederick Graff, the engineer of Philadelphia's Fairmount Works, criticized the 1,600,000 gallons per day capacity of Spot Pond as too small to meet Boston's needs and expressed doubt as to whether the source could supply even this much during dry seasons.[29] In a more detailed 1834 report to the city, engineer Loammi Baldwin concurred in these criticisms. Baldwin estimated Boston's water needs for the present and near future at about 5,000,000 gallons per day, more than three times the Treadwell figure of ten years before. Dismissing Spot Pond as too small to supply this demand, Baldwin instead called for development of Farm, Shakum, and Long Ponds about eighteen miles west of the city at a much higher initial capital expenditure.

Despite Graff's criticisms and Baldwin's report, private investors expressed no interest in making the larger capital investment needed to build such a system.[30] Demand for water, they believed, would grow too slowly for the large initial investment needed to develop Long Pond to ever be profitable. In a report prepared for the city in 1836, engineer R. H. Eddy followed through on this logic to recommend a strategy of incremental development.[31] The capacity of Spot Pond, Eddy maintained, did suffice to meet Boston's immediate needs. As demand increased, Eddy advocated damming up Mystic Pond to keep out the tide and pumping water from this low-level source into the city. Given the willingness of private investors to risk their own capital on a system of this type, backers of private development argued that municipal ownership in general, and of Long Pond in particular, would constitute a wasteful and financially irresponsible expenditure of public funds.[32]

By contrast, it was poor service and shortages rather than risks that money might be wasted by initially investing in overly elaborate facilities that government ownership advocates most feared. Advocates of municipal ownership rejected the definition of water as primarily a product to be purchased by private consumers at their option. Serving public needs, they argued, justified waterworks investments over and above what could be recouped through charges to private consumers. In particular, they maintained, the people of Boston had an interest in an abundant supply of water for public goods such as fire protection, flushing streets, sewerage, and ornamental fountains. Provision of an abundant supply of water at low charges to private consumers was also needed, many municipal ownership advocates argued, to protect the public health.[33] The positions taken by government ownership advocates on the question of whether to use Spot or Long Pond as a source of water reflected their beliefs that broad public interests would be served through provision of generous supplies of water. As the population of Boston rose and the limitations of Spot Pond became more apparent, government ownership advocates increasingly united behind the Long Pond alternative.

Interestingly, even advocates of a privately owned waterworks seemed to accept the position that specialized capital investments made solely to supply public goods should be owned by the municipality. Thus, soon after the fire of 1825, Boston began to invest municipal funds in the construction of cisterns in various parts of Boston for the purpose of storing water for putting out fires. Unlike a waterworks, these cisterns clearly supplied only a pure public good. The decision that these cisterns should be publicly owned was made quickly and apparently as a matter of course.

In the more complicated and controversial case of waterworks, however, some advocates of municipal ownership did find it necessary to think through and justify their position that public goals could be better accomplished under direct municipal ownership than through some sort of contractual arrangement with a private firm. In making their points, advocates demonstrated a keen awareness of the kinds of issues and problems classified in this volume under the heading of "transaction costs." Mayor Josiah Quincy, for example, justified his preference for municipal ownership on the grounds that "there are so many ways, in which water may be desirable, and in such a variety of quantities, for use, comfort and pleasure, that it is impossible to provide, by any prospective provisions, in any charter granted to individuals for all the cases, uses and quantities, which the ever increasing wants of the population of a great city, in the course of years may require."[34]

Potential problems in enforcing good performance by a private firm attracted attention as well. In this regard, Quincy cited the danger that a private firm, "through cupidity, or regard to a false economy, may have an interest not to exercise the works upon a sufficiently extensive scale, with permanent materials."[35] At the same time, however, active supervision by the municipal government to prevent this outcome also posed risks. If the municipal government attempted to exercise too close a supervision over a private firm, a city council committee feared, there would be danger "of collision between different interests, and of delay in the prosecution of the business which, if undertaken, ought to be completed as speedily as is consistent with the durability of a structure designed for the benefit of posterity as well as ourselves."[36] Nor did the option of reimbursing a privately owned waterworks for furnishing specifically public goods represent a promising solution. Because a private firm could not raise capital at nearly so low a rate of interest as could the municipal government, the committee asserted, costs of private provision would be excessive. This alternative also came in for criticism on transactional grounds. In particular, the committee expressed doubt as to whether the municipal government would be able to reach an acceptable bargain with a private firm as to reimbursement for the specialized investments needed to supply public goods.[37]

Until the end of 1845, the dispute between private and municipal ownership advocates would swing back and forth inconclusively, with each side stymieing the other. Municipal ownership advocates repeatedly succeeded in blocking plans for private development, but found their own plans stymied by lack of sufficient political backing to take on the debt needed to construct a public system. Thus, on June 30, 1836, the City Council Water Committee divided on the ownership issue, a majority supporting private development, a minority opposing. The public ownership forces countered with a successful effort to put the issue up for referendum. At the referendum, held on August 22, 1836, the voters of Boston endorsed the principle of municipal ownership by the overwhelming majority of 2,107 to 136. No private development could proceed in the face of this rebuff. Instead, the city council appointed a new water committee to investigate the issue over the winter of 1837. This committee supported municipal ownership, but the members split as to whether Spot Pond or Long Pond would be the best choice. Reflecting this division, the city submitted a petition to the Massachusetts legislature on April 7, 1838, asking for permission to introduce water into the city from either Spot or Long Ponds. The legislature adjourned before taking up the petition and during the 1839 session, opponents succeeded in blocking legislative approval altogether.

The accession of Mayor Jonathan Chapman in 1840 dealt the cause of municipal ownership a further blow. Basing his opposition on financial grounds, Chapman blocked any new city efforts for a municipally owned waterworks.[38] Encouraged by these setbacks to public ownership plans, private investors returned to the initiative. The old Aqueduct Company modestly expanded its system and replaced many of its old wooden pipes with metal ones. As a result of these improvements, the number of water-takers served by the system increased from 1,500 to 3,500 over the years 1838 to 1845. During 1843 and 1844, private investors also renewed efforts to build a waterworks drawing on Spot Pond. As was the case in previous years, however, municipal ownership advocates managed to block these plans.

The stalemate finally ended in 1844–45 with municipal ownership advocates winning a decisive victory. Emboldened by improvements in municipal finances, reconstituted city council water committees issued reports during the summer of 1844 settling on Long Pond as the best source of water and calling for the city to build a system. On November 9, 1844, a commission appointed by the council elaborated upon these conclusions, issuing a report making a more detailed case for use of Long Pond on the basis of more liberal (and in hindsight, more accurate) estimates of Boston's present and future water needs than those put forth by Spot Pond/private ownership advocates. The voting public apparently found these arguments convincing. By a margin of 6,260 to 2,204, the voters of Boston passed a proposition calling for a municipally owned waterworks drawing on Long Pond as a source in a referendum held on December 9, 1844. After lengthy hearings, the Massachusetts legislature granted Boston the powers needed to actually build the waterworks subject to the hurdle of one more referendum.

This grant initiated the climactic and final act of the dispute. In their effort to block passage of the Long Pond referendum, advocates of private development attempted to draw on concerns over concentration of power as well as economic arguments. A municipally owned waterworks, they asserted, would be run by a group of unelected and unaccountable water commissioners with despotic powers. To ease any misgivings that a private firm might abuse its position, Spot Pond backers reiterated their offer that the firm be set up as a mixed private-public enterprise with the city owning one third of the stock. Under their plan, rates would be set by the mayor and aldermen of the city subject to the provision that profits not be allowed to slip below 6 percent or above 10 percent on the moneys invested. These points made an impact on the electorate despite their earlier approval of the Long Pond project. At the referendum held on May 19, 1845, Boston voters defeated the Long Pond proposition by a narrow margin of 3,999 to 3,670.

Long Pond advocates, however, quickly regrouped. To better mobilize public support for the project, they organized Ward Water Unions throughout the city. Even more importantly, they gained the support of a prestigious expert for their cause. On June 25, 1845, the city council's Joint Standing Committee on Water turned to John B. Jervis, the famous chief engineer of New York's Croton Aqueduct, to evaluate whether the Long or Spot Pond projects would better serve Boston's needs. Released on November 18, 1845, Jervis's report provided a crushing vindication to Long Pond advocates. A water supply from Long Pond, Jervis maintained, would serve Boston's needs more generously, and in the long run more cheaply, than any other alternative. While Spot Pond would only be capable of providing the city with 1,500,000 gallons of water per day (an amount clearly inadequate to meet the city's current needs) at a cost of about $637,000, according to Jervis, Long Pond would be able to provide more than four times as much water (about 7,500,000 gallons per day) at an estimated cost little more than twice as high (about $1,350,00).[39]

On March 30, 1846, at the request of the city, the Massachusetts legislature passed a new water act giving Boston the necessary powers to build a waterworks using Long Pond as a source. On April 13, 1846, the question was put up for vote by the electorate of the city for the last time. The municipal ownership proposal passed overwhelmingly by a margin of 4,637 to 348. With these political hurdles overcome, the task of actually building Boston's municipal waterworks proceeded quickly. Control of the project was vested in a three-member water board appointed by the city council. The board in turn hired engineer John B. Jervis to oversee construction. Ground for the waterworks was officially broken on August 20, 1846, with such luminaries as ex-president John Quincy Adams in attendance. Humble Long Pond itself gained a new name in honor of the occasion. To give the source of Boston's water a title commensurate with its new importance in the life of the city,

Boston to the Rescue!!

The Voters of Boston

Opposed to the creation of a close Corporation of Water Commissioners, with high salaries, offices for life, and despotic power—Opposed to the project of introducing animalcules from Long Pond, five years hence, at a cost of $5,000,000—Opposed to an addition of one third to the taxes, in 1844.—And

In favor of the immediate introduction of pure water from Spot Pond or Charles River, in a quantity sufficient to supply 100 gallons a day to each of the 10,000 houses which Boston proper contains, and to as many more, at an average cost of half the sum charged in New York, and without the New York water tax of $675,000 a year.—Are invited to repair to the Polls as soon after 12 M. this day, Monday 19th, as may be, and vote

AGAINST THE WATER ACT,

By depositing a Ballot marked

"NAY!!"

S. N. DICKINSON & CO., Printers, Boston.

Broadside exhorting Boston voters to turn down a proposal for a government-owned waterworks. *Courtesy of the Massachusetts Historical Society.*

Mayor Quincy announced that Long Pond would henceforth be known as Lake Cochituate. This "original Indian" name, according to Adams, could be literally translated to mean "an ample supply of pure and soft water, of a sufficient elevation to carry into the City of Boston, at a moderate price."[40] The waterworks was completed a little more than two years later and on October 25, 1848, the municipal government mounted a great civic celebration to mark its debut.

The day of celebration began with the ringing of church bells and the firing of cannons and concluded with a gathering of an estimated 50,000 to 100,000 citizens on Boston Common. Following speeches by the mayor and other dignitaries, water sprang forth from an eighty-foot fountain, the gas lamps along Tremont Street came on, and an explosion of fireworks filled the sky. During the day itself, an organized pageant of Boston society paraded down the city's streets. The range of professions and social groups symbolically represented encompassed respectable society. Along with assorted dignitaries and public officials came members of different trades in full regalia, floats depicting their occupations, schoolchildren, Harvard professors, Harvard students, fire companies, militia companies, and members of temperance societies.

From printing presses carried on floats, compositors and pressmen distributed a "Song for the Merry-Making on Water Day" to the crowd. Although not immortal as literature, the following excerpt from the song nicely illustrates the mixture of practicality and exhilarating civic idealism with which the waterworks was regarded:

> *Away, away with care to-day*
> *There's naught but joy before us;*
> *A gladsome shout from the mass goes out,*
> *And we will join the chorus. . . .*
> *The thirsty mart feels through its heart*
> *The mighty current quiver,*
> *Through streets and lanes, in iron veins,*
> *A subterranean river.*
> *Unseen it comes to all our homes,*
> *To cheer the high and lowly;*
> *Like gifts from heaven, unknown when given,*
> *But through their influence holy. . . .*

And ever may we bless the day
When Boston's sons and daughters,
Came up elate to celebrate
The Advent of the Waters.[41]

The hoopla was not misplaced. From the first, the new Cochituate waterworks furnished water to a far greater number of customers than had the old Aqueduct Company system. As noted, the Aqueduct Company served at most 3,500 customers as of 1845. Just eight years later, by contrast, the new Cochituate Waterworks furnished water to as many as 18,170 customers.[42] By 1870, 31,500 customers took water from the Cochituate Waterworks.[43] As time went on, Boston residents used the newly abundant and reliable supplies of water furnished by Cochituate in an increasing variety of ways.

At first, in most dwellings, running water meant one or two cold water taps and possibly a sink. Hot as well as cold running water, bathtubs, and water closets (flush toilets) remained rare luxuries. Thus, although there were 18,170 water-takers in Boston as of 1853, there were fewer than 2,500 water closets. During the years that followed, however, people chose to have an increasing variety of flush toilets and other water-using fixtures installed. By 1869, Boston water-takers had more than 7,200 bathtubs and 20,600 flush toilets installed in dwellings, hotels, and businesses. Livery stables and industrial plants were large users of water also. Some manufacturers even used the energy in the running water supplied by Cochituate as a source of power for machinery.

Indeed, although the new Cochituate Waterworks dwarfed the old Aqueduct Company system in scale, the very avidity with which Boston residents consumed water soon made for strains. Whereas the Long Pond system had been planned on the basis of an average daily water consumption of 7,500,000 gallons per day; average daily consumption in 1854 already amounted to 8,542,000 gallons.[44] Late in 1864, levels of water in Lake Cochituate fell so low that the aqueduct relied upon to supply the city threatened to be left high and dry altogether. Waterworks officials exhorted Boston citizens to conserve water, banned the use of hand hoses, and hired twenty inspectors "to examine all the water fixtures throughout the city and to report each day at the office any waste that might be discovered, and also all leaks."[45] But although the measures succeeded in staving off immediate catastrophe, levels of water consumption again began to rise during the years that followed.[46]

The Cochituate Water Board repeatedly expressed its alarm concerning these trends. The situation was particularly intolerable, reports of the board asserted, because much of the water was not even being put to good use or any use at all. Due to carelessness on the part of consumers and the proliferation of poorly designed and installed water fixtures, the board fulminated, Boston found itself threatened with water shortages even as large and increasing quantities of the precious liquid were being left to run to waste.[47] Indeed, even when the system threatened to run dry in 1864, the Cochituate Water Board proclaimed its faith that "we have no doubts whatever but that the supply of water is ample for years to come if used in a liberal but proper manner."[48]

But in seeking to check what they believed to be feckless and profligate water consumption on the part of Boston residents during the 1850s and 1860s, waterworks officials found themselves frustrated by both technological and political obstacles. At least in principle, for example, waterworks managers believed that the most effective and equitable means of checking waste would be to meter all customers. With meters in place, the prevailing system of flat yearly rates for water could be abandoned and consumers could be charged for water on the basis of quantities consumed.[49] Charging for water in this way, an 1864 report asserted, "is the only sure way to prevent a continual waste, as consumers give their fixtures more attention when they are paying for any leakage."[50] And the Cochituate Water Board did impose meter rates on increasing numbers of hotels, factories, and other large water consumers during the 1850s and 1860s. Unfortunately, the high cost of water meters themselves, managers believed, rendered metering all but the largest customers far too expensive to be practicable. While annual water charges for most small consumers amounted to less than ten dollars, one report noted, the cost of procuring and installing a single water meter amounted to about fifty dollars. "Consequently the expense [of metering all consumers] at present cost would nearly consume the [the waterworks'] income."[51]

At the same time political obstacles arose when the Cochituate Water Board attempted to check waste by preventing installation of fixtures that consumed large quantities of water. The most egregious offender in this regard, the board believed, was the hopper water closet. Unlike other types of water closet, water continued running through a hopper unless it was turned off after each flush. In practice, users often forgot to take this extra step or chose not to do so. As a consequence, the quantities of water run through a single "hopper" could be prodigious. "In many instances," one report declared, "the owners of a single hopper-closet are using, or rather wasting, at a cost to them of only *five dollars* per annum, as much water as the manufacturer uses whose yearly water-rate amounts to some hundreds of dollars."[52] Boston residents, however, liked their hopper water closets. Indeed the very features of the hopper closet that the Cochituate Water Board found to be objectionable were viewed as advantages by some users. Unlike other types of water closet that shut off after each use, hoppers could be safely installed in unheated rooms or back buildings and left with the water running to prevent pipes from freezing. Hopper closets could also be installed more cheaply than alternatives.

In this context, elected officials in Boston paid greater heed to Boston citizens' desires to keep their hopper closets than to Cochituate Water Board denunciations of the fixture. At regular intervals during the 1850s and 1860s the Cochituate Water Board called for the imposition of prohibitively high charges on hopper closets or for their banning altogether. Just as regularly, the Boston City Council blocked the board. Indeed, the number of hoppers actually increased from fewer than 700 in 1853 to more than 16,100 in 1873. Calls on the part of the Cochituate Water Board to impose licensing requirements on plumbers to prevent the installation of poorly designed and leaky water fixtures were also repeatedly turned down by the city council during this period.

Unexpected problems also arose in the realm of water for fire protection. Design and maintenance of fire hydrants represented a particularly persistent area of difficulty. "A good part of the original hydrants were so defective in their construction," a Cochituate official asserted in the mid-1860s, that he did not "consider it economy to repair them." Nor were original hydrants of "a size to correspond with the requirements of the steam engines of the Fire Department."[53] More insidious problems also arose. In particular, the iron pipes originally installed for water distribution during the late 1840s and early 1850s proved vulnerable to a kind of hardening of the arteries. Even as central areas of Boston became more built-up and fire risks increased, thick encrustations of rust built up in many distribution pipes and reduced the ability of the system to deliver the large quantities of water required for effective protection.

Waterworks officials became increasingly aware of these problems during the late 1850s and early 1860s and did take steps to address them. A trial installation of a short length of bitumen-lined and it was hoped rustproof pipe, for example, was made in 1858. In 1863 new fire hydrants were installed on Beacon Street in the heart of Boston and about a fifth of a mile of six-inch pipe was replaced with 12-inch. The installation was rendered necessary, the Cochituate Water Board reported, "on account of the great number of new buildings erected on that street, requiring more water than the 6-inch pipe could deliver, and also in case of fire in that vicinity."[54] Using funds contributed by the fire department, large numbers of independent fire reservoirs were also connected up to the water distribution system during the 1860s.

Nevertheless, rhetoric concerning fire risks in Cochituate Water Board annual reports dating from the 1850s and 1860s exhibited little sense of urgency and had something of a smug and self-satisfied quality about it.[55] And many initiatives themselves were of a rather modest and exploratory nature. On October 18, 1865, for example, members of the water board visited Charlestown and "witnessed a very satisfactory trial of the 'Lowry' hydrant playing five streams of water at the same time, to the height of fifty or sixty feet."[56] But despite the imprecations of fire chief Charles Damrell, the board did not choose to have such hydrants installed in large number. Nor did the board undertake the large-scale program of pipe replacement and enlargement recommended by the fire chief with increasing urgency from the mid-1860s onward.[57] Perhaps not surprisingly, members of the Cochituate Water Board did not view the threat of fire as seriously as did the fire chief nor did they take kindly to his criticism of their system.

Unfortunately, the threat of serious conflagration proved all too real. On the evening of November 9, 1872, a fire broke out in Boston's densely packed warehouse district. By the time the fire burned out a day and a half later, sixty-five acres of commercial and warehouse buildings had gone up in flames. Deficiencies in water supply were not the only reasons the fire proved so difficult to control. Fire engines arrived late to the scene because of sickness among the horses, streets in the area were narrow and crooked, and the buildings themselves were extremely fire-prone. But the small size of water mains in the area, rust in the mains, and poorly designed hydrants did greatly contribute to the problems by making it virtually impossible for water to be pumped high enough for the spread of flames from rooftop to rooftop to be prevented.[58]

Serious as the problems and contentions described here were, they need to be placed in the perspective of broader areas of consensus. Despite disagreement as to steps that should be taken to check waste of water, for example, the Cochituate Water Board shared with elected officials a commitment to extending waterworks facilities to those who desired service. When Boston's municipal government began work on the Cochituate system back in 1846, the old Aqueduct Company's distribution system consisted of not more than forty miles of water mains. Under municipal ownership, by contrast, the system of distribution mains measured 96 miles in length as of 1850 and 152 miles as of 1869. In association with Boston's annexation of Charlestown, Roxbury, Dorchester, West Roxbury, and Brighton, the Cochituate Water Board laid an additional 168 miles of water main between 1869 and 1876. For service in elevated areas, new pumping plants, standpipes, and other improvements were also made during the late 1860s and early 1870s.[59]

Even while continuing to denounce waste on the part of consumers, the Cochituate Water Board also began to take steps to enhance water supplies during the mid-1860s. For the purpose both of storing surplus waters from Lake Cochituate for use in times of shortage and of ensuring continued distribution of water in the city even in the event of an accident to the aqueduct, the board and its engineers directed the construction of a large new storage reservoir at Chestnut Hill between 1865 and 1870.[60] Planning for large-scale development of new supplies to furnish the water believed necessary for prospective and hoped-for urban growth began during the early 1870s. New sources of water were needed, an 1874 report asserted, not only to forestall future shortages but to prevent Boston from being left behind in competition between cities for new economic and industrial development: "The adoption of any policy which shall restrict the supply of water for all legitimate uses," the report stated, "will be a mistaken and unfortunate one." In particular, "the fear of an insufficient supply would tend to restrict and dwarf a great many industrial establishments in a very large degree, and possibly lead to their location elsewhere." In sum, the water board felt "that a great and growing city like this cannot afford to endanger its progressive prosperity by failure to take the proper action to secure its continuance."[61]

To prevent such a dire outcome, the Cochituate Water Board began construction of a new system of dams and reservoirs on the Sudbury River in 1875. Largely completed in 1878, the new development boosted the capacity of the waterworks to sixty-two million gallons per day.[62] To prevent a recurrence of the kind of disastrous fire that took place in 1872, the Cochituate Water Board also undertook extensive reconstruction of existing distribution facilities. The board replaced large numbers of old rust-encrusted water pipes with larger conduits lined with coal-tar to prevent rust encrustations.[63] The board also placed large numbers of Lowry hydrants throughout the city. Contention between fire chief Damrell and the Cochituate Water Board did not cease altogether with these steps. Perhaps for reasons of technological chauvinism, for example, the board chose not to construct the auxiliary salt water fire protection system called for by Damrell. But, even according to a critical account by historian Christine Rosen, "the Cochituate Water Board seems never to have reverted to its old practice of blatantly ignoring the needs of fire fighting in the inner city."[64]

The overall result was that by the end of the 1870s Boston was served by a waterworks far more extensive in scale than that of the original Cochituate system. As the population of Boston and its environs grew and water use increased, expansion continued. Indeed, during the 1890s, waterworks development burst the physical and jurisdictional bounds of the municipality of Boston itself. In 1895, the state of Massachusetts enacted legislation absorbing Boston's Cochituate Water Board into a new Metropolitan Water District formed to serve the entire urban region. To meet projected and hoped-for regional growth, the district completed a new reservoir on the Nashua River about forty miles west of Boston in 1906. During the 1930s, the Metropolitan Water District began tapping water from the Swift and Ware Rivers almost seventy miles west of Boston. In 1946, the gigantic Quabbin Reservoir was completed. Thirty-nine square miles in area, eighteen miles long, and holding 412 billion gallons of water, Quabbin is one of the largest water supply reservoirs in the world and a dominant feature of the landscape of central Massachusetts. Construction of the facility increased the safe yield of the Metropolitan Water District from 133 million gallons per day to 330 million gallons per day.[65]

Viewed in the perspective of these developments, the main legacy of Boston's turn to government ownership of waterworks in the 1840s does not lie in the physical facilities constructed at that time. Indeed, with the passage of years, most of these facilities have been superseded one way or another. Rather, under municipal ownership, a set of institutional arrangements were put in place and people put in charge with the resources and motivation to invest on a large scale in development of facilities to both serve and facilitate urban growth. Problems occurred but so did shifts in policy and learning from experience.

Private and Municipally Owned Waterworks in San Francisco

Ownership and development of waterworks in San Francisco during the middle and later years of the nineteenth century proceeded quite differently than in Boston. When Boston turned to municipal ownership of its waterworks during the mid-1840s, the city was already about two hundred years old. At the time, however, really rapid population growth in Boston was only just beginning. During Boston's years of greatest population growth from 1850 onward, the city was served by a government-owned waterworks. As can be seen in the preceding account, threats of shortage occasionally loomed even after the municipal government acquired ownership. Controversies also arose at times about pricing for consumer services and the character of facilities needed in order to adequately protect against fire. In comparison to what went on during the 1830s and 1840s, however, large-scale waterworks development in Boston under municipal ownership proceeded in a relatively smooth and uncontentious fashion.

The relative smoothness of Boston's waterworks development over the years 1850 through 1900 stands out in even sharper relief when events in that city are compared with those in San Francisco. Unlike in Boston, water supply and distribution facilities remained in the hands of a private firm during San Francisco's years of most rapid population growth. Private waterworks development in San Francisco also took place under a far more highly elaborated and varied set of institutional and legal arrangements than in Boston. These included franchise contracting during the early years of waterworks development and a species of municipal rate regulation later on. Arrangements for provision of specifically public services such as water for fire protection also differed. Although Mayor Josiah Quincy and others in Boston did engage in speculation concerning whether arrangements could be devised under which a privately owned waterworks received reimbursement for investments devoted to public purposes, the question remained strictly hypothetical. In San Francisco the recourse was attempted.

The results can most charitably be characterized as mixed. On the one hand, quite extensive development of supply and distribution facilities did take place at times. On the other hand, the history of waterworks development in San Francisco was also far more crisis-ridden and contentious than in Boston, where development took place under government ownership from the late 1840s onward. Controversial issues at different times in San Francisco included the legal validity of initially specified franchise terms, investment in new facilities to support and anticipate future urban growth, the price of water to consumers, and terms of compensation for provision of specifically public services. As suggested by transaction cost analysis, change, uncertainty, and measurement difficulties presented major obstacles to the devising of workable franchising and franchising arrangements.

San Francisco experienced its first water crisis as the result of a population explosion brought on by the gold rush of 1848. The number of people in the city increased from fewer than one thousand at the beginning of 1848 to as many as thirty thousand in 1850 and continued to grow thereafter. As a result, local springs, wells, and brooks were unable to meet water supply needs and residents had to rely on high-priced water-carters. Dysentery was reported to be widespread among new arrivals and the city itself suffered a series of devastating conflagrations.[66] As was the case in many other American cities during their early years, municipal officials in San Francisco accepted private initiatives to build a waterworks as the best means available to address such problems.

To a much greater extent than in Boston and in most other American cities during the early years of the nineteenth century, however, San Francisco sought to set specific and rigorous franchise terms as a means of ensuring that a privately owned waterworks would furnish water to consumers at a fair price and make adequate investments to serve public as well as private needs. The tool failed. At the beginning, franchise sanctions proved to be of little use for forcing a private firm to provide good performance in the face of its incapacity to do so. By the end of the 1870s, franchising had broken down entirely in a haze of legal ambiguity and divided state and local jurisdiction.

San Francisco issued its first waterworks franchise to the locally organized Mountain Lakes Water Company in 1851. No competitive bidding for the franchise occurred, but Mountain Lakes saw enough potential profit in the project for the firm to accept a grant containing a number of rigorous provisions designed to protect the public interest.[67] Within a year after it received the contract award, however, Mountain Lakes began to complain of inability to raise capital under the terms imposed by the city. As the difficulties seemed genuine (and no waterworks could be constructed without capital), the common council acquiesced to the firm's petition for a more lenient arrangement.[68] The company proved successful enough in attracting capital under this new franchise to begin construction, but unexpected difficulties in construction and financial shortfalls continued to plague the project.[69] Nevertheless, in the absence of any alternative, the city repeatedly granted the firm extensions on the franchise deadline for completing the project.

In the end it was not the legal compulsion of franchise provisions, but a proposal by the newly organized San Francisco City Water Company that gave the municipal government a means to escape from the bind. Its faith in Mountain Lakes finally exhausted,[70] San Francisco granted a waterworks franchise to the new firm in August of 1857. Following a less ambitious construction strategy than that used by Mountain Lakes, the San Francisco City Company quickly brought a system into operation. By the summer of 1860, the firm had laid more than fourteen miles of pipes and supplied about 600,000 gallons of water daily to consumers in the more densely populated parts of the city.

The franchise obtained by the San Francisco City Waterworks, like that of the Mountain Lakes venture, was a fairly elaborate document and contained many provisions designed to protect the city's interests. To ensure adequate system development, the franchise required the San Francisco City Company to construct a waterworks with a capacity of at least two million gallons of water per day. To protect against monopolistic price exploitation while ensuring the company's ability to raise money, the franchise provided for rate regulation by the municipal government on a generous rate of return basis—24 percent per year on cash invested for the first five years and 20 percent thereafter.[71] The franchise also contained some more problematic provisions. Like the Mountain Lakes franchise, it required the water company to provide water for most public purposes free of charge without making any reference to the investment to be made by the company for that purpose. The franchise also contained expiration provisions with poor incentive properties. Upon the expiration of the franchise after twenty years, the works would revert to the city without compensation to the company but, if the city wished to buy the works before that time, the franchise provided for the price to be worked out by arbitration.

In practice, continued urban growth rendered rigid franchise terms (even when enforced) rapidly obsolete as guarantors of good performance. Over the years 1860 through 1880, San Francisco's population more than quadrupled, from fewer than 57,000 to about 234,000. Because of this growth, the franchise requirement that the waterworks have a minimum capacity of two million gallons per day quickly lost whatever meaning it may once have had as a performance specification. The private waterworks found the market for water sufficiently attractive as to invest in system expansion beyond that specified in the franchise but improvements took place slowly and supplies and access to water remained more limited and less reliable than in many other major American cities.[72] In addition, conflicts between local and state legislation created great difficulties in enforcing even those franchise requirements that did remain relevant—resulting ultimately in the breakdown of franchise control altogether.

The conflicts had their origin back in 1858, when George Ensign, owner of a small spring in San Francisco, obtained a franchise from the California legislature to run pipes through the streets of the city. Because of the small quantity of water supplied by the spring, the franchise did not include normal provisions as to free supply of water for public purposes. Nor did the franchise contain an expiration date. In 1860, some of the early backers of the San Francisco City Waterworks Company left that firm, took over the more favorable Ensign franchise, and began development of water supplies in San Mateo County, south of the city. Organized as the Spring Valley Water Company, the firm introduced this supply into the city in 1862. For a short period, the Spring Valley and San Francisco City companies engaged in active competition for domestic consumers, but in 1865 the Spring Valley company took over the San Francisco City firm.

Two years later, the Spring Valley Company ceased its former practice of supplying the city with water for public purposes free of charge (as specified in the San Francisco City franchise) on the grounds that the Ensign franchise obtained by the company in 1860 did not require it. The city responded by suing the company. The litigation proceeded for ten years, punctuated by a complex series of suits, countersuits, and appeals by both parties. Finally, in 1877, the California Supreme Court issued a ruling holding that *neither* the Ensign or San Francisco City franchises had any validity. The general state waterworks law of 1858, the court held, entirely superseded both franchises.[73]

The inadequacies of existing service, the ineffectuality of franchise control, and legal conflicts with the water company all played a role in spurring efforts by San Francisco to acquire a municipally owned waterworks during the early 1870s. As was the case in Boston, advocates saw municipal ownership as the best means of serving public interests in the provision of abundant water for fire protection, sprinkling streets, and flushing sewers. Extension of pipes to areas of the city not yet served and the provision of water to the poor free of charge constituted additional reasons for public ownership cited by advocates.[74]

This push for municipal ownership failed. In a move that would be bitterly recalled in future water disputes in San Francisco, Spring Valley outmaneuvered the city in 1875 by purchasing for itself a reservoir property in the Calaveras Valley less than two weeks after San Francisco announced its intention to utilize the site source of supply for its proposed municipal system. The city responded by opening negotiations for the purchase of the Spring Valley system, but the two sides failed to reach agreement.[75] In response, the city began condemnation proceedings against Spring Valley during 1878, but this effort was quickly brought to a halt by an opinion of the city attorney that the provisions of the state act providing for condemnation of the Spring Valley property, as well as those permitting the city to construct its own water system without purchasing that of the incumbent company, both violated the state constitution.

In the wake of the disintegration of franchise control and the failure of municipal ownership initiatives, the California State Constitution of 1880 set up a sort of regulatory regime. To the biennially elected San Francisco Board of Supervisors, the constitution gave the right to set water charges to private consumers as well as the price that would be paid by the municipality itself for the use of water for public purposes such as fire protection. Against this, Spring Valley's continued control over investments needed to serve city growth represented a potent bargaining chip against the threat of rate cuts deemed unfair by the waterworks. Because Spring Valley (to a much greater extent than electric utilities or cable television firms) could still make money even if it provided poor service and failed to extend its distribution network, the firm could withhold investment as a bargaining tool against government-ordered rate cuts without greatly damaging its own interests.

At times during the years that followed, the city and the water company did manage to devise workable quid pro quos. In 1882, for example, the Board of Supervisors initiated a $2.50 per month payment to the water company for each fire hydrant placed by the city. In exchange for this payment, Spring Valley began to install larger water mains in some areas of the city to better meet fire protection needs. Spring Valley, however, did not consider the compensation sufficient to carry on an ongoing program of mains replacement adequate to serve the growth of the city and, by 1895, it had become apparent to municipal officials that additional investments would be needed.[76] In response, the Board of Supervisors raised the hydrant rate from $2.50 to $5.00 per month, in return for which the water company embarked on a new program of water mains replacement for the purpose of meeting fire protection needs.[77]

In general, during the 1880s and 1890s, the municipal government pursued a policy of moderate rate reduction that did not threaten the financial viability of Spring Valley. Average cost per thousand gallons of water decreased from twenty-eight cents in 1880 to twenty cents in 1900, according to company figures, while returns to stockholders increased substantially.[78] The water company, in turn, pursued an investment policy that, although conservative and risk-averse in the making of large capital investments to support and anticipate future growth, resulted in system construction catching up to and keeping pace with existing urban development.[79] As a result of this policy, per capita water consumption over the period 1880–1900 increased from fifty-four to seventy-four gallons per day.[80]

Nevertheless, relations between city and water company remained contentious, the level of trust low, and each side vulnerable to opportunistic behavior on the part of the other. Water company officials criticized the power of the Board of Supervisors to set rates as unjust and potentially oppressive because of that body's political accountability to the purchasers and consumers of water.[81] Against what they perceived to be unfair use of this power, water company officials at times showed little hesitation in brandishing their power over investment decisions. In an 1881 communication to the Board of Supervisors, for example, the president of the company responded to a threatened rate cut as follows: "This corporation is organized for profit, not for benevolence. The effect of reduction must be either to force it to discontinue its business, or to compel an economy in its expenditures which will result in insufficient protection to health and property."[82] The Board of Supervisors thus faced an ever-present implicit or explicit threat of an investment strike by the water company.

The board was also disadvantaged in that it possessed inferior access to information concerning water rates than did the company, and faced several difficulties in processing what information it could obtain. Whereas Spring Valley was represented before the city by executives (such as company president Howard and chief engineer Schussler) who devoted their full professional attention to the affairs of the waterworks, served for long tenures, and defined the form in which information was presented; the Board of Supervisors experienced a high degree of turnover.[83] Placing the Board of Supervisors at a further disadvantage, members served only part-time, had an enormously variegated set of responsibilities, and had little staff support.[84] As a result, while Spring Valley was required by law to provide the supervisors with all relevant information needed for regulation, the supervisors had limited means (and time) to independently examine the facts provided by the company or to question their interpretation. At times, mayors and supervisors did express their distrust of information furnished by Spring Valley. These officials, however, possessed neither the resources nor the sustained commitment needed to put together a factual challenge to the firm's contention that the high price of water in San Francisco resulted from the unique difficulties of the city's hilly terrain and semi-arid climate.[85]

A resurgence of calls for municipal ownership during the 1890s reflected growing dissatisfaction with perceived weaknesses in municipal control. Citing "fictitious valuations" by the Spring Valley Company and its "exorbitant" charges, for example, Mayor Sutro called for construction of a municipally owned waterworks in his 1895 inaugural speech.[86] As further reason for municipal ownership, advocates cited widespread beliefs that the rate-setting process itself engendered corruption and dishonesty. An 1897 Board of Supervisors committee report made this point as follows:

> These annually recurring investigations by the Board of Supervisors are popularly believed to be schools for perjury, in which men, who during the rest of the year, are regarded as honorable business and professional men, appear before the public in the role of fraudulent concealers of facts, special pleaders, and falsifiers.
>
> And when the investigations are completed and the rates for the year are fixed, the belief becomes deeply impressed on the public mind that a "Solid Seven" or a "Solid Nine" have once more been bribed to violate their ante-election pledges and to betray their constituents. The moral effect of all this upon the community is necessarily pernicious.[87]

A municipal plant, advocates believed, could provide consumers with cheaper water, not only by eliminating these sources of inflated charges, but because the city could obtain financing more inexpensively than could a private firm.[88] Advocates also argued that only through municipal ownership could property owners be made to pay their fair share of costs for fire protection. Because of the political difficulty of raising property taxes in San Francisco during the late nineteenth century, particularly for the purpose of paying money to so unpopular and unaccountable an entity as the Spring Valley Water Company, hydrant payments in San Francisco remained very low. As a consequence, water consumers actually subsidized large property owners, who enjoyed a disproportionate benefit from investments in main enlargements made for fire protection purposes. Municipal ownership, advocates believed, constituted the only politically feasible means to shift this burden to property owners.[89]

Accommodation between San Francisco and the Spring Valley Water Company broke down entirely over the years 1897 through 1903. As each side took steps to defend itself against what it perceived to be opportunistic and unfair behavior on the part of the other, a stalemate developed that served the interests of neither. San Francisco, under the leadership of reform Mayor James D. Phelan and his successors, sought to protect the city against what officials saw as the water company's continued monopolistic exploitation by ordering substantial cuts in water rates, performing (for the first time) an independent valuation of Spring Valley's property, and taking steps to acquire a municipally owned plant with or without purchase of the existing system.

City-ordered cuts in charges to private consumers amounted to 13 percent in 1898, 10 percent in 1900, and an additional 7 percent in 1902.[90] The Board of Supervisors reduced hydrant payments as well, despite previous implicit agreements with Spring Valley to maintain existing charges in return for water company investments in system improvements. Released in 1901, city engineer Grunsky's valuation of the Spring Valley system struck a further blow against the company. Compared to the approximately $45,500,000 Spring Valley claimed as the worth of its property, Grunsky placed the water system's value at only about $24,250,000.[91] This valuation not only provided a justification for even further city rate cuts, but furnished a basis for negotiating municipal purchase of the system at a low price.

San Francisco had taken its first major step toward municipal ownership in 1898 with the passage of a new city charter pronouncing in favor of municipal ownership of all public utilities and committing the city to specific steps for the acquisition of a municipally owned waterworks through original construction, condemnation proceedings, or a negotiated purchase. By 1902, the city's efforts to acquire its own waterworks had become increasingly focused on gaining access to the prime reservoir site furnished by the Hetch Hetchy Valley in Yosemite National Park in the Sierra Nevada. Located about 150 miles from the city in a protected watershed, a reservoir at Hetch Hetchy could be developed to provide a quantity of water sufficient to serve the growth of San Francisco indefinitely.[92] Selection of the site marked a major departure from Spring Valley's strategy of incremental development of nearby water sources and conservatism in making large capital investments. For many years, at least in part for bargaining purposes, municipal officials left undecided the question of whether they would actually purchase Spring Valley's system or construct duplicate storage facilities and a distribution system as well.[93]

Spring Valley responded to these threats by slashing capital investments in system improvements needed to serve the growth of the city and by initiating litigation to overturn both the city's rate cuts and its valuation figures.[94] In a 1908 speech to stockholders, Spring Valley president A. H. Payson defined the position of the firm during this period as follows: "The City, during the ten years or so which must pass before a Sierra supply can be had, cannot get water except through the Spring Valley Water Company. The company cannot keep the City supplied during this time without making large investments, and the money for these investments cannot be had from private sources without such radical change in the relations between the City and the company as will offer reasonable security for a continued and fair return on the present value of the property . . . as also some assurance that . . . it will not . . . be thrown back on the owners' hands when the City brings in its own supply."[95]

Lack of investment slowed development of new neighborhoods and seriously hampered the capacity of the water system to meet the increased fire protection demands created by new building construction.[96] The conflagration that followed the San Francisco earthquake of 1906 brought the dangers of the situation dramatically into relief. In addition to extensively damaging the Spring Valley system, the earthquake rendered it virtually useless for fighting the fires that followed.[97] Although subsequent investigation showed that neither company nor city could have foreseen the severity of events that led to this system failure, the disaster clearly underlined the need for major system improvements.

The stalemate between city and company, however, continued to block such investment. On May 19, 1910, for example, the Board of Fire Underwriters sent a notice to the Board of Supervisors "urgently" warning of inadequate water pressures and supplies for fire protection in large portions of the city's Western Addition and Mission districts. "Until a proper supply is developed," the notice warned, "every building added during the wonderful growth of the city will increase the danger of conflagration."[98] In a report issued over the summer of 1910, the National

Board of Fire Underwriters described the Spring Valley system as one barely functioning at the limit of its developed capacity.[99]

The stalemate between city and water company was eventually resolved but it took a long time. As was the case in Boston, the provision of specialized capital investments by the city for solely public goods purposes proved to be the least controversial and most easily accomplished step. Two years after the 1906 conflagration, the voters of San Francisco approved a $5,500,000 bond issue for city construction of an auxiliary water system for fire protection that would include a system of cisterns in the central areas of the city, high-pressure water mains for fire protection, duplicate pumping stations that could be used to supply the mains with salt water in case of emergency, and two fire boats for the same purpose.[100]

The effort to acquire an entire municipally owned waterworks faced considerably greater obstacles. Although San Francisco was riven by many forms of political and social conflicts during the period, most of the city's voters supported the project, as did all major newspapers and business organizations. At the same time, however, the Hetch Hetchy Valley was one of the outstanding natural features of Yosemite National Park and undertaking the project required the permission of the United States Department of the Interior. San Francisco's efforts to obtain this permission added a new dimension to an already complex set of conflicts over waterworks development. On top of the old set of contentions between the municipality of San Francisco and the Spring Valley Water Company, the city's prospective inundation of the Hetch Hetchy Valley sparked one of the first of the twentieth century's great national environmental controversies. Project supporters asserted that supplying water to a growing city represented a far more important public interest than preserving a few campsites, meadows, and waterfalls that would only be visited by a few people anyway. Opponents of the city's plans were disparaged as sentimental "cat's paws" in the witting or unwitting service of the greedy and monopolistic Spring Valley Water Company. An editorial laid before members of the United States Senate in a special December 2, 1913 Washington edition of the *San Francisco Examiner* expressed this perspective as follows: "The campaign carried out against the proposition to allow San Francisco to get a supply of mountain water from the Hetch Hetchy Valley . . . is nothing more than a corporation campaign to maintain the grip of an oppressive and inadequate private water monopoly upon the city of San Francisco."[101] Without hesitation, the editorial identified the growth of San Francisco that would be made possible by Hetch Hetchy with both broader public interests and individual aspirations: "thousands have San Francisco as their goal. There they expect to make their homes. But what hope have they of establishing themselves and their families in a city where the suburbs are denied water or where home seekers are met with water famine notices declaring that a great thirst is impending and that drought has claimed the city for its own."[102]

Some preservationist opponents of Hetch Hetchy, by contrast, contested this identification of economic with broader public interests taken for granted by the project's backers. Influential preservationist John Muir expressed his disdain in religious terms: "The temple destroyers, devotees of ravaging commercialism, seem to have a perfect contempt for Nature, and, instead of lifting their eyes to the God of the mountains, lift them to the Almighty dollar. Dam Hetch-Hetchy! As well dam for water-tanks the people's cathedrals and churches for no holier temple has ever been consecrated by the heart of man."[103]

The fight over Hetch Hetchy briefly noted here is of great historical significance in its own right and can be viewed as something of a harbinger of future environmental conflicts in the United States. At least in immediate terms, however, the advocates of municipal ownership and natural resource development won and the advocates of preservation lost. With passage of the Raker Act in December of 1913, the United States government granted the municipality of San Francisco permission to dam up the valley of the Hetch Hetchy for use as both a water supply for the city and for electric power development. San Francisco's municipal government soon began work on building the system. Because of a variety of financial and construction delays, however, the first water from Hetch Hetchy was introduced into the city only in 1934.

In the meantime, the disposition of the Spring Valley properties still had to be worked out. Because of the economic waste involved in building a duplicate system, and because Spring Valley possessed the best available sites for storing large quantities of water near San Francisco, municipal acquisition of the Spring Valley distribution plant and reservoirs was the preferred option. Unfortunately, this plan faced the stumbling block of the valuation issue, as had the problem of rate regulation earlier. Even when city and company officials succeeded in negotiating a price for the Spring Valley property, San Francisco's electorate repeatedly refused to grant the two-thirds majority needed to carry the bond issues to finance the purchase. The bond issues foundered on arguments that the price of the properties was too high, that incurring additional debt to purchase Spring Valley might endanger the financial viability of the Hetch Hetchy project, and that the Spring Valley system was so decrepit that the property was not worth purchasing in any case. The Board of Supervisors and Spring Valley did succeed in actually negotiating a purchase price for the waterworks in November and December of 1909. The price, $35,000,000, represented a compromise—considerably above the value of about $24,400,000 placed by the city engineer but considerably below the $40,000,000 claimed by Spring Valley.[104] Unexpectedly, however, incoming Mayor P. H. McCarthy declared against the bond issue, citing both the danger that passage would result in Hetch Hetchy exceeding the city's bond limit and the poor condition of the Spring Valley property.[105] At the referendum held in 1910, enough San Francisco voters found such arguments persuasive to prevent the bond issue from receiving the two-thirds majority needed for passage by a close margin.

With the ascension of Mayor Rolph in 1912, city officials again began to work toward a municipal purchase of Spring Valley. Controversy, however, continued. Put before the voters in 1915, 1921, and 1927, bond issues for the purchase of Spring Valley obtained majority support each time but fell short of the two-thirds proportion required. As was the case in 1910, opposition focused on the inadequacies of the Spring Valley system, allegations that the purchase price was too high, and fears that acquisition would endanger Hetch Hetchy. Finally, as completion of Hetch Hetchy drew near, a bond issue for purchase of Spring Valley won approval of the required two-thirds margin of the city's voters in 1928.

As it became clear that San Francisco was committed to eventually buying the property, some investment by Spring Valley in system development did resume over the course of this period. As early as 1913, Spring Valley felt confident enough that the city would not construct a duplicate system to begin work on its Alameda storage project to increase water supplies. But investments remained limited and main extension policies were very conservative.[106] The impasse between city and company began to further unravel with the assumption of jurisdiction over water rates by the California Railroad Commission late in 1915 and a court ruling two years later finally settling the rate litigation begun in 1903.[107] The commission made an effort to address the problems of rate-making and arranging for capital investment in a 1920 decision. The decision set a valuation on the Spring Valley properties of $37,000,000, ordered the company to carry out its future development plans with a view toward eventual incorporation into the Hetch Hetchy system, and specified that future work by the company would be added to the price that would be eventually paid by the city. On the basis of this decision, Spring Valley gave the city a ten-year purchase option for its plant at the $37,000,000 price specified, with provision for an additional $1,000,000 payment for system improvements in the meantime.

As a kind of halfway house between private and governmental ownership, the arrangement proved cumbersome at best. For any expansion of water supply and distribution facilities to take place at all required either steep rate increases so that amortization could take place quickly or detailed case-by-case-negotiations to ensure Spring Valley that its expenditures would be reimbursed by the city when it finally bought the system. In 1922, for example, Spring Valley agreed to bring water from Alameda County into San Francisco by renting a conduit built by the city that would eventually be used by the Hetch Hetchy system. But costs to consumers were high. To stay within the price limit specified by the city's purchase option, the Railroad Commission granted Spring Valley a 20 percent rate increase to finance the needed expenditures for the project.

Only for the most desperately needed water supply facilities were such awkward and costly agreements reached at all. As during earlier years, investment in water distribution continued to lag.[108] Genuine resolution came only in 1930, when San Francisco's municipal government purchased the Spring Valley outright. With this purchase, San Francisco finally joined the ranks of other major cities in the United States with a municipally owned waterworks. Municipal control of water supply and distribution did not come cheaply. For purchase of the Spring Valley facilities alone, the municipal government paid about $41,000,000. Another $64,000,000 went toward municipal construction of the Hetch Hetchy

Dam and Reservoir, faculties for the conveyance of the water and for the electric power generation and transmission facilities developed as part of the system. But even with a reduction of 10 percent in 1934, water rates proved sufficient to support operation and debt service on the project.

Private and Municipally Owned Waterworks in Seattle

Located, like San Francisco, on the west coast of the United States, Seattle rose to prominence as an urban center more recently than did either San Francisco or Boston. Indeed, the settlers who established Seattle landed at the site only in 1853 and the city has yet to celebrate its bicentennial. In Seattle, as in San Francisco, controversies over government versus private ownership of waterworks took place during the later years of the nineteenth century—well after such issues had already been resolved in Boston. Private waterworks development, however, was not nearly so drawn out a process in Seattle as in San Francisco. As in Boston, Seattle's municipal government acquired ownership of the city's waterworks during the early stages of a period of rapid urban growth and expansion.

Not surprisingly, given its relatively brief experience with private ownership, Seattle's municipal government did not experiment with nearly so wide a variety of franchising and regulatory arrangements as did San Francisco's. But, as in San Francisco, municipal officials in Seattle did put in place arrangements designed to recompense its privately owned waterworks for making investments in facilities devoted to specifically public purposes such as fire protection. Here, too, unfortunately, the recourse failed and severe service problems arose.

The history of waterworks development in Seattle can be said to have its beginnings during the 1870s. Although few people lived in the nascent urban center as yet, the place was already growing and at least some of its inhabitants had great hopes for the future. Henry Yesler and other leading Seattle businessmen came before the Seattle City Council in May of 1876 and offered to build and operate a water supply and distribution system for the community in return for an exclusive twenty-five year franchise, "jurisdiction over all streams and sources from which their supply of water may be obtained," and a specified monthly rate of two dollars per faucet. As a means to ensure compensation for investments made for fire protection, the entrepreneurs also called for the levy of a three-mills property tax assessment to be paid directly to their firm.[109]

For Yesler and his partners, private business enterprise and involvement in public city building initiatives easily blended together. Yesler had been a resident of Seattle since 1853; his community activities included establishment of the settlement's first sawmill and construction of its first meeting hall, real estate development and speculation, and service as the city's first mayor in 1869.[110] But however impeccable Yesler and his associates' civic credentials may have been, the prospect of granting to a private firm a direct claim on tax revenues as well as legal monopoly over water provision proved too much for many Seattle residents and the proposal quickly went down to defeat. Even while acknowledging the need for public subsidies and expressing support for the development of a waterworks of some kind, an editorial in Seattle's *Daily Pacific Tribune* framed the issues as follows: "No well-wisher of Seattle would like to have its people burdened and ground down for twenty-five long years with an oppressive measure of any sort even to escape the ills now so threateningly overcharging us. If that time is too long, cut it short; if the three-mill tax is too heavy, reduce it; if the other privileges asked are too exclusive, tone them down. . . . All other cities either subsidize their water companies, or own the waterworks themselves, and Seattle must do the same."[111]

About five and one-half years later, Seattle did begin issuing waterworks franchises to private firms. This time, however, the municipal government employed a different and far more laissez-faire approach. Rather than awarding the kind of exclusive grant requested by Yesler and his associates, Seattle issued a number of nonexclusive twenty-five-year waterworks franchises on request to individuals and firms. The franchises represented little more than a license to go into the water business. They contained no requirements as to quality of water furnished to private consumers, extension of mains, or provision of specifically public services. Nor did the they afford recipients any legal shelter from competition.

Whether Seattle officials expected recipients of these franchises to compete with one another and build duplicate distribution systems is unclear. In any case, however, such competition did not arise. Most of the recipients owned small springs and streams and confined their activities to the construction of small local systems designed to serve the domestic water needs of neighbors. Only two companies built systems that can properly be classified as waterworks—the Spring Hill Water Company and the Union Water Company. The two companies constructed their systems in different areas of the city and did not compete with one another despite the absence of legal barriers in the way of doing so. Spring Hill controlled by far the larger of the two systems, and quickly emerged as a de facto monopoly in Seattle's commercial center and in the locales in which the bulk of the city's people lived.

Recognizing the dominant position of Spring Hill, the city council passed a rate-setting ordinance soon after the company began operation. In 1884, Seattle and Spring Hill also reached agreement on terms under which the company would be compensated for fire protection investments. The contract provided for Seattle to pay Spring Hill a flat fee of $7.50 per month for each fire hydrant installed on the company's mains. In return, Spring Hill agreed to keep the company's "mains and machinery in repair so that the said city shall be supplied at all times with a sufficient amount of water and at such pressure and force at each of said hydrants as to be sufficient and available for effective use in case of fire."[112] It is possible that this arrangement might have worked if Seattle's growth had continued at the relatively modest pace of preceding years but it was during the 1880s that Seattle's rise to prominence as a major urban center began. From 1880 through 1890, the population of Seattle increased more than tenfold, from 3,533 to 42,837.

The Spring Hill Water Company did take some steps to cope with this growth. To improve the capacity and reliability of its system, for example, the company built a five million gallon storage reservoir in 1887 and 1888. As the inhabited areas of the city began to stretch further during the 1880s, Spring Hill also extended some distribution lines. Nevertheless, large areas of Seattle remained completely without access to piped-in water supplies. Furthermore, investment in facilities required for protection against fire also lagged. Much of the company's distribution system, for example, consisted of two and one-half inch pipe. Not much bigger than a garden hose, such pipe may have been adequate to supply ordinary domestic consumption but was of little use for fire protection. Even in central areas of the city served by larger water mains, the system's ability to cope with large-scale conflagration remained in doubt. According to an 1888 report prepared by Seattle's fire chief, for example, pressures in the Spring Hill system's mains were generally sufficient to cope with small fires. Overall capacities, however, would not suffice, the report predicted, in the event of an "extensive conflagration" requiring many streams.[113]

An all-too-graphic demonstration of the inadequacies of the Spring Hill system took place about a year after the release of this report. On June 6, 1889, Seattle burned down. Starting in the basement of a store, the conflagration quickly burned through Seattle's heart, leaving virtually no buildings intact.[114] The efforts of the fire department to fight the blaze fell short largely because of the inadequacy of the water supply. According to an account in the *Seattle Daily Press* for June 7, 1889: "There were numbers of willing firemen, but from the first the water was at a provoking low pressure. The firemen fought mightily, but vainly."[115]

Decisions for municipal waterworks ownership followed hard on the heels of this disaster. At an election held on July 8, 1889, the citizens of Seattle voted by the overwhelming margin of 1,785 to 51 to issue bonds of up to one million dollars to acquire the Spring Hill system and to build a municipally owned waterworks. In a last-ditch bid to stave off municipal takeover, president Gatzert of Spring Hill admitted that the waterworks had performed inadequately in containing the June fire but excused the failure on the grounds that the company could not afford to make system improvements so long as the city might establish itself as a competitor. As an alternative to municipal ownership, Gatzert proposed that the city extend the duration of his company's franchise in exchange for the firm investing in system improvements. Perhaps not surprisingly, the city refused Gatzert's proposal and after some haggling over price, purchased the Spring Hill system for $352,000.[116] The city followed up this transaction with the purchase of the much smaller Union Water Company system during the summer of 1891. Public health rather than fire protection concerns played the major role in motivating this latter and far more modest purchase.[117]

The rapidity and decisiveness with which Seattle turned to municipal ownership cannot be attributed to the great fire alone. As early as 1888, elected officials in Seattle were proposing construction of a municipal waterworks as a means to obtain more abundant supplies, higher-quality

View of Seattle after the fire of 1889. *Courtesy of the Seattle Museum of History and Industry.*

fire protection, extension of service throughout the city, and flushing of streets and sewers to reduce "surface filth" believed to threaten public health. By offering abundant supplies and promotional rates, officials asserted, a municipally owned waterworks could also be used to induce manufacturers to locate in the city.[118]

Fears as well as hopes concerning Seattle's future economic prospects also played a role in driving calls for municipal waterworks ownership. Seattle was isolated from more populated regions of the country by distance and hostile terrain; the city's prospects for growth during the 1880s and 1890s depended not only on the promotional, trading, and city-building activities of local entrepreneurs and public officials but on attracting capital and investment from outside. Local elites welcomed such investment and indeed worked hard to attract it. At the same time, however, ongoing battles to obtain vital railroad connections to the east during the 1870s and 1880s also left many Seattle leaders highly suspicious of the motives and good intent of distant capitalists. In this context, an 1888 report by the Seattle Common Council called for the city to acquire its own waterworks not only as a means to obtain better service but as a kind of insurance against outsiders gaining control of a resource deemed vital to the survival and growth of the community: "We ought not to be dependent in the matter of water supply, which may be called the life blood of a city, on the caprice or rapacity of any corporation. . . . The stocks of these companies have been up to the present time mainly owned by our own citizens, and this has been a measure of protection. But we have no guarantee for the future that this stock will not pass into foreign hands, who will not scruple to exact from us all that the business will bear and their charters authorize." [119]

On the whole, the turn to municipal ownership in Seattle substantially met the expectations of its advocates. During the years immediately following the takeover, the municipal government extended water distribution far more aggressively than had the Spring Hill Company. By December 31, 1891, the municipal government had extended the twenty-six miles of distribution main laid by the Spring Hill Company into a system of sixty-one miles. By the end of 1892, the system had reached ninety-two and one-half miles. As in Boston, the city's fire chief criticized some of the facilities initially developed under municipal auspices as inadequate for fire protection needs, largely because of the continued presence of pipe four inches and under. But even he acknowledged that under municipal ownership, provision of water for fire protection was far superior to that of early years. According to the report of the fire department for 1892, the expansion gave "a water supply for fire protection to a large district heretofore without that protection. There is still room for this branch of the service to be extended, and we would recommend that more hydrants be placed in the central portion of the city and that all four inch water mains . . . be replaced with larger ones, as the water supply for fire purposes from these mains is insufficient." [120]

Great increases in water consumption accompanied the expansion of the waterworks. Over the years 1890 through 1893 alone, average daily consumption of water increased from about 4,100,000 gallons per day to about 4,900,000 gallons. Faced with the prospect of indefinite increases in the cost of pumping water from Lake Washington and likely pollution problems, Seattle turned to the mountains for a gravity-fed supply of water from a protected watershed. In association with this decision, a second public-private ownership controversy briefly arose in Seattle during the fall of 1895. The controversy concerned whether Seattle should itself construct and own a gravity-fed system from the Cedar River or permit a private firm to construct the works and sell both water to the municipal government for distribution in the city and hydro-power to private consumers. Opponents of municipal construction argued that the city's present water supply from Lake Washington was adequate and that the city could not afford to risk taking on any more debt, even in the form of revenue bonds backed by water rates. Supporters of municipal ownership cited both the profitability of the publicly owned system to the municipal government and suspicions that if a private firm were permitted to develop Cedar River it might uses its monopoly position to choke off the city's development. These arguments won out, with the citizens of Seattle opting for municipal construction in a referendum held on December 10, 1895.

In 1901, Seattle completed construction of an aqueduct to the Cedar River twenty-five miles southeast of the city. The pipeline had a capacity of more than twenty-two million gallons per day, more than twice the average daily consumption of about 8,700,000 gallons during 1900. While the system quickly needed expansion because of the enormous increase in Seattle's population from 81,000 in 1900 to almost 240,000 in 1910, the basic pattern of development had been set. With comparatively little controversy, the citizens of Seattle voted in March of 1908 to approve a bond issue of $2,250,000 for the construction of a second pipeline for Cedar River water. The pipeline was completed on June 21, 1909, giving the water system a total capacity of 66,000,000 gallons per day.

Shifts in waterworks pricing and financing also took place. As in San Francisco, the municipal government initially relied on water rates alone to recoup the costs of waterworks acquisition, construction, and operation. Writing in January of 1893, however, superintendent of waterworks Wilson criticized this sole reliance on water rates as an unfair subsidy by water consumers to property owners. "Thus far, our financial policy has been based on the theory that the consumer or ratepayer, is the only person benefited by a water supply, but this is far from being a true view of the case. . . . Every acre of land within the city limits has a higher value by reason of the fact that the city owns a water supply capable of extension over the entire area, as rapidly as means will justify. Every insurance rate in the city is lower by reason the adequate fire protection, made possible by hundreds of hydrants, maintained with constant pressure and supply." [121]

As a way to make property owners pay their fair share, Wilson proposed cutting water rates by about a third and imposing a "general water tax" of three cents for every hundred feet of property. Although the proposal was seconded by the mayor, the municipal government did not carry out this recommendation. Three years later, however, a new charter for the city was adopted, under which local improvements could be financed through the levy of special assessments on the property benefited. Over time, Seattle's municipal government took advantage of this provision to shift to property owners a portion of the costs of waterworks extension and expansion. As of January of 1914, such special assessments accounted for about a third of the capital cost of Seattle's waterworks plant, exclusive of real estate.[122]

Conclusion

As can be seen in the preceding accounts, the histories of waterworks ownership and development in Boston, San Francisco, and Seattle were far from identical with one another. In Boston, private waterworks development took place on a modest scale during the early decades of the nineteenth century. In San Francisco, by contrast, the Spring Valley Water Company undertook relatively large-scale waterworks development over a span of decades stretching from the 1850s and 1860s through the 1920s. Indeed, the system ultimately developed by Spring Valley far exceeded in scale that of the original Cochituate system developed by Boston's municipal government. In Seattle, private waterworks development also took place during the later years of the nineteenth century, but for a far shorter period than in either Boston or San Francisco. The regulatory, franchising, and contracting arrangements under which private waterworks development took place in each city also differed, as did the exact sequence of events that brought about turns to municipal ownership.

Nevertheless, resemblances are unmistakable. Although initial development took place at different times, private firms initially operated waterworks in Boston, San Francisco, and Seattle alike. Although regulatory, franchising, and contracting arrangements differed, arranging for provision of specifically public services and for investments believed necessary to accommodate growth made for severe problems in all three cities. And in all three cities, such problems played roles in driving turns to municipal ownership. Under municipal ownership, waterworks problems did not magically disappear. In all three cities, however, turns to municipal ownership were accompanied by increased investment in facilities and improved provision of specifically public services.

Nor were these patterns unique to Boston, San Francisco, and Seattle. During the early decades of the nineteenth century, for example, relationships between private water companies and municipal governments in other rapidly growing major east coast cities such as New York City and Baltimore were equally if not more contentious than in Boston. In these locales, also, private waterworks firms demonstrated a distinct lack of eagerness to invest large sums of money in system expansion. According to historian Nelson Blake: "The companies laid their pipes through the districts that promised the largest returns and left the poorer or more remote districts without a supply. The larger the cities grew, the more serious this lag in providing an essential service became. Moreover, the companies naturally gave priority to the needs of their private customers. Some provision, though rarely adequate, was made for fire hydrants; water for other important civic purposes was usually not available."[123] As in Boston, turns to municipal ownership in New York City and Baltimore went hand-in-hand with expansive development of supply and distribution facilities. New York City's great Croton system, for example, completed during the summer of 1842, revolutionized water provision in that city in many of the same ways as did completion of the Cochituate in Boston.

Later in the nineteenth century, the sorts of conflicts and problems that prompted municipal ownership in both San Francisco and Seattle also arose in other cities. In Houston, for example, historian Harold Platt reports, "the quality of service provided by the [privately owned] waterworks remained far below any other utility," during the latter part of the nineteenth century. Houston's water company drew its supplies from an increasingly polluted nearby bayou, exercised great conservatism in extending its distribution system into new neighborhoods, and maintained a "niggardly attitude toward replacing obsolete distributive pipes," depriving firefighters of adequate water pressures.[124] Because of the limited availability of water for fire protection, Houston property owners could not obtain fire insurance without paying a special tariff. An actual fire in August 1894 that destroyed the Saint Joseph Infirmary and killed two nuns further underlined the seriousness of the situation. Similar problems arose in Los Angeles as that city's population began to increase during the later years of the nineteenth century. The water company serving Los Angeles, critics alleged, charged unduly high prices for serving private consumers and failed to provide the quantities and pressures of water needed to protect against fire dangers.

In both Houston and Los Angeles, more expansive system development took place and provision of public services improved once waterworks came under municipal ownership. In Houston, the municipal government took over the city's waterworks in 1905 and immediately began to invest in improvements and extensions to the water distribution network. To reduce waste, a program to install water meters was also initiated.[125] In Los Angeles, the municipal government took over the city's waterworks in 1901 and initiated an even more radical set of changes. Municipal officials in Los Angeles viewed ambitious waterworks development as a key to the future growth and greatness of the city. The municipal government rebuilt supply and distribution facilities, cut rates to consumers dramatically, and still managed to make a profit from sale of water.[126]

These steps, however, were but a prelude to construction of one of the most epic and controversial developmental public works efforts of the early twentieth century—the Owens Valley project. The enterprise involved capture by Los Angeles for its own use of river and later ground water in the Owens Valley about 240 miles away from the city. With completion of the Owens River Aqueduct in 1913, any threat of water shortage in Los Angeles was instantly transformed into a reality of water surplus. The immediate result, for which canny land speculators were already well prepared, was a land boom in the San Fernando Valley as Los Angeles annexed the area and opened it up to irrigated agriculture. As the area became urbanized during the years that followed, the Los Angeles Department of Water and Power continued to single-mindedly and sometimes ruthlessly devote itself to the task of capturing for the city the large quantities of low-cost water believed necessary for the growth of Los Angeles and its regional economy.

The histories of waterworks development in Boston, San Francisco, Seattle, and other cities presented here can be viewed from more than one perspective. Most obviously, they can be seen as accounts of municipal government assertiveness in the face of economic and transaction cost problems in arranging for private waterworks to furnish important public services and to make the investments needed to accommodate urban growth. Whiggish as it may appear, such a perspective does have a degree of validity. But there is more to the story than this. On the one hand, attributes of waterworks technology shaped and constrained the workings of ownership, regulatory, and franchising arrangements in American cities. But on the other hand, political and institutional arrangements also played roles in shaping the technology. Problems that drove municipal governments to acquire their own waterworks and to invest aggressively in system development once they did so were not merely technical in nature. The reluctance and inability of municipal governments to regulate and restrict property owners and consumers also contributed. The difficulties faced by the Cochituate Water Board in attempting to convince residents of Boston to conserve water are illustrative. Whatever the abstract merits of the case, politically, developing new sources of supply and beefing up distribution arrangements represented a path of lesser resistance in Boston during the 1860s and 1870s than attempting to cajole or coerce the residents of the city into not wasting water.

When American waterworks experiences are compared with those in western European cities, the significance of constraints and limits on governmental authority in the United States in driving aggressive waterworks investment stands out in even sharper relief. In the United States, municipal governments were generally reluctant to enact or enforce anything more than the most modest of building regulations in the face of protests by affected property owners and interests in the building industry.[127] In the absence of strong and consistently enforced regulation, American cities came to rely heavily (if not always successfully) upon their fire departments and waterworks to quench the large numbers of fires that inevitably broke out and to protect themselves against large-scale conflagration.

In France, Great Britain, and other western European countries, by contrast, local and national governments relied heavily upon building codes and regulations concerning land use to fulfill a range of urban, esthetic, and even symbolic goals. In France, building codes specifically for fire protection purposes had their roots in exercise of the royal prerogative. A 1607 enactment by Henri IV, for example, required owners of property on main thoroughfares (legally the property of the king) to obtain governmental permission in order to build houses. Government officials used this requirement to exercise at least a modest supervision of the fire safety of the buildings constructed in the larger towns of France. In 1783, a royal decree established height restrictions for houses in Paris based upon the methods of construction and the width of the streets. Although these rulings were based on arbitrary royal authority, they were incorporated into the legal codes of French cities after the Revolution.[128] In England, the imposition of strict building codes dates back to proclamations and acts of Parliament in 1666 after a great fire destroyed the bulk of the built-up area of London. The acts limited the use of wood in building and set strict height limits for buildings that depended on the width of streets.

Such regulation contributed to the shaping of urban environments less fire-prone than their American counterparts and less dependent on networked systems of water supply and distribution as a consequence. When fires did occur, blazes did not generally spread to large areas even in the absence of well-developed water supply and distribution networks. Up until the last decades of the nineteenth century, for example, many parts of London enjoyed only intermittent water supplies. When fire broke out in such areas, efforts to quench the blaze could not even begin until water company representatives arrived to open the necessary valves. Despite the resulting delays, London experienced far less severe fire losses than did many American cities with far better developed water supply and distribution networks.[129]

It is easy to discern a degree of irony in all of this. Municipal governments in American cities had neither the power to impinge on established property interests nor the sort of access to the national treasury drawn upon by Haussmann and his successors to remake Paris. Yet it was in part because of this very lack of power that municipal governments acquired waterworks and developed systems on a far more extensive scale in than did their western European counterparts.[130] Reluctance to exercise power in one domain made for increased pressures to do so in another.

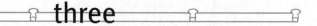

three

Electric Utilities

ON MAY 26, 1898, THE VOTERS OF SAN FRANCISCO approved a new municipal charter declaring it to be "the purpose and intention of the people of the City and the County that its public utilities should be gradually acquired and ultimately owned by the City and County."[1] Although turnout for the special charter election was light and the margin of approval narrow, victory for charter revision represented a remarkable political achievement for San Francisco's wealthy reform mayor James Phelan. After years of effort, Phelan and his allies had managed to marshal an unlikely coalition of leading businessmen represented by the Merchants' Association, neighborhood improvement groups, and some labor leaders in support of a new vision of urban governance. A new world of greater prosperity and a richer quality of life for the citizens of San Francisco could be brought into being, the reformers promised, through higher taxes, increased spending on public improvements and education, and the imposition of civil service requirements and administrative reforms. Municipal ownership of both electric utilities and waterworks represented important elements of the reformers' vision. "Civil Service Reform and City ownership," Mayor Phelan promised, "not only will give better service at lower cost, but it will eliminate from the City Hall the constant presence of a corrupting power, and will enlist in the cause of good municipal government those citi-

74

zens, otherwise worthy, who as directors, stockholders and mangers of public corporations, selfishly, if not criminally encourage or connive at fraud and rascality."[2]

Although municipal involvement in a bitter waterfront labor dispute had split Phelan's reform coalition by the end of 1901, San Francisco's major newspapers and leading businessmen remained solidly committed to plans for a municipally owned waterworks during the years that followed.[3] And in the face of the numerous obstacles and setbacks recounted in the previous chapter, the municipal ownership forces eventually triumphed and San Francisco finally obtained a publicly owned waterworks during the 1930s.

The outcome was quite different in electric utilities, however, despite commitments to public ownership in the city charter, the construction by San Francisco of a hydroelectric generating plant as part of its Hetch Hetchy water project during the 1920s, and federal prohibitions on power sales from that plant to a private utility.[4] San Francisco's elected leaders did pursue efforts to acquire a municipally owned electric utility during the 1920s and 1930s. In sharp contrast to the case in waterworks, however, municipal policy was inconsistent, major newspapers and business groups were opposed, and the city's plans repeatedly failed to gain the required margins of support when referenda were held. Calls for government ownership are still heard, but distribution of electricity in San Francisco remains in the hands of the privately owned Pacific Gas and Electric Company.

As shall be seen, many aspects of San Francisco's experiences with electric utility development were unique. The defeats experienced by municipal ownership advocates, however, were not. Historically, the evolution of government involvement in electric utilities has resembled that in other networked systems in the United States far more closely than has been the case in waterworks. Whereas almost every major city in the United States had a government-owned waterworks by the first decade of the twentieth century, ownership of electric utilities, like that of gas manufacturing and distribution systems, railroads, and telephone and telegraph networks, remains largely private.

Along with survival of private ownership came shifts in the locus of governmental authority and decision making. As in waterworks, a large share of the policy making "action" in electric utilities initially took place at the municipal level. To a far greater degree than in waterworks, however, state governments increasingly came to restrict roles played by municipalities and to themselves assert forms of authority over electric utilities and other networked systems. Imposition of forms of state regulation over electric utilities in particular dates from 1887 in Massachusetts and from 1907 in Wisconsin and New York. By 1935, regulatory commissions possessing the authority both to limit rates charged by private utility firms and to protect the enterprises against duplicative competition had been put in place in thirty-seven states and the District of Columbia.

At least in part, the trend can be understood as a product of Progressive Era faith in apolitical administration and in the uses of professional expertise to reconcile public and private interests. Municipal governments, advocates of regulation asserted, functioned over too confined a geographic area, lacked the expertise, and were too easily influenced by narrow private interests to be entrusted with either oversight or operation of great public utility enterprises. By contrast, advocates averred, the best features of both government and private ownership of industries with "natural monopoly" attributes could be preserved if the right sort of state regulation was put in place. Under regulation, it was claimed, the initiative and enterprise characteristic of private ownership could be maintained even as impartial and professional regulatory agencies protected the community against both monopolistic abuses and the waste and inefficiency arising from unsustainable and duplicative competition.[5]

Whatever regulation's apolitical pretensions, however, its history has been awash in politics. Heartfelt calls for reform and good government, jockeying for position among interest groups, and attempts on the part of utility firms themselves to secure and advance their goals all played roles in affecting outcomes. For proprietors of electric utility firms, state legislatures and regulatory agencies generally represented a far friendlier forum in which to advance their cause than the municipal governments of the locales in which the bulk of their consumers lived. And as many historians have noted, industry leaders did in fact openly and covertly lobby for imposition of restrictions on municipal jurisdiction over electric utility firms and for establishment of forms of state regulation during the late nineteenth and early twentieth centuries.

Additional features of the story stand out in sharp relief when the history of public policy toward electric utilities in the United States is compared with that of waterworks. As in waterworks, hard-fought battles over private versus government ownership took place in many American cities. Private electric utility firms, critics alleged, saddled consumers with unduly high prices and exercised unduly great influence over the political system. On the whole, however, it is not the presence but the relative absence of day-to-day problems and controversy that is most conspicuous when the histories of waterworks and electric utilities are compared with one another.

As noted in chapter 2, issues of service quality and problems in arranging for the provision of specifically public goods played major roles in driving municipal governments to oust private waterworks firms in rapidly growing major American cities during the nineteenth and early twentieth centuries. In electric utilities, by contrast, problems in these domains did not arise to nearly the same degree. Nor, with important exceptions, did private electric utility firms in major urban centers come under attack to the same extent as did their waterworks counterparts for failing to invest in facilities believed necessary to serve economic growth. Comparison of the roles played by market discipline and of factors suggested by transaction cost analysis suggests some of the reasons for these differences. In the case of waterworks, market discipline on private firms was fairly limited under even the best of circumstances. Furthermore, whatever market discipline resulted from availability of local sources of water tended to decline as cities increased in size. In electric utilities, too, there was far from unlimited competition in many of the markets served and complaints of monopoly exploitation often arose. To a far greater extent than in waterworks, however, the presence of inter-product competition and other forms of market discipline meant that proprietors of electric utility firms found it to be in their own interests to furnish good quality service and to pursue aggressive marketing and investment policies.

Many electric utilities got their start as suppliers of illumination higher in quality than that of available alternatives but also far more expensive. Over time, however, electric utility firms found that they could profitably break out of this narrow market niche by cutting costs, exploiting new technology, and marketing their product to an increasingly diverse array of domestic, commercial, and industrial customers. Incentives for entrepreneurial vigor and for aggressive investment in system expansion arose from a number of quarters.

During the 1880s and 1890s, when electric utility supply and distribution networks were just beginning to be developed, entrepreneurs seeking to make their fortune in the new industry faced an unpredictable competitive environment rich with opportunities to lose as well as to make money. Limited economies of scale coupled with public policies designed to encourage competition lay at the root of much of this insecurity. Because the voltage of the direct current used by lighting companies during the 1880s and early 1890s could not be easily "stepped up" or "stepped down" to match the requirements of consumers, different types of generators had to be used for different kinds of consumption. Arc lights (used for street lighting and other large spaces), incandescent light (used in homes and offices), and traction uses each had to be supplied by different sets of wires and generating units. In the incandescent lighting and small power markets, economies of scale were further limited by the small size of the distribution areas that could be served by the low voltages of the systems developed by Thomas Edison.[6]

At the same time, municipalities in the United States typically issued nonexclusive franchises to electric utility firms that neither imposed significant constraints with respect to price or quality of service to private consumers nor furnished a significant degree of protection against competition. For the specifically public good of street lighting, cities sought to assure themselves of the benefits of competition by putting up for bid short-term one to three year contracts. So long as such policies remained in place, the small size of generating facilities combined with the relatively low costs of stringing wire as compared to laying pipe meant that risks to incumbent firms from duplicative competition were greater in electric utilities than in waterworks.

As would be expected on the basis of the discussion of natural monopoly in chapter 1, a single firm usually dominated in any given area and episodes of competition rarely persisted for long. Nevertheless, price wars and costs incurred in buying out competitors could be a source of financial strain on even the most dominant of electric utility firms during this period. Short-term contracting for street lighting presented particular risks. Although, in practice, incumbent firms were almost never displaced, loss of a street light contract could mean loss of virtually the entire value of a company's investment in physical plant. In addition, even when electric utility firms succeeded (as they usually did) in beating off threats posed by duplicative competition through merger or other means, they still had to contest for market share with well-entrenched gas utility firms and with large consumers who could economically generate their own electricity.[7]

That electric lights could furnish a higher quality and more versatile source of illumination than gas was already apparent by the middle of the 1880s. For many years, however, technological constraints on economies of scale prevented electric lighting companies from exploiting this superiority to gain a monopoly in the markets they served. Well into the first decade of the twentieth century, gas companies continued to hold onto large portions of the lighting market in major cities through price cutting and the introduction of such innovations as the Welsbach mantle. Constraints on scale economies also enabled large consumers such as department stores and office buildings to economically generate rather than purchase electricity.

To survive, let alone grow, in the face of these varied competitive threats, electric utility firms had to furnish a product of high reliability and to keep costs as low as possible. Competitive vulnerabilities arising from limitations on economies of scale also helped to spur technological change. Only by overcoming constraints on scale economies could electric utility entrepreneurs profitably expand their businesses and conquer new markets. During the late nineteenth and early twentieth centuries, some of the most brilliant inventors and best-organized research and development enterprises of the day devoted themselves to attacking the technological bottlenecks that lay in the way of generating, transmitting, and distributing large outputs of electricity at a low price.

A crucial first step, the introduction by Westinghouse of single phase alternating current, came during the late 1880s. The major advantage of Westinghouse's innovation over the direct current generated by Edison plants was that voltage could be easily "stepped up" for economical transmission and then "stepped down" again for use by customers. This meant that individual alternating current generating plants did not have to be built adjacent to major centers of demand in order for a large area to be served. Over the course of the 1890s, the introduction of such innovations as polyphase alternating current made it possible for alternating current to be used for an increasing variety of purposes such as running motors and energizing arc lights. At the same time, rotary converters made it possible for independently constructed direct and alternating current networks to be fed off the same generating plant.

Largely in place by the first decade of the twentieth century, these developments in turn laid the technological groundwork for the economical provision of larger distribution areas by electric utility firms and for the increased exploitation of economies of scale in the generation and transmission of power. Particularly during the first decades of the twentieth century, the industry enjoyed explosive growth. Indeed, over the years 1907 through 1937, the annual output of electricity generated by private utility firms in the United States increased almost twentyfold from less than six billion kilowatt-hours to almost 110 billion kilowatt-hours.[8] With increased production came declining costs. Progressively larger and more efficient generating units, the replacement of reciprocating engines by steam turbines, and the use of higher steam pressures in boilers all made for lower costs and increased economies of scale in producing electricity. At the same time, the introduction of progressively higher voltages in electricity transmission permitted larger quantities of power to be transmitted over longer distances at higher efficiencies.[9]

With interesting exceptions, reduced competition between electric utility firms accompanied these developments. Growth of scale economies rendered entry by new electric utility firms more difficult even while encouraging mergers between existing companies to avoid large-scale, expensive, and unprofitable duplication of expensive capital investments in generation and distribution facilities. Reductions in price made possible by improved economies of scale (as well as technological improvements in lamp efficiencies) gradually reduced the competitive threat to electric utility firms from gas companies as well. Although gas lighting remained in use by many domestic consumers well into the second decade of the twentieth century, the costs of electric street lighting had been so reduced by 1900 that competition from gas companies for street lighting business had virtually disappeared. In a few cities, mergers between gas and electric companies eliminated this competition altogether.[10]

Nevertheless, powerful forms of market discipline on electric utility firms remained. Even in the absence of direct competition, capacity utilization needs and growth in economies of scale during the early decades of the twentieth century continued to provide incentives for electric utility firms to furnish high-quality and reliable service and to aggressively extend their networks and develop new markets. Because electric utilities could not store significant amounts of power for future use, maintaining the ratio of average to peak consumption—load factor—at a high level was of critical importance for utilities to obtain satisfactory remuneration from their increasingly large-scale and expensive capital facilities.[11]

In order to balance the nighttime demand for illumination and increase their load factor, electric utility firms began to make vigorous efforts to increase the use of electricity for household tasks during the early years of the twentieth century. Electric utility firms also began to compete more aggressively in the markets for industrial power and traction. In developing these later markets, electric companies faced competition from potential purchasers who were also capable of generating their own electricity and sometimes found it economical to do so. To succeed, electric utility firms had to provide service of high quality and reliability and to design their rate structure in such a way as to set prices low in off-peak markets with high-demand elasticities.[12]

At least in densely populated urban areas, these forms of market discipline meant that protection of consumer interests never depended upon the efficacy of franchising and regulatory arrangements in electric utilities to nearly the same extent as in waterworks. Nor did arranging for the provision of specifically public goods such as street lighting present the sorts of transaction cost difficulties that so bedeviled relationships between municipalities and privately owned water companies.

Like that of water for fire protection, provision of public illumination by electric utilities was carried out through fixed and networked distribution facilities that possessed natural monopoly attributes to a substantial degree. Even when short-term contracts with provisions for competitive bidding were employed, therefore, municipalities and privately owned service providers typically found themselves enmeshed in long-term relationships. In electric street lighting, as in water for fire protection, these relationships were characterized, at times, by conflicts between municipalities and privately owned service providers and allegations of monopolistic abuses and corrupt practices. Under contrac-

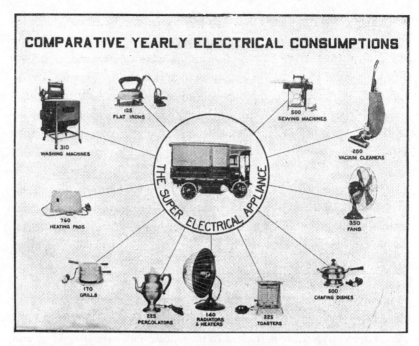

COMPARATIVE YEARLY ELECTRICAL CONSUMPTIONS

125
FLAT IRONS

500
SEWING MACHINES

310
WASHING MACHINES

280
VACUUM CLEANERS

THE SUPER ELECTRICAL APPLIANCE

760
HEATING PADS

350
FANS

170
GRILLS

500
CHAFING DISHES

225
PERCOLATORS

140
RADIATORS
& HEATERS

225
TOASTERS

This illustration from the 1923 Proceedings of the National Electric Light Association shows how electric utility firms viewed the potential of different appliances to increase electricity consumption. From this perspective, the electric truck was indeed desirable, a "super appliance" needing large outputs of electricity to charge batteries. Because most battery charging would take place at night when other electricity demands were relatively low, the vehicles were also highly desirable from a load management perspective. Despite utility campaigns to promote the vehicles, however, they never became popular.

tual arrangements little different from those characteristic of water for fire protection, however, municipal governments and privately owned service providers found it possible to arrange for service quality to be maintained and increases in demand accommodated with relatively little difficulty and conflict.

An analysis of factors suggested by transaction cost analysis can help in understanding why increased demand could be accommodated so much more easily in street light contracting than in water for fire protection. In this regard, I pay particularly close attention here to issues encountered in measuring output and monitoring quality. Unlike the case of water for fire protection, the output of public illumination being furnished by a privately owned service provider could be specified with reasonable precision in terms of a readily observable and easily measured unit—the number of street lamps operating on a given night. At the same time, the quality of the illumination being furnished could be literally discerned with the naked eye and easily monitored on a day-to-day basis, at least in a gross way, by policemen and even ordinary citizens reporting lamp outages. Poor quality or unreliable service was not only immediately and indisputably apparent to municipal officials and members of the public but could be easily sanctioned in an incremental and ongoing way simply through contract terms that provided a set penalty for each lamp outage.[13]

In addition, even massive increases in demand for street lighting could be accommodated without having to renegotiate the terms of the simple per-lamp pricing structures employed. The number of street lamps operating in a city was a fairly good index of the actual output of public illumination being furnished. Costs per lamp generally declined as output increased. Cities and electric utility firms could (and did) dispute what constituted a fair price per lamp as costs of labor and material changed, technology improved, and economies of scale increased. But so long as the price per lamp remained at a level equal to or higher than average costs, even the most opportunistic and unprincipled purveyor of electric street lighting services would have been foolish to either refuse to accommodate growing demand (for which it would be rewarded) or to skimp on quality of service (for which it would be easily caught and penalized).

Brief accounts follow of the history of electric utility development and public policy in Boston, San Francisco, Seattle, and other American cities. The accounts will discuss trajectories of electric utility development in the different locales, experiences with contracting for specifically public services such as street lighting, and roles played by these experiences in shaping the politics of ownership and regulation. As shall be seen, there has been great variation in electric utility technology, markets, and public policy in Boston, San Francisco, Seattle, and other American cities. At the same time, distinct patterns can be discerned.

In Boston, as in most other cities in the Northeast and the Midwest, for example, coal-fired generating stations located fairly close to the centers of demand continued to furnish the bulk of the electricity consumed well into the 1920s. In both San Francisco and Seattle, by contrast, hydro-generation played an increasingly important role from the early decades of the twentieth century onward. Politics and public policy also varied from place to place. In Boston, for example, state regulation over electric utilities dated from virtually the birth of the industry and the municipal government's main point of contact with electric utility firms lay in the domain of street light contracting. By contrast, state regulation over San Francisco's electric utilities was only imposed in 1915 and the municipal government consistently enjoyed far more freedom of action and legal authority than did its Boston counterpart.

As noted, movements for municipal ownership of electric utilities went down to defeat in most major American cities, including both Boston and San Francisco. But there are exceptions. Cleveland, Los Angeles, and Seattle are among the major American cities in which municipal governments did acquire their own electric utility systems during the late nineteenth and early twentieth century. Awareness of such exceptions is valuable in and of itself as a corrective to an overly deterministic view of the history of the industry. At least in Seattle, the triumph of municipal ownership can be attributed in good part to particularities of local circumstances, politics, and personalities. At the same time, however, the outcome can also be understood in terms of common themes developed previously in the discussions of both waterworks and electric utilities in the United States.

Public Policy and Electric Utility Development in Boston

For virtually the entire history of the industry, electricity in Boston has been generated and distributed by private firms under state regulation. The state legislature established a three-member board appointed by the governor to oversee pricing, service quality, and entry in the gas industry in 1885. With extension of its jurisdiction to electric utilities in 1887, the body became known as the Massachusetts Board of Gas and Electric Light Commissioners. By statute, the Board of Gas and Electric Light Commissioners had authority to protect consumer interests by ordering reductions in rates or improvements in service quality in response to written complaints by twenty or more consumers or the mayor of a city.[14] In a bid to prevent overcapitalization and resulting pressures to increase consumer charges, the board acquired jurisdiction over the issue of securities by Massachusetts gas and electric companies as well during the 1890s.[15]

This turn to state oversight took place at a time of considerable instability and change in the gas and electric lighting industries. Gas lighting had a long history in Boston, with public illumination of streets and parks dating from the 1820s. By 1880, the city was contracting with six different private firms for over ten thousand gas lamps and twenty-four hundred oil lamps. The firms enjoyed a secure existence. Each served a different area of the city and there was no direct competition between them.[16] The coming of electric street lighting during the early 1880s, however, meant an end to this relative security from competitive pressures.

The Brush Company initiated the use of electric arc lamps for public illumination in Boston during 1881 by setting up a small demonstration plant in the heart of the city at Scollay Square. The demonstration succeeded spectacularly. The arc lamps gave off a light many times brighter than that furnished by gas and could illuminate large spaces far more brilliantly. Boston's superintendent of lamps described the public response to the new form of lighting in an 1883 city report as follows: "it seems that all at once the public have become convinced that heretofore Boston has been a poorly lighted city. . . . The reasons advanced by the many petitioners for these lights vary according to the localities in which it is desired to place them, but all seem to unite upon one common ground, and that is, that they are a great benefit and protection to those whose business or pleasure requires that they should walk the streets after dark; and, in accordance with the oft-repeated statement, that a 'city that is well lighted is well policed,' an urgent demand is made for more light."[17] This sort of public acceptance inspired Boston to contract with the Brush Company in February of 1882 to supply up to one hundred of the new lamps. Later in the year, Boston awarded similar contracts without competitive bidding to the New England Weston Company and the American Electric and Illuminating Company. But although they obtained these first contracts easily, electric utility entrepreneurs soon faced a world filled with competitive pressures and potential hazards to their investments.

While electric lighting represented a potent new source of competition to gas, the threat did not go entirely in one direction. The arc lights did have disadvantages. They cost more than gas to illuminate an equivalent area and were too bright to be used in small enclosed spaces at all. For many years after electric lighting technology was first introduced, gas and oil continued to play an important role in lighting Boston's streets as the companies cut their prices and introduced such innovations as the Welsbach mantle. Of most pressing concern to street lighting entrepreneurs, however, were threats that investments in fixed facilities would be rendered entirely valueless by duplicative competition or municipal ownership initiatives.

These latter threats were not merely theoretical. Many people both inside and outside Boston's government during the 1880s and 1890s believed that unless ongoing competition between electric utility firms could be maintained, government ownership represented the only means of preventing rapacious and monopolistic privately owned service providers from exploiting the public. By contrast, advocates of regulation and members of the Massachusetts Board of Gas and Electric Light Commissioners believed that duplicative competition threatened public as well as private interests. Such competition, they maintained, would inevitably prove short-lived, result in uneconomic duplication of facilities, and eventually bring about higher rates to consumers.[18] At the same time, advocates of regulation rejected the view that government ownership represented the only viable approach to protecting public interests in the absence of competition. Under enlightened state regulation, they maintained, no insuperable obstacles lay in the way of reconciling the interests of the public and those of privately owned monopolies.

Even if regulation meant some loss of autonomy with respect to price and quality of service, thoughtful executives in both the gas and electric utility industries could support its imposition. Speaking in 1885 before the New England Gas Association, the superintendent of the Boston Gas Company described the efforts of his industry to cope with competitive threats by influencing state policy as follows: "The proposal for a Commission is practically, if amended as proposed by us—that no company which shows the figures, and accedes to the recommendations of the Commissioners, shall be troubled by competition; for the assent of the Commissioners must be given to enable the institution of a rival works, and that permission would not probably be obtained."[19]

In at least some respects, state policy did evolve in ways hoped for by utility firms. The Board of Gas and Electric Light Commissioners did not exercise a rigid supervision over utility rate structures or profits and only rarely found occasion to order reductions in the charges set by electric utility firms. Over the nineteen-year period 1888 through 1907, for example, the board ordered individual utility firms to reduce their charges in only seventeen instances.[20] While the board's very presence may have exercised a restraining influence on pricing practices, utility rates of return as reflected in dividend payments continued to vary widely after the imposition of regulation. Annual dividends declared by Massachusetts utilities in 1903, for example, ranged from nothing in some rural communities to 10 percent by the Edison Company of Boston and 18 percent by the company serving Worcester.[21]

In other domains, however, regulation's limits did not rebound to the advantage of privately owned service providers. Despite the hopes of utility executives and some rhetoric by regulators themselves, regulation played only a modest role in insulating privately owned service providers against many competitive threats. While the Board of Gas and Electric Light Commissioners did consistently turn down applications from isolated plants for permission to run their wires across streets so that they could sell their surplus power in competition with the city's established utility firms, it did not have the authority to prevent firms already established in a locality from competing with one another.[22] On occasion, such competition represented a real threat to Boston's electric utility firms.

The first threat of this sort arose in 1887, the year in which state regulation was imposed. In an effort to bring down prices, Boston put its street lighting contracts out for bid. Recognizing the threat to price levels and fixed investments if competitive bidding for short-term contracts took place, the electric companies responded by colluding with one another. They submitted identical tenders at the sixty-five cents per lamp per night price they were already charging.[23] Soon after, the firms merged outright, forming the Boston Electric Light Company.

More seriously, an episode of actual competition broke out in 1889 when a firm called the Suburban Electric Light Company bid against Boston Electric for contracts to light some neighborhoods of the city. To exploit this unusual outbreak of genuine competition, Boston's mayor threw out the bids presented by both companies as too high. The tactic succeeded. After it became clear that the municipality might actually purchase its lights from Suburban, Boston Electric cut its bid for furnishing service under a five-year contract from fifty cents per lamp per night to the limit of forty cents per lamp per night set by the mayor. Suburban responded by submitting an even lower bid, but the city (in a decision that aroused much controversy at the time) decided to stick with the incumbent firm rather than risk the potential disruption, legal problems, and duplication of facilities that could result from making a switch. Soon after, Boston's existing electric firms jointly bought out the Suburban Company.

Two firms now dominated Boston's electric utility industry. Initially, the firms refrained from competing with one another. Founded in 1886, the Edison Company predominantly furnished incandescent lighting to private customers, while Boston Electric concentrated on arc lamps for the illumination of large spaces and had a monopoly on electric street lighting. As time went on, however, the two firms exploited new technologies to invade one another's markets. Over the course of the 1890s, Boston Electric made use of newly developed alternating current technology to compete with Edison for the incandescent and power customers upon which that company depended. At the end of the decade, Edison still dominated these markets but the gap between the two firms had narrowed considerably. At the same time, Edison began to directly compete with Boston Electric for private arc lighting customers, although the firm refrained from any effort to obtain city street lighting contracts. This competition, too, however, did not persist for long. The episode ended in 1902 with the takeover of Boston Electric by the Edison Company.

Whether more duplicative competition would have occurred in Boston in the absence of state-imposed restrictions on entry cannot be known with certainty. Even if more competition had occurred, however, it is reasonable to infer based upon experiences in other cities that any additional episodes would have proven short-lived and that technological and economic factors played the greatest role in driving consolidation. Nor did imposition of regulation entirely forestall threats presented by municipal ownership initiatives. Indeed, accusations that electric utility firms not only charged monopolistic prices but exercised an overly great influence on local and state politics played a role at times in spurring such initiatives. Private ownership and state regulation, however, both survived. The very influence of the utilities over state policy making of which municipal ownership advocates complained accounted in substantial part for this outcome.

In particular, utility firms won a real increase in state protection in 1891 with passage by the Massachusetts legislature of an act prohibiting a municipality from acquiring its own electric utility without buying out the facilities of the incumbent firm at a "fair market value" to be determined by an arbitration process if the two sides could not agree.[24] The law also imposed major procedural hurdles in the way of municipal ownership initiatives. Before a municipal government could generate and distribute electricity, approval by a two-thirds vote of each branch of the city council and by the mayor was required for each of two consecutive years. After such approval was obtained, the proposal then had to be submitted to a referendum.

The most important reason for the failure of municipal ownership initiatives, however, was that Boston's electric utility firms found it to be in their own interests to furnish service of good quality, cut prices, expand distribution networks, and develop new markets. Competitive pressures arose from a number of sources. As late as 1900, Boston still contracted for more than 8,600 gas lamps and 2,500 naphtha lamps for its streets.[25] Indeed, the city of Boston did not abandon its last gas lights until 1909. For potentially lucrative business from large customers with steady demands, isolated plants also represented a serious source of competition well into the first and second decades of the twentieth century.[26] While competition from gas and from isolated plants declined in importance during the first decade of the twentieth century, growing economies of scale in production and the need for efficient capacity utilization continued to create incentives for electric utility firms to furnish reasonably reliable service and to engage in active efforts to increase consumption through price cutting, extension of distribution plant, and promotional initiatives to develop off-peak markets.

Electric utility firms in Boston responded aggressively to these competitive pressures and incentives for expansion. Over the years 1887 through 1909, for example, the number of customers served by Edison Electric Company of Boston increased from five hundred to over thirty thousand and the capacity of its generators from forty to over seventy-six thousand kilowatts. The firm expanded its distribution area, over the course of the period, from a small area of downtown Boston to an expanse of over five hundred square miles encompassing the entire city as well as many nearby communities.[27] In 1909, Edison Electric found it profitable to cut by 25 percent the electric rates previously charged in Newton, Brookline, Chelsea, and Waltham as it added these suburban communities to its system. Marketing initiatives included the opening of an elaborate appliance exchange in 1907 and the initiation of a major promotional campaign in 1911 to encourage the use of electric vehicles.

Edison also mounted a series of "old house wiring campaigns" to encourage as yet unserved residents to become electricity consumers. Under these plans, the Edison company furnished low-cost financing for the wiring of homes and arranged for independent contractors to perform the work under a standard fee schedule. Aggressive efforts to market electricity, including voluntary price cuts to small consumers, renewed house-wiring programs, and campaigns to increase the use of electricity for sign advertising, industrial heating, and other commercial uses continued during the 1920s.[28]

For electric street lighting, contracting factors also played a major role in spurring good performance even after threats of inter-product and duplicative competition had almost completely disappeared. Less than a page long, Boston's very first contract for electric street lighting signed in 1881 was short and simple in form. It provided for Boston to pay the Brush Company sixty-five cents per lamp per night with the municipality responsible for determining acceptable quality of service.[29] The contract could not remain entirely unmodified as the number of electric street lamps in Boston increased from fewer than fifty in 1881 to more than thirty-six hundred in 1900 and over eighty-six hundred by 1918. Specification of service attributes, for example, did become more detailed. But visual observation remained the foundation of the system and prices continued to be set on a per-lamp basis with specified penalties for outages.

Unlike the case of water for fire protection, however, growing demands and improvements in technology could be accommodated without a drastic increase in the complexity of the basic structure of the contracts employed or the need for detailed case-by-case negotiation. As

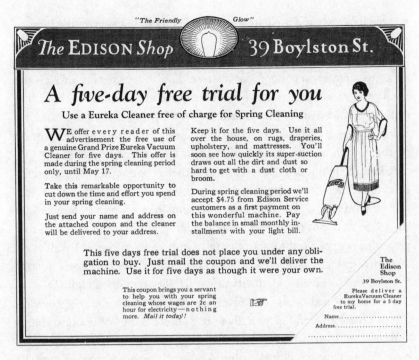

The Edison Electric Company even sold appliances to consumers to conquer new market niches for electricity. *Photograph courtesy of the Archives of Boston Edison, an NSTAR Company.*

time went on, possibilities for competition became more remote, duration of contracts increased, and procedures for setting prices increasingly resembled those found in state regulation. In 1899, the municipality and the electric company negotiated a ten-year contract in which the firm agreed to reduce its street lighting prices below those initially specified if arbitrators should determine that the firm's rate of return for furnishing the service exceeded 6 percent per year.[30] The agreement reached between the city and the electric company in 1909 took the movement toward regulation a step further by providing for contract renewal without even the pretense of a bidding procedure. The contract also provided for street lighting prices to be cut as costs of provision declined.[31]

Like the state regulation imposed in 1887, these arrangements allowed prices to be adjusted to adapt to changing conditions. Here as elsewhere, however, the Progressive hope that disinterested experts would be able to adjust and mediate public and private interests on the basis of exact and scientific formulas proved unrealized. Thus, even when the Massachusetts Board of Gas and Electric Light Commissioners did order an approximately 9 percent cut in street lighting charges in 1918 on the basis of contract arbitration procedures, the explanation for the ruling explicitly conceded the impossibility of setting an exactly fair rate of return because of difficulties involved in determining the exact proportion of the company's investments that should be considered as being allocated for street lighting.[32] Nevertheless, these contracting arrangements functioned far better than did their counterparts in waterworks. Prices for arc lamps dropped from sixty-five cents per lamp per night during the 1880s to about thirty-five cents per lamp per night in 1900 and to a price that worked out to about twenty-four cents in 1918.[33] By all available accounts, any problems that did occur with the service were quickly noticed and resolved and quality and reliability remained high.[34]

In the context of such relatively good performance in the provision of both consumer and specifically public goods, claims of political abuses and monopolistic pricing (whether true or false) simply proved insufficient to mobilize a political coalition powerful enough to overcome the substantial procedural and financial hurdles that lay in the way of municipal ownership. Concerns with political corruption also cut both ways. If a municipality was too corrupt to properly oversee street light contracting, opponents of municipalization could ask, how could such a government be entrusted to own and operate its own facilities? Even many people who believed that the Edison Company did charge overly high prices, accepted the situation as a lesser evil or believed that reform of state regulation represented a more promising remedy than outright government ownership. In a 1925 veto message, Boston Mayor James Curley (a political figure not unacquainted with some of the more interesting possibilities of municipal patronage) expressed this perspective as follows: "The real remedy for excessive lighting rates is at hand and needs only the assistance of an aroused public sentiment. The election of the public utilities commission by the people, or the election of a governor who would reconstitute the commission by the appointment of an entirely new membership would undoubtedly result in a reduction of rates and would avoid either a wasteful duplication of electric lighting plants or the taking of the present Edison plant at an enormous expense and possibly an inflated valuation."[35]

Public Policy and Electric Utility Development in San Francisco

As was the case in Boston, the dazzle of Brush arc lights marked the debut of electric utility service in San Francisco. The first electric utility in San Francisco, the California Electric Light Company, began operation in 1879 as a small supplier of arc lighting to commercial customers. The firm initiated service with an installation composed of a total of two Brush arc light dynamos with a combined capacity of twenty-one lamps.[36] From this modest beginning, production and consumption of electricity increased rapidly over the next two decades. As in Boston, however, prices remained high and markets were constrained by technological limitations on economies of scale in generation and transmission during the early years of electric utility development.

Similarities in the roles played by government can also be discerned. During the early years of the industry, municipal governments in both San Francisco and Boston constituted important consumers of the illumination services furnished by electric utility firms. For fledgling electric utility firms in both cities, whether or not one received a municipal street lighting contract could mean the difference between corporate life or death. But while government was important as a consumer, government as a regulator or planner was not. In Massachusetts, state regulators did enjoy a degree of legal authority over the electric utility industry from 1887 onward. But in practice, state regulators played only a minimal role in either setting rates charged by private utility firms or in preventing firms from competing with one another. In San Francisco, neither state nor local officials made even a pretense of regulating rates charged by electric utility firms to private consumers during the 1880s and 1890s.

Nor did impossible-to-surmount legal barriers lie in the way of duplicative competition. Prior to 1898, the municipality of San Francisco did give the California Electric Light Company and successor firms a degree of protection against competition of this kind by refusing to grant pole rights to other companies. But this protection was incomplete because under the terms of the California state constitution, any company had the right to lay conduits under the streets or to stretch wires between buildings. A superior court ruling by Judge J. M. Seawell on November 16, 1898, eliminated even this legal impediment to competition altogether by requiring the city to grant pole permits to all electric utility firms on equal terms.

In this context, California Electric and successor firms faced many obstacles as they strove to secure and expand markets for the electricity generated in central plants and distributed over wire networks. As in Boston, well-established gas lighting companies had already been in business for many years when electric lighting was first introduced during the late 1870s and early 1880s. For many years thereafter, gas companies continued to retain a large proportion of the illumination market. As late as 1896, for example, the city of San Francisco still contracted for more than 5,100 gas lamps, compared to fewer than 650 of the far brighter electric arcs.

For the business of the largest and potentially most lucrative customers, isolated plants too represented a significant source of competition. Rather than purchase current from utility firms, many large users of electricity—such as the Mills Building, the Baldwin Hotel, the California Hotel, the Spreckels Building, and the Phelan Building—found it more economical to generate their own power during the 1880s and 1890s. The largest consumers of all, San Francisco's electric street railways, generated their own power well into the 1920s. These threats were compounded at times when independently owned electric utility firms sought to sell power to each others' customers despite the natural monopoly attributes of distribution systems.

As did its Boston counterparts, California Electric and successor firms responded to threats and pressures from competitive suppliers of electricity and gas by merger—when they could—and by cutting prices—when they had to. Usually, episodes of duplicative competition ended with the absorption of the interloping firm by California Electric and its successors. The outcome of the first such episode was fairly typical. The competition began in 1887 with the formation of the Electric Improvement Company. The new company was a scrappy and tough competitor running its wires over building roofs and through basements in the absence of a city permit to erect its own utility poles. To obtain business the Electric Improvement Company cut rates, offered free wiring, and even put in an unsuccessful bid for the 1888 city street lighting contract. The incumbent firm dealt with the threat, first by cutting its own rates, and then by buying out the interloper in 1892.[37]

The exact sequence of events in San Francisco, however, differed markedly from that in Boston. As noted, supply of electricity in Boston during the 1880s and 1890s was dominated by two leading firms, the Boston Electric Company and the Edison Electric Company. Although the firms initially served separate markets, they increasingly competed with one another for both lighting and power customers as time went on. In San Francisco, by contrast, one leading electric utility firm consistently overshadowed all rivals. Backers of the California Electric Company successfully forestalled the rise of an Edison system as a competitor by arranging to acquire exclusive local rights to the Edison patents for themselves in 1891. As part of this maneuver, the California Electric Company was reorganized under the name of the Edison Light and Power Company. Competition from San Francisco's gas company for provision of illumination was dealt with similarly. Whereas gas companies competed with electric utility firms for lighting customers in Boston well into the first decade of the twentieth century, the Edison Company and San Francisco's leading gas company merged into the San Francisco Gas and Electric Company in 1896.

As in Boston, the coming of the twentieth century ushered in a period of growth, change, and regionalization in provision of electricity in San Francisco. Production and consumption of electricity grew rapidly, exceeding 345,500,000 kilowatt-hours in 1914 and 532,100,000 kilowatt-hours in 1922. In San Francisco, as in Boston and other major American cities, electric utility networks had become deeply integrated into the fabric of day-to-day urban life by the 1920s. By this time, major uses of electricity included not only commercial, residential, and street lighting, but also heating and cooking, manufacturing, and electric railway consumption.

Changes in the structure and organization of the electric utilities serving San Francisco also took place, in ways that differed quite substantially from those underway in Boston during the same period. In Boston, the main change in industry structure took place in 1902 with the merger of the Boston Electric and Edison Electric companies. During the years that followed, the new enterprise cemented its dominance over electricity production and consumption in the city of Boston and expanded distribution into nearby suburban areas also. Economies of scale and improved load factor were realized by increasing the size and efficiency of generating units, using new technology such as rotary converters to supply both alternating and direct current distribution networks, and by aggressively marketing electricity for an increasingly wide array of purposes. But electricity continued to be produced by coal-fired generating units located in relatively close proximity to consumers.

In San Francisco and northern California, by contrast, entrepreneurs took advantage of regional geography and improved means of long-distance power transmission to exploit opportunities not available to utility firms in Northeastern cities such as Boston. The richest markets for electricity and power in northern California lay in the Bay Area cities of San Francisco, Oakland, and their environs. Pumping for irrigation in the great Central Valley of California also represented a potentially rich power market. Fuel for generating power within these areas, however, was quite expensive and hard to come by. Up until the first decade of the twentieth century, for example, utilities in San Francisco found it necessary to fuel their generating plants with coal imported from Australia.[38]

Just to the east of the Central Valley of California, however, lay the enormous water powers of the Sierra-Nevada. Starting in the late nineteenth and early twentieth centuries, entrepreneurs began to build up regional electric utility networks that linked together these cheap sources of power supply in the mountains with the rich power markets of the Central Valley and the Bay Area. Entrepreneurs Eugene J. de Sabla, Jr. and John Martin in 1895 played a particularly important role. Seeking cheap power for mines in which they had an interest, de Sabla and Martin developed a small, 6,100 kW power plant on the South Yuba River near Nevada City, California. Encouraged by the success of this facility, the entrepreneurs obtained financing from Romulus Riggs Colgate and embarked on the development of additional power plants in the region. In 1899, de Sabla and Martin and Colgate incorporated the Yuba Electric Power Company and developed the Colgate power plant on the Yuba. The plant supplied electricity not only to local mines and industries but to customers in Sacramento located more than sixty miles away.[39]

With backing from Eastern bond firms, de Sabla, Martin, and Colgate formed the Bay Counties Power Company in 1901. The company built a high-voltage transmission line 140 miles long from the Colgate plant on the Yuba to Oakland, where the cheap power was used to operate the city's streetcar system. During the years that followed, the Bay Counties Company interconnected its hydroplants in the Sierra Nevada, absorbed other companies, and began to serve an increasingly wide range of customers along the route of its transmission line and in Oakland itself.[40] In 1903, de Sabla and Martin merged the Bay Counties and several other utilities into the California Gas and Electric Company. Companies acquired included electric and gas utilities serving Sacramento and the Standard Electric Company, which operated its own hydroplant in the Sierra Nevada and transmitted power to the Bay Area over its own transmission line. In a complicated set of financial transactions orchestrated by the New York brokerage firm N. W. Halsey & Company, the California Gas and Electric Company in turn merged with the San Francisco Gas and Electric Company to form the Pacific Gas and Electric Company in 1905. The new regional utility operated on a huge geographical scale. As noted, Boston's electric utility served a densely populated area of about five hundred to six hundred square miles during the first decades of the twentieth century. The Pacific Gas and Electric Company, by contrast, supplied an area of about 37,000 square miles.[41] But despite the great geographical scale on which it operated, the Pacific Gas and Electric Company did not dominate distribution of electricity in San Francisco to quite the same degree as did its Boston counterpart.

In the absence of governmental restrictions on duplicative competition, new companies continued to build their own electrical supply and distribution networks in San Francisco. The City Electric Company, founded in 1907, was the most successful of the new entrants. The firm rapidly acquired a large commercial and industrial business and by 1910 earned almost a third as much revenue from the sale of electricity in San Francisco as did the Pacific Gas and Electric Company.[42] During the years that followed, the same regional geography that contributed to the growth of Pacific Gas and Electric also lent an additional impetus to competition.

As noted, San Francisco represented the richest and most concentrated market for power in all of northern California. For a firm with large quantities of hydropower to sell, gaining access to this market could be worth the costs of acquiring or developing its own distribution system. And this is precisely what happened. To gain a distribution outlet in the city, a large hydroproducer called the Great Western Company purchased San Francisco's City Electric Company in 1911. In subsequent years, Great Western absorbed other, much smaller electric utility firms in San Francisco. Great Western continued to compete with Pacific Gas and Electric in some districts of the city until the two firms finally merged in 1930. The result of this merger was the complete elimination of duplicative competition in San Francisco. For the remainder of the twentieth century, Pacific Gas and Electric continued to enjoy a monopoly on the distribution of both gas and electricity to private consumers in the city.

Whether episodes of competition between electric utility firms harmed or benefited consumers in San Francisco is open to question. Ultimately, costs of duplicated facilities may have been passed on to consumers. Nonetheless, consumers clearly did reap immediate benefits in at least some instances. The experiences of San Francisco's municipal government with the provision of electric street lighting are illustrative. As in Boston, competition between electric utility firms for street lighting contracts made for real, if sporadic, price discipline. On the two occasions when more than one company competed for the contract (once in 1888 and a second time ten years later), prices did indeed decline, although the incumbent firm retained the contract. More typically, however, the incumbent company alone submitted a bid and prices remained the same. For private consumers, the effects of competition between electric utility firms were geographically as well as temporally uneven. During a "rate war" that occurred from 1901 to 1903, for example, maximum charges for small consumers of electricity ranged from \$0.035/kWh in areas with competing distribution systems to \$0.11/kWh in areas where one firm enjoyed a monopoly. With the merger of the two largest competitors in 1903, maximum charges to small consumers regained their former level.

Public policy toward San Francisco's electric utilities began to move away from total laissez-faire during the final years of the nineteenth century. As noted, San Francisco adopted a new municipal charter in 1898 calling for eventual government ownership of all of the city's public utilities. But (unlike the case of waterworks during the same period), San

Francisco's municipal officials did not find abuses by electric utility firms sufficiently important to spur them to translate their rhetorical support for municipal ownership into immediate action. Instead, the San Francisco Board of Supervisors began to exercise its powers under the state constitution to set maximum prices for gas and electricity charged by utility firms.

From the perspective of privately owned service providers, this turn to municipal regulation potentially represented a sort of worst of all worlds. On the one hand, utility firms continued to enjoy no legal protection against duplicative competition. On the other hand, those charged with setting rates were directly elected by a population composed almost entirely of purchasers of gas and electric service. Such democratically elected rate setters, many utility executives believed, could not be trusted to exercise authority with due regard for the interests of privately owned service providers. At the same time, reformers who decried utility influence on municipal politics were not satisfied either. While the Board of Supervisors did exercise its authority to order cuts in electricity rates, occasions for corruption may have actually increased with the growth in municipal authority. During 1906, for example, fifteen of the sixteen members of the San Francisco Board of Supervisors took a bribe from the Pacific Gas and Electric Company in return for lowering gas prices to $0.85 per 1,000 cubic feet rather than to $0.75, as called for by the Union Labor platform on which they were elected.[43]

In this context, sources of political support for the imposition of state regulation over public utilities in California were quite similar to those in Massachusetts more than twenty years before. Progressive reformers led by Governor Hiram Johnson hoped that state regulation would eliminate the corruption arising from utility involvement in politics, while preventing both monopoly exploitation and unfair rate discrimination by utility firms. Such reformers conceived of regulation as a means to draw upon professional and apolitical expertise to reconcile the interests of consumers and privately owned service providers. At the same time, leading utility executives believed that credible state regulation would protect their firms against what they believed to be extortion by corrupt municipal officials, stave off calls for outright municipal ownership, and limit threats presented by duplicative competition.[44] Electric and gas utility firms not only supported regulation in California but played a leading role in lobbying the state legislature to bring it about. In 1910, the Pacific Gas and Electric Company, the Pacific Lighting Company, and the Los Angeles Gas and Electric Company set up committees to lobby the state legislature for the imposition of state regulation.

Reflecting the strength of this political coalition between Progressives and utility firms, the Public Utilities Act extending Railroad Commission jurisdiction to electric utilities passed both houses of the California legislature by unanimous vote on November 28, 1911. The law gave the Railroad Commission authority to set electric utility rates on its own initiative, grant or deny firms "certificates of necessity and convenience" as to whether they could enter markets, set conditions of service (a nonissue in the case of electricity), and investigate and approve securities issues. Under the initial legislation, the powers of the Railroad Commission did not extend to cities (such as San Francisco) that chose to retain their own regulatory authority. In 1915, however, this restriction was removed and the Railroad Commission gained jurisdiction over San Francisco's electric utilities as well.

The California Commission, like its counterpart in Massachusetts, regarded duplicative competition as harmful and exercised its powers in many cases to prevent electric utility firms from entering areas already served by existing companies.[45] In San Francisco, as in Boston, the commission could not order the existing firms to cease competing with one another (although in 1923, the commission ordered both the Pacific Gas and Electric and the Great Western companies to establish uniform prices and cease to charge lower rates in those areas where they maintained duplicate systems), but it did have the authority to prevent new firms from entering the market. Although consolidation was a long-standing trend in the electric utility industry in any case, it is possible that this policy on the part of state regulators contributed to the fact that no major efforts by new firms to enter the San Francisco electricity market took place after the imposition of regulation.

In most respects, however, neither municipal nor state regulation seems to have greatly affected investment and pricing choices made by San Francisco's electric utility firms. As in Boston during the early decades of the twentieth century, it was not particular regulatory decisions but increasing technological economies of scale in generation and transmission, the need to maintain high load factor, and demand elasticities that played the major roles in spurring San Francisco's electric utilities to make the investments needed to increase output, extend distribution networks, and provide consumers with good-quality service.

With the possible and significant exception of charges to small consumers, neither municipal nor state oversight seems to have played a major role in driving a decline in price. While it is possible that under the city's regulatory regime, utility executives may have had reason to fear draconian rate cuts, in practice electric utilities found it in their own interests to sell power to many consumers at prices lower than the maximums specified by the Board of Supervisors. In 1911, for example, the Pacific Gas and Electric Company had the legal right to charge customers from $.05 to $.09 per kilowatt-hour, depending on the amount of electricity consumed. To the very smallest consumers the company charged the legal maximum. But to many larger consumers, the firm charged prices much lower. As a result, average revenue received by the company in 1911 amounted to only about $0.04 per kWh—a figure less than even the very lowest price specified in the city's rate scale.[46]

During the 1920s and 1930s, state regulation proved to be little more constraining to utility firms. Like the Board of Gas and Electric Light Commissioners in Massachusetts, the California Railroad Commission did not attempt to rigidly restrain utility profits to a given rate of return.[47] Writing in 1916, commission stock and bond expert Paul A. Sinsheimer described California's policy as one that permitted liberal returns to stockholders and bondholders to secure an "ample and steady flow of investment money into the coffers of the public utility corporations for reinvestment in the public service of the State."[48] The commission's dealings with the Pacific Gas and Electric Company exemplify the workings of this policy. On the basis of an elaborate two-year investigation, in 1923 the commission placed a valuation on the physical property of the company of $109,724,000, compared to $170,711,000 claimed by the firm. Although their valuation amounted to about a third less than that claimed by the company, the commission ordered rate cuts amounting to only about 10–12 percent. As it turned out, company profits actually *increased* following the rate cut because of growth in demand and declines in cost of production. Despite this increase, the commission did not find it necessary to order additional rate cuts in the years that followed to constrain the utility's rate of return to a given percentage of its physical valuation.[49]

San Francisco experienced a politically potent resurgence of calls for municipal ownership of its electric utilities during the 1920s and 1930s. The renewed calls arose in connection with the question of how best to dispose of the hydroelectric power generated as part of the city's Hetch Hetchy water project. In giving San Francisco the right to build its Hetch Hetchy water and power project in Yosemite National Park, the United States Congress had included a provision in the Raker Act of 1913 specifically prohibiting the city from selling any of the power generated to a corporation for resale.[50] With acceptance of the act, federal law as well as municipal charter provisions now committed the city to municipal ownership of its electric utilities. But, with the completion of the Moccasin hydroplant in 1925, and with no city-owned distribution system yet in existence, San Francisco and the Pacific Gas and Electric Company negotiated an "agency contract," in which the firm agreed to take all the power generated by the city for the sum of two million dollars per year. Announcement of the arrangement aroused a firestorm of protest. All of the supervisors who voted for it were turned out of office at the next municipal election.

For the next fifteen years, contention over whether distribution of electricity in San Francisco should be in public or private hands played an important part in the political life of the city. Advocates of municipal ownership argued that private utility firms exploited their monopoly status to charge overly high prices and that state regulatory commissions were ineffective and dominated by utility firms. Indeed, according to former mayor James Phelan, placing oversight of electric utilities in the hands of the California Railroad Commission did not solve the problem of utility influence in politics but merely shifted the locus of corruption to the state level.[51]

Other factors also drove calls for municipal ownership and helped to give the movement its impetus. Unlike the case in Boston, controversy centered not just on the behavior of privately owned service providers but on the disposition of power generated by city-owned facilities. The agency contract with Pacific Gas and Electric not only violated the Raker Act, municipal ownership advocates maintained, but represented a virtual giveaway of a public investment that had already been made. In 1942 testimony before the U.S. Congress, Supervisor McSheehy made this point: "we are selling our power, generated in Hetch Hetchy to the Pacific Gas & Electric Company for about $2,000,000 and they, in turn, are selling it to the consumers in San Francisco for $10,000,000."[52]

A municipally owned distribution system, advocates argued, could charge consumers lower prices for electricity and still earn sufficient revenues to support itself and to feed money into the municipal treasury.[53] These results could be achieved under municipal ownership because of the city's ability to obtain capital at a lower cost than that available to a private company and because, under private ownership, consumers in San Francisco unfairly subsidized customers outside the city where distribution costs were higher.[54]

To some of the most vocal advocates of municipal ownership, however, cutting costs to consumers and reducing utility influence on politics were not in themselves the most important considerations. They believed that municipal ownership of electric utilities, like that of waterworks, was essential for the city's growth. In particular, they were convinced that a municipally owned electric utility in San Francisco was needed as an economic development tool to stem the relative decline of the city as compared to other West Coast centers such as Los Angeles and Seattle, which already had their own plants. With the savings available under municipal ownership, and freedom from Railroad Commission prohibitions on rate discrimination, San Francisco could follow the lead of these other cities and use the provision of cheap electricity as a means to attract industrial development. In a 1923 speech to the Commonwealth Club, Phelan declared: "These utilities, in the hands of the city, are not subject to the State Railroad Commission, which otherwise has jurisdiction over quasi-public or private utility corporations; so special inducements in the way of low rates can be offered to business and population which seek location there. . . . The rates are not superimposed upon the city by a foreign body. Owning the utility itself, it can fix its own rates, and when a man comes along who offers to bring a factory which will give employment and make business for the city . . . it is in a position to grant him facilities."[55]

At least in this case, however, arguments concerning economic development failed to rouse the support of a political coalition sufficiently powerful to spur the city to make the expenditures needed to acquire a plant. Under the terms of the San Francisco charter, bond issues to construct or acquire a municipal distribution system had to be submitted to the voters of the city at referendum.[56] Eight times over the years 1927 through 1941, the city put before the voters bond issues for the construction and/or acquisition of a municipal distribution system in San Francisco. All failed. In 1927 and 1928, the first two bond issues did receive a majority, but not the two-thirds vote required for passage. With the onset of the Depression, the issues fared even less well. Of the six bond issues put before the voters from 1930 to 1941, not one received even majority support.

Opponents of municipal ownership directly attacked the claim that San Francisco could distribute power at a lower cost than the existing private firms. Distribution of electricity by the city, opponents maintained, would be more likely to increase prices and/or taxes than to reduce them. Factors likely to contribute to this result included higher-than-predicted costs of property acquisition and financing, inefficient municipal management, and higher operating costs by the municipality because of the loss of scale economies resulting from the breakup of the private systems. Given these doubts as to whether a city-owned plant would really cut power costs, San Francisco business leaders saw no reason to rally to municipal ownership as a tool for economic development. In a 1941 statement, the San Francisco Chamber of Commerce made the case against municipal ownership:

> Unless the Pacific Gas and Electric Company is willing to sell its property to the city at the prices used by the city in its Plan Nine, that property can only be acquired by condemnation proceedings and in that case there may be a delay of five or more years before the price to be paid can be definitely known.
>
> What assurances have we what prices will be five years hence? What assurances have we that the proposed bonds can be floated five years hence at the proposed interest rate of 3 per cent?
>
> As the ultimate price goes up, the promised profits go down. These promised profits depend upon a revenue based upon the city charging the same rates for electricity which are now charged by the private company. The Plan Nine assures no relief to the rate payers and its assurances of tax reductions may prove illusory to taxpayers.[57]

CALL BULLETIN

Take It and Like It

By Parks

Mr. Ickes seems determined to make San Francisco shoot the works for purchase of the P. G. & E. distributing system here, even though it blows the municipal head off. Mr. Ickes, of course, need not worry about that!

SAN FRANCISCO
JUNE 9, 1941

Both opponents and supporters of municipal ownership of San Francisco's electric utility distribution system brought political as well as economic arguments into play. This 1941 editorial cartoon attacks Secretary of the Interior Harold Ickes for his attempts to enforce the electricity sales provisions of the Raker Act and to encourage the municipal government to purchase Pacific Gas & Electric's distribution facilities. *Courtesy of the* San Francisco Examiner.

These sorts of risks, opponents argued, were simply not worth taking because, under existing arrangements, San Francisco already enjoyed adequate service, prices lower than those in most other American cities, and the protection to consumers afforded by state regulation. In a 1923 speech before the Commonwealth Club, electrical engineer Louis Leurey said: "There can be but two charges made against the present service of the public utility companies which would warrant their immediate dispossession: Either their service is inadequate to meet the demands of domestic and commercial customers or the rates for service are exorbitant. The answer to the first possibility is that the public utility companies have worked out an interconnected power network that has challenged the admiration of the nation. . . . The movement to tie one power plant to one city for all time is like setting the clock of electrical progress backward for twenty years. The second possibility of onerous rates is disposed of when it is realized that these rates are set by the Railroad Commission of California with full knowledge and power to protect the public interest."[58]

Faced with lack of voter support to construct a municipally owned system and a court order invalidating the city's "agency contract" with Pacific Gas and Electric, San Francisco turned to other arrangements to dispose of the power generated by its hydroelectric plants. In 1943, the city began to sell its power to a large government aluminum plant at Riverside. Two years later, San Francisco worked out a set of slightly more complex arrangements that still remain in effect. To supply municipal needs for street lighting, mass transit, public buildings, and the airport, San Francisco and Pacific Gas and Electric agreed to have power wheeled over the company's lines. Under the terms of the plan, the company receives an amount of power from Hetch Hetchy equal to that used in supplying the city's needs. The rest of the power is disposed of through continued sales to large industrial plants outside San Francisco and to the Modesto and Turlock irrigation districts. Otherwise, as in Boston, distribution of electricity in San Francisco remains in the hands of a private utility firm subject to regulation over rates by a state utility commission.

The Growth of Private Electric Utilities and the Turn to State Regulation in Other Cities in the United States

Many differences can be cited in trajectories of utility development in and around Boston and San Francisco and in the evolution of public policy toward these systems. Sources of power relied upon for the generation of electricity and the scale of the generating and distributing networks actually developed during the first decades of the twentieth century differed substantially in the two cities, as did the role of the municipality as an independent actor in setting policy. In the context of these sorts of differences, commonalties in utility development and public policy in Boston and San Francisco stand out all the more sharply.

Thus, while San Francisco experienced more duplicative competition than did Boston in the distribution of electricity, such competition in both cities tended to be highly episodic, and its benefits mostly confined to larger consumers and those located in more central areas. State regulation came to San Francisco much later than to Boston, but in both cities influential utility executives as well as many good government reformers supported its imposition. In important respects, regulation functioned similarly in the two cities as well. In both, regulation furnished existing electric utility firms with a degree of protection against entry by competitors but otherwise imposed few constraints on the character of physical plant, the quality of service, or even the levels of profits. Nevertheless, private electric utility firms found it in their interests under this regime to invest generously in generating and distribution facilities in urban areas, provide generally reliable service, and to charge consumers steady or declining prices.

This pattern of development was broadly typical of that in most other major cities in the United States as well. As in Boston and San Francisco, a multitude of firms typically furnished service during the early years of the industry and occasional episodes of competition occurred. In Chicago, for example, thirty central station companies generated and distributed electricity inside the city limits as of 1893. The firms competed against well-established gas companies, isolated plants built by large consumers, and one another in neighborhoods where distribution systems overlapped. Philadelphia, too, freely granted franchises for electric utility firms to operate in the same territories, leading to episodes of duplicative competition. During the 1880s, for example, the Brush and the United States companies shared virtually identical territories in the center of the city and actively competed with one another until a merger was arranged in 1886. Milwaukee, too, granted large numbers of nonexclusive franchises. By 1889, six companies operated in the central area of the city and some blocks were served by three or even four firms. As in Boston, however, episodes of duplicative competition usually proved short-lived. Even in the absence of state regulation, complete consolidation in most cities dated from about the same time as in Boston. In Chicago, for example, the Edison and Commonwealth companies (both controlled by Samuel Insull) had obtained a virtually complete monopoly on the electric utility industry in the city by 1896—well before the imposition of state regulation. In Philadelphia, consolidation was complete by 1901; in Detroit, by 1900; and in Milwaukee, by the end of 1896.[59]

As in Boston, legislation establishing state regulation over electric utilities typically had the support of influential utility executives as well as that of many reformers. Utility executives who played a leading role in lobbying for state regulation during the early twentieth century included Samuel Insull of Chicago and Alex Dow of Detroit. State regulation had the support of influential utility officials in Pennsylvania as well. In 1916, the chief spokesman of the Philadelphia Electric Company praised the state's law as "the most perfect and complete upon the statute books of any state, and with the provisions of which we are in most sincere and hearty accord."[60]

In some instances, alliances between utility executives and reformers concerned with good government made for strange bedfellows. In Wisconsin, for example, the imposition of state regulation was supported by both Henry Payne, vice president of Milwaukee Electric Railroad and Light, Republican boss, and anti-Progressive, and by leading Progressive (and governor) Robert LaFollette. At the national level, such alliances reached their high-water mark during the spring and summer of 1907, with the issuance of two reports advocating state regulation: one by the National Civic Federation (an organization in which reformers, academics, and business leaders all played important roles) and one by the Committee on Public Policy of the National Electric Light Association, the trade association of the electric utility industry. The National

Civic Federation report advocated regulation as a means of preventing utilities from abusing their monopoly positions and of reducing the occasion for utility corruption of municipal officials. The N.E.L.A. Committee on Public Policy, led by Samuel Insull and Alex Dow, supported regulation as a means for utilities to escape threats posed by municipal ownership initiatives, more hostile regulation by city officials, and duplicative competition.[61]

Outcomes have not been entirely homogeneous, however. As shall be seen in the discussion of events in Seattle, technological trajectories of utility development, the persistence of duplicative competition, and the impetus and strength of movements for government ownership did vary in some instances over the years 1880 through 1940. In electric utilities, as in waterworks, beliefs that privately owned service providers furnished poor service or acted in ways that jeopardized the prosperity and growth of a city could precipitate the formation of a political coalition powerful enough to put municipal ownership in place.

A Sort of Exception: Public Policy and Electric Utility Development in Seattle

In Seattle, as in other cities in the United States, the early years of electric utility development were shaped by local circumstances and marked by local idiosyncrasies. In broad terms, however, public policies toward electric utilities in Seattle and trajectories of technological development initially proceeded along paths more or less similar to those in the urban centers described previously. Here, as elsewhere, municipal officials during the 1880s and 1890s believed in the value of direct competition among privately owned service providers for protecting public interests and put in place franchising practices that reflected these beliefs. But as in other cities, many municipal officials and politically influential citizens came to be dissatisfied with this strategy as time went on and some called for outright government ownership. The outcome of these calls for change, however, was radically different in Seattle than in most other urban centers in the United States.

During the first decade of the twentieth century, municipal ownership advocates in Seattle succeeded in spurring the city to build up its own electricity supply and distribution facilities and to sell power to residential, commercial, and industrial consumers. However, this turn to government ownership did not bring about the complete elimination of private supply and distribution of electricity in Seattle. While the last episode of direct competition between privately owned electric utilities in Seattle ended with a merger in 1912, competition between the private and municipal systems continued for decades. The story of how these events played out over time is a fascinating one, rich with drama and conflict and worthy of being recounted for its own sake. At the same time, analysis of this unique case can lead to a deeper understanding of more typical outcomes in waterworks as well as electric utilities.

In Seattle, as in other American cities during the late nineteenth and early twentieth centuries, debate over the ownership and regulation of electric utilities centered around complaints of monopolist pricing and concerns with concentrated political and economic power. But, to a far greater extent than in San Francisco or in any of the urban centers discussed previously, economic prospects for the city as a whole were seen from an early date as depending upon appropriate resolution of these issues. Remote from the country's main centers of population and commerce, Seattle was still a small city of less than one hundred thousand people as late as 1900. Business and civic leaders, however, believed that cheap electricity generated by nearby water powers and transmitted over high-voltage power lines could rapidly transform Seattle into a great manufacturing and commercial center. With cheap power and the limitless resources of the Great Pacific Northwest at her command, boosters believed, Seattle could one day rival Pittsburgh as a manufacturing center and New York City as a great emporium of trade.

Belief in electricity-driven visions of metropolitan greatness was not necessarily synonymous with advocacy of government ownership. As early as 1895, plans for linked water power and manufacturing developments were already being proposed by private entrepreneurs and by 1900 privately generated hydroelectric power was actually being transmitted to Seattle. In this context, some civic leaders argued that the threat of scaring off the outside capital needed for realization of the boosters' visions made it particularly important that private investors enjoy a free hand in developing utility facilities. On the whole, however, beliefs that the right sort of electric utility development was essential to economic growth played a more important role in driving people into the municipal ownership camp than out of it.

Private electric utility firms, many Seattle citizens believed, simply could not be trusted to pursue electric utility development in the ways needed to advance the growth of the city. Populist Alderman T. Eugene Jordan expressed this concern with regard to an 1895 plan by entrepreneur Edward Ammidown to develop the water and power resources of the Cedar River thirty miles from Seattle. "At Renton, instead of Seattle would I place my dynamos. With options on a few thousand acres of land and town lots . . . I would offer such inducements in cheap power for manufactories to locate there . . . as would not only build a rival to Seattle in an incredibly short time but would irresistibly draw to that new city even what factories Seattle now has on the waterfront."[62]

Such fears may appear exaggerated in retrospect. They did, however, have a basis in the experiences of Seattle citizens and members of the local business community whose own prosperity depended upon city growth. These experiences were not only in electric utilities. Seattle's trauma with private waterworks development has been described in the previous chapter. Past experiences with railroad development bore an even closer resemblance to Jordan's nightmare vision. For cities of the American West during the late nineteenth century, obtaining high-quality railroad connections could literally be a matter of urban life or death. In the case of Seattle, however, the interests of local landowners and businesspeople in railroad access did not coincide with those of the Northern Pacific Railroad, which enjoyed a monopoly on service to the region for many years. Because it owned the site and could thereby profit from land speculation, the railroad chose virtually uninhabited Tacoma rather than Seattle as its West Coast terminus.

In the face of the Northern Pacific's preference for development of its own new settlement, the effort to obtain a high-quality railroad connection to the east was a major preoccupation of Seattle's businessmen and civic leaders during the 1870s and 1880s. Their plans were repeatedly frustrated, however, and even occasional successes did little to increase faith that the goodwill of distant capitalists could ultimately be relied upon. During the early 1880s, for example, financier Henry Villard took control of the Northern Pacific in a complicated series of transactions and actually began building a spur line from Tacoma to Seattle. When Villard lost control of the railroad in January of 1884, however, all work on the spur line was canceled and the Northern Pacific reverted to its previous policy of promoting development in Tacoma rather than in Seattle.[63]

But it was on the basis of experiences with electric utilities themselves that the battle for municipal ownership was primarily fought. By the turn of the century, a whole series of events and conflicts had left many citizens and public officials with little faith in either the ability of the municipal government to exercise effective oversight over privately owned service providers or in the public-spiritedness of the firms themselves. As in other cities, the impotence of measures designed to prevent the emergence of monopoly itself represented a source of irritation to some municipal officials and members of the public. Over the years 1883 through 1893, Seattle awarded electric utility franchises to a total of eight different firms. All of the franchises were nonexclusive, gave each firm the right to serve the entire city, ran for terms of twenty-five years, and contained no provisions as to prices to be charged, extension of wires, or quality of service.[64] As in other cities, occasional episodes of competition did occur, but the absence of legal barriers to entry did not suffice to prevent one company from maintaining a dominant position.[65]

Founded in 1886 as the Seattle Electric Company, the dominant firm began service modestly with two Edison dynamos, each capable of supplying current to up to six hundred lamps. As Seattle was still quite a small city at the time and local sources of capital were limited, the ability of Seattle Electric and other local utility firms to expand their supply and distribution facilities depended in great part upon their access to Eastern sources of financing. Backed by Edison interests from the beginning, Seattle Electric was relatively well positioned in this respect. Thus, over the years 1890 through 1892, the firm was able to draw upon an infusion of Villiard capital from the East to buy out its largest competitor, the Home Electric Light Company. In its new incarnation as the Union Electric Company, the firm continued to pursue aggressive and usually successful efforts to absorb potential rivals or otherwise prevent them from competing. Particularly galling to municipal officials was an 1895 incident in which Seattle granted its street lighting contract to a competing firm and the incumbent company responded by buying out the interloper.

In Seattle, as in other cities, charges that privately owned service providers exploited their monopoly position to charge overly high prices for electricity played a major role in spurring calls for municipal ownership. As early as 1890, for example, conservative Republican Major Rinehart of the Seattle Board of Public Works issued an extensive report calling for a municipally owned electric utility as a means for the city to reduce its disproportionately high costs for street lighting. Fourteen years later, in 1904, the local Democratic party platform similarly expressed support for acquisition of a municipally owned electric plant as a means to bring to private consumers "just rates for light and power."[66]

More unusually, complaints concerning the quality and availability of the service furnished by Seattle's privately owned electric utility also played a part in prompting calls for government ownership. Poor-quality street lighting represented a particular irritant, although for reasons largely not of the contractor's making. Whereas other cities such as Boston and San Francisco relied predominantly upon arc lights for their street illumination, Seattle, for reasons of economy, contracted for extensive numbers of the much dimmer incandescents. Also for reasons of economy in public expenditure, Seattle wrote into its streetcar franchises provisions requiring those companies to provide street lamps along their routes free of charge. Not surprisingly, the companies did not display a great deal of energy in living up to this particular franchise requirement. As a result, many areas even along streetcar lines remained unlighted despite persistent complaints by city officials.[67] For some private citizens, obtaining electric service of any sort presented difficulties as well. With a population of but eighty thousand in 1900, turn-of-the-century Seattle was a far smaller and less densely populated city than either Boston or San Francisco. Many electric utility firms did not find it in their interest to extend service to areas outside the city center and not located directly along streetcar lines.[68]

The most important difference between Seattle and most other American cities of the late nineteenth and early twentieth centuries, however, was that monopolistic abuses on the part of privately owned service providers were seen as endangering the city's economic prospects. In calling for the establishment of a municipal electric utility, for example, a 1902 resolution by the Seattle Chamber of Commerce made the connection between monopoly supply of electricity, high rates to consumers, and the threat of economic strangulation thus:

> Under the existing conditions, Seattle is at the mercy of one company which does not hesitate to take advantage of its monopoly. . . . An exorbitant charge is made to factories . . . a charge far in excess of what is taxed in Tacoma or Everett for a similar service.
>
> This condition of affairs could not last 24 hours had the city a municipal lighting plant ready to furnish power or light at a minimum of cost. It would prove a great equalizer of expenses in this line, and would remedy one of the most aggravating handicaps manufacturers and users of electric power have to contend with in Seattle.[69]

Allegations that monopoly and its defense on the part of privately owned service providers led to political abuses were also closely associated with hopes and fears concerning the role of cheap power in spurring economic development. Interestingly, it was an episode of rivalry between privately owned service providers that brought concerns with utility political influence to center stage. Seattle grew rapidly during the first decade of the twentieth century and by 1910 its population had vaulted to almost 240,000. As Seattle outdistanced contenders such as Tacoma for regional urban supremacy, the city itself came to represent the most important prize in a contest between private firms to gain control of distribution outlets for electricity generated by nearby water powers. Over the years 1898 through 1903, especially, efforts to influence the political system—and allegations that competing firms were pursuing such efforts—represented important tools in the struggle.

Ownership of the firms involved lay in the hands of East Coast equipment manufacturers and consulting firms. During the years 1899 and 1900, the Stone and Webster partnership of Boston, in combination with General Electric interests, consolidated all of Seattle's streetcar and electric utility firms into the Seattle Electric Company. Through acceptance of stock and bonds in return for provision of services and equipment, Stone and Webster and General Electric also owned large holdings in many other utility firms in the region. Over the course of the decade that followed, they began to take steps to consolidate these relatively small firms and gain control over the supply and distribution of electricity throughout the Puget Sound region and western Washington state. At the same time, firms backed by the Pittsburgh-based Westinghouse Corporation were engaged in a similar effort.

The contest for Seattle began in earnest in 1898 when the Westinghouse-backed Snoqualmie Falls Power Company requested permission from the municipal government to build its own distribution system in the city. Well-known and influential local attorney James Burke represented Snoqualmie before the city council. Nevertheless, the franchise Snoqualmie received contained a number of provisions unfavorable to the applicant. Unlike the franchises held by Seattle Electric, the Snoqualmie document prohibited rate increases, required that the company pay a 1 percent tax on gross receipts, and forbade rate discrimination between similar classes of customers. City officials maintained that inclusion of these franchise terms represented a genuine (if belated) effort to protect public interests against exploitation by privately owned service providers.

Backers of Snoqualmie cried foul. They claimed that the franchise terms were really imposed at the behest of the incumbent service provider, which still relied upon more expensive power generated at local steam-generating plants and feared the competition. Allegations that the incumbent supplier was manipulating the political system to its own ends gained greater plausibility in 1902 when Seattle Electric was granted a new fifty-year franchise without any of the restrictions with which Snoqualmie was hedged. The award prompted a public outcry and set in motion a grand jury investigation. Some of the testimony was damning, if not entirely unmotivated by self-interest. In particular, the son of the president of Snoqualmie claimed that back in 1898 city council members had demanded a bribe in return for being granted a more favorable franchise and that his father had refused to accede to this corrupt and improper act of extortion.[70] The grand jury itself painted its findings in purple if ungrammatical prose, claiming that the Seattle Electric Company "has obtained its franchises through fraud, debauched public officials, and whenever it has loomed up in our investigation has exhibited the earmarks of the unlawful and shameless use of money to accomplish its ends."[71] Although the grand jury's indictment of leading citizen and Seattle Electric president Jacob Furth was ultimately dropped, the odor of scandal surrounding utility franchising in Seattle remained.

Efforts by Snoqualmie to use the political system and the courts to set back the plans of its rival also attracted criticism. During the winter of 1899, the Washington Power and Transmission Company (a firm closely associated with Stone and Webster) announced plans to build its own hydroelectric facilities on the Cedar River upstream from Seattle's projected water supply. Snoqualmie responded in a rather devious fashion. Citing a supposed danger that drinking water might be contaminated by the power development, agents of Snoqualmie living in Seattle brought suit against the municipal government to prevent it from completing its Cedar River water supply system. The hope was that the city in turn would be forced to bring suit against the Washington Water Power development or be prompted to simply buy the site so as to prevent construction of the desperately needed waterworks from being delayed. The gambit succeeded. Seattle did buy the Washington Water Power site.

The overall effect of these maneuvers, however, served the interests of neither firm. Rather than restoring faith in the possibilities of competition between private firms in the electric utility industry, the rivalry between Seattle Electric and Snoqualmie reinforced existing fears concerning control of local service providers by distant and unaccountable corporations and financiers, indifference to even the most fundamental of public interests, and corruption and subversion of the democratic political processes. Combined with concerns over economic development, the results were the emergence of a far wider base of political support for construction of a municipal electric utility in Seattle than was the case in any of the cities discussed previously.

The initial steps resembled those taken in San Francisco. In 1896, the voters of Seattle approved a new municipal charter. Like the charter approved in San Francisco two years later, the document put in place such good government reforms as a municipal civil service even as it called for city ownership of all utilities as a long-term goal. But unlike the case in San Francisco, where concerns over water supply still dominated, Seattle actually took immediate steps to obtain its own electric utility. The 1896 charter provided for a referendum to be held on actually building a municipal lighting plant at the first election after completion of

Seattle's Cedar River water system. The waterworks was completed in 1901 and a $590,000 bond issue for construction of a city-owned hydro-plant on the Cedar River was placed before the people at the March 4, 1902 election. While the election itself was hotly contested, all of the leading candidates for mayor supported municipal ownership, as did that portion of the business community represented in the Chamber of Commerce. The bond issue passed overwhelmingly, with 7,973 citizens voting for the measure and 1,466 voting against. Two and a half years later, and in a more lightly attended election, a majority of citizens who voted approved the expenditure of an additional $250,000 for expansion of the generating plant and for construction of facilities for distribution of power to private consumers as well as for street lighting.

Construction of a small 2,400-kilowatt generating plant on the Cedar River was actually completed by the city late in 1904. Current for street lighting began to be supplied in January of 1905, with service to private consumers initiated in the fall. The municipal system grew rapidly during the years that followed, with voters passing bond issues for expansion of supply and distribution facilities in 1906, 1908, and 1910. The number of customers served by City Light increased from about five hundred in 1905 to about fifteen thousand five years later. By 1911, generating facilities had been installed by City Light with a rated capacity of about 13,500 kilowatts.[72] Despite the role played by industrial development concerns in prompting the establishment of the system, the primary beneficiaries were small consumers and municipal street lighting. The municipal utility proved far more receptive than its privately owned counterparts to calls for distribution lines to be extended into relatively lightly populated residential districts and the greatest price cuts were for small consumers. Investments in street lighting were also a high priority and by 1911, City Light was advertising Seattle in its boosterish annual reports as the "best lighted city in America."

Overall, the period 1900 through 1910 was one of great promise to those who believed in cheap hydroelectricity as an engine of growth and in Seattle's future as a great metropolis. The city's population increased from fewer than 90,000 to almost 240,000 over the course of the decade. By 1910, Seattle had clearly outdistanced Tacoma and even Portland as the leading entrepôt of the Pacific Northwest. By the decade's end, hydro-power introduced by private as well as publicly owned service providers in 1903 and 1904 had already brought about economies in the costs of generating electricity unavailable in less-favored regions. Manufacturing industries such as shipbuilding had gained a foothold. The potential for future development of hydroelectric resources was clearly enormous.

After years of frustration and scandal, municipal efforts to encourage competition between private electric utility firms also appeared to be bearing fruit. Most important was that, in the wake of the 1903 grand jury report described previously, the city finally removed from the Snoqualmie Electric franchise the provisions its managers had found objectionable. At least in the short term, these policies appeared to succeed. Snoqualmie rapidly built up its own distribution system in the areas of Seattle with the most concentrated demands and began to actively compete with Seattle Electric, primarily for commercial and industrial business. As a consequence of this emphasis, Seattle Electric and Snoqualmie together supplied about two-thirds of the electricity consumed in Seattle as of 1910, even though the firms served fewer than half the customers. At the same time, the municipal system's rate-making and extension policies ensured that small consumers were able to obtain service and share in at least some of the benefits of competition.[73]

Although some people called for outright government ownership of all utilities, municipal officials during this period defined the value of City Light primarily in terms of its competitive and price-setting role as one among many service providers.[74] In this context, the municipal utility appeared to enjoy broadly based public support. Bond issues for expansion were approved by wide margins with the support of most of Seattle's newspapers, organized labor, middle-class reformers, and such business associations as the Chamber of Commerce and the Manufacturers' Association. Nevertheless, controversy over the development and governance of electric utilities did not entirely disappear. Not all citizens or members of the business community approved of the municipality's role as purveyor of electric power.

One major newspaper, the *Seattle Times*, actively crusaded against the enterprise. The *Times* opposed municipal ownership of electric utilities as a matter of principle. Municipal provision of electricity, the *Times* maintained, represented a socialist and un-American arrogation of power on the part of municipal government and constituted an opening wedge for more vicious forms of tyranny. In addition, the newspaper maintained, the municipal utility's management was incompetent and dishonest. The newspaper's writers conceded that municipal ownership might have brought about lower rates for consumers. The benefit was illusory, however, coming at the cost of higher taxes, with the subsidies hidden by accounting tricks.

On the other side, allegations of undue utility influence over municipal government continued to resonate. The continued power of these matters to arouse public controversy was revealed in 1910 with the election of Republican Hiram Gill as mayor. Gill selected former Seattle Electric Company employee Richard Arms for the newly created position of superintendent of lighting. Six months after the appointment was made, the muckraking *Seattle Star* was running banner headlines charging that the appointment of Arms was the product of a deal between Gill and the Seattle Electric Company. The newspaper alleged that in order to protect his former employer, Arms was turning down lucrative power supply contracts and seeking to destroy the municipal utility from within. In the view of many of Seattle's more solid citizens, such business influence over politics was directly linked with the Gill administration's tolerance of gambling, prostitution, and other forms of moral degradation.[75] Although collusion between Arms and Seattle Electric was never conclusively established, the combination of concerns with public immorality, improper business influence over government, and possible threats to City Light were sufficiently potent to bring about the recall of Gill, the resignation of Arms, and the election of real estate agent George Dilling as mayor on a reform platform.

During the years that followed, patterns of utility development and utility politics began to shift as private and government-owned utilities both took aggressive steps to realize scale economies and to reach for the brass ring of monopoly. In 1912, Seattle's two competing privately owned electric utilities were consolidated, along with other local firms, into the newly formed Puget Sound Traction, Light, and Power Company. Like Seattle Electric, the new firm was incorporated in Massachusetts and managed under the auspices of Stone and Webster. The Puget Sound Company blossomed into a truly regional power supply system. The most concentrated center of demand for electricity remained in Seattle but by the end of the 1920s, Puget generated power at widely dispersed hydro and steam facilities and distributed electricity over a broad swath of western and central Washington state. As was the case with electric utilities elsewhere in the country during this period, growth was rapid, with power-generating capacity increasing almost two and a half fold between 1911 and 1928.

Managers of Seattle's municipal electric utility attempted to pursue a similar path. The dominant figure here was J. D. Ross. Hired back in 1903 as chief electrical engineer for the municipal light plant, Ross had testified against Superintendent Arms at the City Council investigatory hearings. After Mayor Gill was recalled and Arms stepped down, the new mayor appointed Ross as Arms's successor. Ross remained in charge of Seattle's municipal electric utility until his death in 1939. A strenuous believer in the gospel of city-building through cheap electricity and in the perfidy of privately owned service providers, Ross was convinced that the municipal electric utility had no alternative but to pursue growth. Aggressive development of electric utility supply and distribution facilities under municipal control was needed, Ross consistently maintained, in order to secure Seattle's destiny as a great metropolis and to bring to her citizens the high standard of living made possible by modern technology.[76] Ross feared that in the absence of such investment the municipal utility would ultimately be crushed by profit-seeking privately owned service providers pursuing their own interests and not those of the community.

The first task, Ross believed, was to expand municipal hydro-generating facilities at its existing site on the Cedar River. The effort failed. Completed in the summer of 1914, a high masonry dam at Cedar Falls was designed to increase the generating capacity of the facility from 10,400 kilowatts to 25,400 kilowatts. Unfortunately, the dam proved useless because of seepage that had been predicted in earlier engineering reports. But although this failure was embarrassing and created short-term difficulties for the municipal utility, the limited potential of the Cedar River was already clear in 1911 and 1912. Even if the Cedar Dam had performed as expected, really large-scale development of the kind envisioned by Ross would still have required entirely new sites.

In the effort to gain access to such sites, it was not poor planning on the part of the municipality but deliberate obstruction on the part of the privately owned utility that created the main problems. In March of 1914, a bond issue needed to finance condemnation of a hydro site at Cushman Lake on the Skokomish River in the Olympic Mountains fell slightly short of the 60 percent majority needed for passage. Three years later, efforts to acquire a larger site received a further setback. In December 1916, the city authorized issuing revenue bonds (not requiring approval of the electorate) for construction of a new hydroplant at one of several sites under consideration by the city. But in the summer of 1917, Ross learned that Stone and Webster had managed to purchase or tie up the rights to all of the sites under consideration. The private firm appeared to have boxed the city in.

Seattle municipal officials responded by turning to the federal government for aid. The largest single hydro resource in all of western Washington lay on the Skagit River in the Washington National Forest. Puget held a temporary permit to develop the river but had yet to actually begin work on a facility. In the summer of 1917, Ross responded to Puget's preemption of the city's planned development sites by cross-filing with the Secretary of Agriculture for a permit on the Skagit. Both company and city officials lobbied intensely in Washington for a favorable ruling. This time, the municipal government prevailed.

Citing the failure of the Stone and Webster-controlled Skagit Power Company to initiate construction of a facility on the river despite permit requirements that it do so, Secretary of Agriculture Houston granted the city's request on December 22, 1917. In January of 1918, the secretary gave the city provisional permission to begin construction of its own facilities. After a number of controversies over financing of the facilities, final permits were granted in 1920. The gorge power house on the Skagit began operation in September of 1924. Work on a second dam designed to stabilize water flows and increase power-generating capacities and furnish flood protection was begun upstream at the Diablo Canyon in 1928 and was completed in the fall of 1930.

To a degree, completion of these facilities represented a fulfillment of Ross's vision for Seattle's municipal electric utility. In particular, development of the Skagit made it possible for Seattle's municipal electric utility to independently generate electric power on a scale approaching that of its private sector counterpart.[77] But by the end of the 1920s, Ross and other leading public power activists were dreaming of far more. Like Morris Cooke in Pennsylvania, they sought to build up a regional publicly controlled super power system that would generate and distribute electricity on a scale far exceeding that of any of the privately owned utilities of the day. Municipally owned utilities such as those in Seattle and Tacoma would be the linchpins of the giant network envisioned.

In practice, however, distribution of electricity by Seattle's municipal utility during the 1920s and 1930s remained mostly confined to the city itself. By 1929 a few extensions had been made to nearby suburbs. But these were limited and of dubious legality under state law in any case. Even inside Seattle, Puget Power and Light did not demonstrate any signs of willingness to withdraw from what remained its largest and most concentrated market despite Ross's belief that vigorous municipal development would ultimately be rewarded with monopoly.[78] Indeed, over the years 1925 through 1929, Puget actually expanded its presence in Seattle, extending distribution lines to many of the far-flung residential districts that had heretofore been the preserve of the municipal utility alone.[79]

The obstacles to regional public power development lay in substantial part at the state level. Like California, Washington extended the jurisdiction of its railroad commission to gas, water, electricity, and other public utilities in 1911. As in California and other states, the commission took the view that the interests of monopolistic privately owned monopoly service providers were not fundamentally incompatible with those of consumers and that competition of any sort in the provision of such goods as electricity ultimately raised costs and harmed the public.[80] Neither municipal ownership of utilities nor municipal competition with privately owned service providers was compatible with this vision.

With the support of privately owned service providers and regulators themselves, a number of initiatives were taken in the state legislature over the years 1911 through 1916 to extend the jurisdiction of the state commission to municipally owned utilities, to prohibit municipal utilities from competing with privately owned service providers unless they obtained permission, and to make it more difficult to use eminent domain to acquire utility property. Municipal officials and home-rule advocates had sufficient influence at the state level to secure defeat of most of these measures in the legislature or at referendum. But a measure was passed in 1915 revoking the authority of municipally owned utilities to extend their distribution networks outside of a city's bounds.

Large-scale regional development of government-owned utilities could not go forward in the face of such a ban and during the early 1920s,

Homer Bone of Tacoma, J. D. Ross, and other public power advocates sought to pull together a statewide political coalition powerful enough to spur the adoption of more favorable legislation. In arguments before the legislature, Bone made the case for a state policy permitting municipal utilities to extend their lines outside their bounds in terms of the injustice of local resources being controlled by outside interests: "To permit Stone and Webster to take the power from our hills which is the heritage of our children is a crime against the coming generations."[81] By contrast, a government-controlled super power network, advocates maintained, would provide cheaper electricity, more vigorously extend service to rural areas, and remove the threat to democracy presented by private utility influence on state as well as local politics. Such arguments succeeded in rallying the support of many urban labor organizations, the state grange, and some reformers to the public ownership camp. But although the initiative received majority support from voters in Seattle and Tacoma, the vast majority of voters elsewhere in the state rejected a 1924 ballot initiative that would have permitted municipal electric utilities to expand beyond the bounds of cities.

Difficulties faced by the measure in the legislature and its ultimate defeat at referendum can be attributed in substantial part to a vigorous lobbying and public relations campaign by private electric utility firms and the secret sponsorship of supposedly independent front organizations. Interestingly, the same concerns with economic development and control by outside interests that had earlier proven so potent in prompting Seattle's decision to develop its own electric utility were now effectively used by private utility representatives to advance their own cause. To residents and businessmen in outlying communities, opponents of super power portrayed the cities of Seattle and Tacoma as self-aggrandizing economic imperialists not to be trusted with control of a regional utility network. Puget Sound Power and Light public relations agent Norwood Brockett made the case as follows: "Once let Seattle and Tacoma get a strangle hold on power and they will never let industries go to Everett and Bellingham. They will make one rate for industries in your cities and another for Seattle and Tacoma."[82]

During the 1930s, plans to expand the role of public power by having Seattle take over some or all of Puget's generating and distribution facilities were also stymied. One set of problems and difficulties arose from the task of simply working out a price for the acquisition. The first proposal made public by City Light was to use condemnation proceedings to acquire Puget's Seattle distribution system and possibly some of the firm's generating facilities as well. Publicly announced in 1929, the plan was quietly dropped in subsequent years as the Depression took hold and realities of the difficulties involved sank in. In particular, it was realized that condemnation proceedings would almost inevitably be long and drawn-out if the company chose to aggressively contest the process. Even if the city won, costs could be highly unpredictable depending upon the ingenuity of the lawyers involved and judges' readings of the tangled arcana of the statute and case law involved in determining fair value.[83]

The abandonment of condemnation proceedings meant that any acquisition would instead have to be carried out through some form of negotiated buyout. In some respects, the coming of the Depression increased the attractiveness of this option to both parties. As the Depression took hold in Washington during the early 1930s and demand for electricity declined, both the municipal and the private electric utilities found themselves under increasing financial stress. With investments and capital structures premised on the sort of growth in demand for electricity that had characterized the previous three decades, both systems found themselves squeezed in a vise of declining revenues and high fixed costs. At least in theory, ending the competition between the systems would have afforded an obvious way to reduce the need for future investment in distribution and generating plants and to cut entirely such ongoing burdens as the need for two sets of salespeople in the same area.

But negotiating a price to divide such present and future spoils of monopoly still presented problems. The fate of a plan publicly proposed by Ross in 1934 and 1935 to buy out the entire company in return for about ninety-five million dollars in City Light revenue bonds illustrates the character of some of these problems. From the perspective of company officers, the price was clearly too low. Bondholders would be recompensed but holders of common stock would get nothing at all. This was not entirely unfair as the stock was paying no dividends at the time. But the company was not bankrupt, shareholders still had a voice, and hopes that at least some value would be regained in the future had not entirely disappeared. Uncertainties as to the future performance of City Light bonds represented an additional source of resistance.[84]

For City Light, on the other hand, public fears that the cost would be too high helped to make this and other acquisition plans proposed during the period a difficult sell to the voters who would have to approve the bond issues. Promises of lower costs to consumers played a prominent role in the arguments of municipal utility officials and local political leaders who sought to rally public support to acquisition proposals.[85] But while it undoubtedly made the economies of consolidation more attractive, the general financial stringency of the Depression also increased fears that any new investment by the city might end up increasing the burdens on already hard-pressed taxpayers.

Fairly or not, recurrent financial crises faced by Seattle's public transit system increased public skepticism, prompting widely accepted claims that the municipality had paid too high a price to acquire the system from Puget Power and Light in 1919. Given widespread belief that Puget's system was over-capitalized and that much of its property was in poor condition, even the 1934 price suggested by the city came under attack from many quarters as too high. The construction by the federal government of its great hydroplants at Grand Coulee and Bonneville on the Columbia River muddied the financial picture further. With cheap federal power soon to be available to the Northwest, argued the critics of the acquisition plans, why bother with attempting to take over Puget's relatively high-cost facilities?[86]

As was the case with the fight over the Bone Bill during the 1920s, concerns with concentrated economic and political power also operated against plans to expand the role of Seattle's municipally owned electric utility. Acquisition by the city, advocates maintained, would eliminate once and for all the baleful influence of Puget Power and Light on local and state politics. But the prospect of a single municipally owned system also aroused fears. Ross himself was a source of controversy. Swept by the tides of electoral fortune, mayors and city administrations came and went over the years 1912 through 1939. No matter who held electoral office, however, Ross remained. From the beginning, Ross closely identified his own fortunes with those of the municipal electric utility and maintained a firm grip on all phases of operations, investment planning, and the hiring and firing of employees. At least from Ross's own perspective, his efforts to maintain tight control over the municipal electric utility and his involvements in politics were primarily defensive in character. If the municipal electric utility was to survive and grow, Ross maintained, interference by politicians and even civil service commissions in operations and planning had to be thwarted. Employee loyalties had to be undivided; one person had to be in control and accountable for results. At the same time, Ross believed, public support for the municipal electric utility had to be aggressively cultivated in the face of wide-ranging public relations and propaganda campaigns undertaken by the private utility industry. Fire had to be fought with fire and Ross played an active role in the establishment of such groups as Friends of City Light during the mid-1920s and the Citizens' Municipal Utilities Protective League in 1930 to rally public support for himself and for pro-City Light candidates.

These efforts succeeded to a substantial extent. Active support from the business community, which had played such an important role in the establishment of the municipal electric utility at the turn of the century, declined in importance during the 1920s and 1930s. Nevertheless, City Light and Ross himself continued to enjoy a substantial degree of popular support and in places adulation—particularly among residents of neighborhoods where the municipal utility had extended distribution lines after the private firm had refused to do so. The potency of this support was most sharply revealed in 1931 when Mayor Edwards fired Ross on the eve of the March 9 municipal election. The backlash in favor of Ross was quick and reverberated through municipal politics. Candidates in favor of City Light were elected and a campaign for the recall of Mayor Edwards, spearheaded by the Citizens' Municipal Utilities Protective League, immediately got underway. At the election, held on July 13, 1931, Edwards was recalled by a vote of 35,659 to 21,839 and the new administration promptly reappointed Ross as head of the municipal electric utility.[87] Ross never again faced a serious threat to his position and he retained it until his death in 1939. But his active role in municipal politics continued to inspire fears of empire-building, not only among outright opponents of municipal electric utility development but among many who supported the concept.

In the case of Ross's 1934 proposal that Seattle buy out the entire private system, fear of dominance by the city remained a potent source of opposition in outlying communities.[88] In part as a result of such sentiment, the plan for a regional buyout was quietly dropped in 1935 and discussion turned again to having Seattle acquire only Puget's local facilities. Here too, however, concerns with potential abuses of concentrated economic and political power continued to play against initiatives for a municipally owned monopoly. A 1935 public statement by the Seattle Real Estate Board made the case: "The Seattle Real Estate Board believes in competition. It is the life of trade. We believe that if we did not have competition that we would have higher rates and less efficiency than now prevails. We believe that if the City had the exclusive monopoly on light and power here, that there is a possibility that our homes would be held for the unpaid light bills of non-paying tenants just as they are being held now for unpaid water bills."[89]

The combined effect of these factors was that despite extensive publicity campaigns conducted by such organizations as Friends of City Light during the mid-1930s, the movement for a merger never really took fire as a popular cause. Supporting the municipal electric utility as a competitor and a sort of political counterweight to the private suppliers was one thing. Putting in place a public or private monopoly for the provision of electricity was seen as another matter altogether, no matter what the putative advantages.[90]

Passions over the development of electric utilities in Seattle perceptibly cooled during the 1940s, partly because the nation's attention was riveted on World War II. Furthermore, none of the figures who succeeded Ross as head of Seattle's municipal electric utility dominated the scene in quite the same way. But controversy over public versus private development of electric utilities did continue and public support for a municipal buyout of Puget's facilities in Seattle remained lukewarm at best. Over time, however, a number of factors drove both municipal officials and company executives to work toward an acquisition on mutually acceptable terms. One of the most important of these was the 1952 expiration of Puget Power and Light's franchise in Seattle. In anticipation of the franchise expiration, the Seattle City Council passed a resolution in 1943 declaring the municipality's intention to eliminate private supply and distribution of electricity inside the city and to expand the municipality's own supply and distribution facilities to carry the load.

The execution of such a policy would have been a grave blow to Puget Sound Power and Light. Not only would revenue from customers in Seattle be lost but investments in distribution facilities to serve them would have been rendered virtually worthless.

But while franchise expiration undoubtedly strengthened the municipal government's bargaining position, Puget was not entirely without negotiating chips of its own. Wartime and postwar material shortages limited the ability of Seattle to build up its supply and distribution network to the extent needed. At the same time, the company had little incentive to invest in its own facilities in the absence of an accommodation with the city. For municipal officials, the prospect of an investment strike was particularly threatening because older dreams of economic growth through cheap electricity finally appeared to be on the verge of realization. During the 1920s and 1930s, boosters' dreams of industrial development driven by cheap electricity had gone unfulfilled in Seattle. Although charges for electricity were some of the lowest in the United States, population growth lagged and numbers of jobs in manufacturing actually declined from their 1919 war-driven peak. The 1940s and 1950s, however, opened up new possibilities. Seattle's economy did not boom in the way that Southern California's did (something for which many of today's residents are deeply grateful) but war and its aftermath meant the end of economic and industrial stagnation. Along the Columbia River, great aluminum plants opened up to take advantage of cheap federal power from the Bonneville and Grand Coulee dams. In the environs of Seattle itself, Boeing emerged as the premier aircraft manufacturer in the world, with employment at its plants rising from four thousand in 1939 to a peak of fifty thousand in 1944. Its employment fell immediately after the war but aircraft manufacturing remained a major industry and the economy of the region continued to grow.

The opportunities and threats created by these circumstances gave strong incentives for both city and company to work out an accommodation. For Puget Sound Power and Light, burgeoning economic development in the suburbs east of Lake Washington meant that the utility could withdraw from the city and still enjoy a growing market for electricity. For Seattle, buying out the utility's facilities rather than attempting to build its own would eliminate a potentially deadly bottleneck to economic development in the city itself. Although public skepticism remained, an agreement was reached in 1949. Seattle would buy up Puget's distribution system inside the city for a price of about $28,500,000. Despite widely publicized predictions of an electrical supply catastrophe unless the deal went through, voters passed a bond issue to underwrite the acquisition by a paper-thin margin of only 750 votes after a recount. The transaction was nevertheless completed on March 5, 1951, and from that date onward, Seattle has had a single municipally owned electric utility.

Conclusion

The politics of growth have been of central importance in shaping public policy toward both electric utilities and waterworks in major American cities. Consistently over time, and in a broad range of circumstances, the greatest threat to the political viability of governance arrangements in both industries came from perceptions by civic leaders and influential business elites that poor service or inadequate investment in system development threatened local economic prospects. In the case of waterworks, difficulties in arranging for privately owned service providers to make such investments represented the most powerful factor driving government ownership movements. In the case of electric utilities in Seattle, as well, such concerns infused discussion and debate almost from the beginning and played a major role in shaping outcomes. In most urban and suburban areas, by contrast, electric utility firms found it was in their own interests to expand output, furnish reliable service, extend distribution networks, and hold prices at steady or declining levels during the early decades of the twentieth century.[91] In the absence of serious complaints over service quality or widely shared beliefs that expensive electricity hindered economic development, campaigns for municipal ownership of electric utilities usually went down to defeat.

Suspicions of unaccountable economic and political power also shaped governance and development in both waterworks and electric utilities. In waterworks, the reluctance and inability of municipal governments to impose stringent building codes and land-use controls on urban property owners played powerful—albeit indirect—roles in contributing to demands for large-scale investment in supply and distribution facilities and for government ownership. In electric utilities, questions of building codes and land use did not arise in connection with system development to nearly the same degree. But suspicions of undue or unaccountable power in the hands of utility enterprises themselves played important roles in shaping outcomes. The way in which municipal governments in large numbers of cities in the United States, for example, almost automatically relied upon private firms for the provision of electricity during the early years of system development can be accounted for in great part by these sorts of suspicions and beliefs. The persistence of often futile municipal efforts to somehow arrange for competition between privately owned service providers can also be understood in these terms. Complicating matters further, suspicions of concentrated power have not always favored privately owned service providers. In turn-of-the-century Seattle, for example, movements for the construction of a municipally owned electric utility were based on both a belief in the value of competition and a desire to check the political and economic power of privately owned service providers.[92]

American federalism, too, has contributed to the complexities of the politics surrounding both waterworks and electric utility development and governance. The existence not only of strong judicial property rights protections but of multiple levels of government authority has created a political world in which privately owned service providers have sometimes been able to beat back threats to their interests by appealing to other levels of jurisdiction. In the case of waterworks in San Francisco, for example, maneuvering in both the courts and at the state level contributed to the survival of private ownership during the 1870s and 1880s. Similarly, the imposition of state regulation over electric utilities was supported in many instances not only by good government reformers contemptuous of what they saw as the corruption and irrationality of political decision making in American cities but by private utility firms themselves seeking to get out from under what they viewed as overly stringent local ownership and rate-setting initiatives.

Here too, however, it has not always been privately owned service providers that benefit. At all levels of government, the exigencies of political and administrative decision making, developmentalist agendas, and suspicions of concentrations of power in official as well as private hands have influenced policy making toward electric utilities in varying ways. Although on balance, the involvement of both courts and state regulators benefited privately owned service providers, federal interventions have often gone in the other direction. Acquisition by San Francisco of its Hetch Hetchy water supply in 1913 and 1914 can be understood in these terms. Similarly, it was only through federal assistance in 1918 and 1919 that Seattle's municipal electric utility was able to expand, outflanking efforts by Puget Power and Light to prevent this.

As noted, shifts in the locus of governmental authority and decision making also took place. By virtue of actually owning systems, municipal governments retained a relatively important role in shaping waterworks policy in most major American cities. In electric utilities, by contrast, a large share of the policy making action moved to the state level during the early decades of the twentieth century. As time went on, the federal government also came to play an increasingly important role in shaping public policy toward electric utilities. At the start, federal interventions into the affairs of the electric utility industry tended to be either limited in magnitude or of a temporary nature. Over the years 1903 through 1930, for example, the United States Bureau of Reclamation built large dams used to generate hydroelectric power. But the projects were carried out as part of the agency's mandate to furnish irrigation water to western farmers and sale of electricity was seen strictly as a revenue-raising mechanism. Indeed, in the case of Boulder Dam, the Bureau of Reclamation did not even own generating plants located in the structure itself. Instead, the power of the falling water was leased to Southern California Edison and the Los Angeles Department of Water and Power and they operated the generators.[93]

The most important federal regulatory initiatives of the period came as emergency responses to power, coal, and war matériel shortages during World War I. In response to the bottlenecks, federal agencies rationed and allocated electric power in major industrial centers. To ensure adequate production of war matériel in one case, the president used his war powers to simply requisition the entire output of the Hydraulic and Niagara Falls Power Company's generating facilities.[94] Although lack of previous planning and investment limited what could be done, federal agencies also used their war powers to stimulate and sometimes force interconnections between independently owned utility firms.[95] Defined as emergency measures, these initiatives were allowed to lapse once the war ended. Nevertheless, the measures constituted important precedents for federal involvement in the electric utility industry and in the economy more generally. In particular, wartime experiences with interconnection suggested to some thoughtful observers that much greater scale economies in the generation of electricity and more efficient use of existing facilities could be obtained by developing the complex institutional arrangements and networks of transmission lines needed to coordinate supply and distribution of electricity on a regional scale. A federally sponsored survey undertaken with the leadership of consulting engineer William S. Murray in 1921, for example, proposed that electric utility networks from Washington, D.C. to Boston be integrated into a single "superpower system" linked together by high voltage power lines.[96]

At the same time, the very success of electric utilities in transforming life in America's cities and suburban areas intensified perceptions of the backwardness of conditions on the nation's farms and inspired calls for the extension of service to rural areas as a means to redress the balance. Bringing the conveniences of electric appliances to the farm kitchen and of electric-powered tools and lights to fields and barns was seen by advocates of rural electrification as a means of revivifying the Jeffersonian values embodied in rural life and of stemming the tide of migration off of the land and into the physically cramped and morally pernicious environment of the great cities.

In their agitation for increased governmental involvement in the electric utility industry during the early and middle years of the 1920s, activists and politicians such as J. D. Ross and Homer Bone in Washington and Morris Cooke and Gifford Pinchot in Pennsylvania brought together these themes. Like the "city-builders" of Seattle during the late nineteenth and early twentieth centuries, they envisioned cheap power as a stimulus to industrial development and increased material prosperity. The emphasis now, however, was on ideals of regional development and the potential for extensive electricity networks to combine the benefits of efficient production with those of dispersal of population and industry. In Pennsylvania, for example, Pinchot and Cooke presented their highly elaborated "giant power" plan as a means to transform the entire society. Under giant power, the state's authority to regulate electric utilities and to charter new firms would be aggressively employed to construct giant mine-mouth generating plants in the bituminous coal regions of southwestern Pennsylvania, to use high-voltage transmission lines crossing the state to send power to eastern demand centers, and to distribute power to farmers through cooperative and mutual companies. The results, according to advocates, would be more effective utilization of coal and other natural resources, cheaper electricity, and the extension of electric distribution lines to the rural and agricultural areas of the state, still mostly unserved. Pinchot defined the stakes as follows: "Giant Power is a plan to bring cheaper and better electric service to all those who have it now, and to bring good and cheap electric service to those who are still without it. It is a plan by which most of the drudgery of human life can be taken from shoulders of men and women who toil, and replaced by the power of electricity." [97]

Calls for electrification to be used as a tool for regional development also attracted attention in connection with the federal government's Muscle Shoals nitrate and power development begun during World War I. Public ownership advocates such as Senator George Norris of Nebraska eventually joined the cause but in this case it was a private entrepreneur who took the lead. In a widely publicized initiative, Henry Ford submitted a proposal in 1921 to take over the partially completed Muscle Shoals facilities and use them as the centerpiece of a new decentralized industrial complex that would bring to the people of the region the advantages of urban life without its demoralizing and corrupting influences.

At least during the 1920s, visions of this sort had little immediate effect on utility development. With the onset of the Great Depression and the election of Franklin Delano Roosevelt as president, however, matters changed. In sharp contrast to his Republican predecessors, Roosevelt supported government ownership initiatives as means to bring electric utility service to rural areas and as regional development tools. Among the most important steps taken was the establishment of the Rural Electrification Administration in 1935. By sponsoring the formation of rural electric cooperatives and furnishing them with low-interest loans, grants, and technical advice, the agency made possible the extension of electric utility service to the countryside on an unprecedented scale.[98] At Muscle Shoals, the deadlock over public versus private development was broken in 1933 with the establishment of the Tennessee Valley Authority. While administration-supported campaigns to establish similar authorities in other river basins went down to defeat, the Army Corps of Engineers and the Bureau of Reclamation did gain authorization to construct large water and power projects on the Columbia River in the Pacific Northwest, the Central Valley of California, and other locales.

Along with its public ownership initiatives, the Roosevelt administration sought to use the powers of the federal government to check the practices of privately owned service providers it believed hindered effective regulation at the state level. The perceived problems arose in part from procedural and legal handicaps.[99] In nearly all states, commissions could not begin cases on their own initiative. In the context of declining costs that characterized the industry, this worked to the advantage of utility firms because of the high costs of initiating and carrying through a complaint.[100] Other constraints faced by regulatory commissions included inadequate staffing, lack of jurisdiction over wholesale interstate power sales, and the likelihood of disruptive, time-consuming, and inconsistent judicial intervention against any regulatory decision opposed by utility firms.[101]

These weaknesses in state regulation came to appear increasingly salient to critical observers during the 1920s, as more and more electric utility firms came under the sway of holding companies and as holding company empires themselves developed increasingly elaborate ties with one another. Thoughtful critics of holding companies acknowledged that the enterprises could bring economies of scale, improved management, and cheap capital to local utility development. But at the same time, control of local utilities by holding companies based in distant cities could render state regulation virtually irrelevant.

In practice, during the middle and later years of the 1920s, holding companies were structured by both utility managers and financiers in increasingly baroque ways and used to channel enormous profits to a relatively few equity holders perched on top of highly leveraged financial pyramids.[102] The onset of the Depression brought down the more fragile and highly leveraged of these structures. Wiped out and deeply embittered as a consequence were many small investors, including those enticed by assorted utility customer ownership campaigns designed to build customer support.[103] Reports by the Federal Trade Commission indicting financial abuses by holding companies and exposes of industry propaganda efforts contributed to the industry's public relations problems.[104]

In 1935, the Roosevelt administration exploited the political openings thus created to run through legislation giving the Federal Power Commission authority to regulate wholesale prices for electricity marketed across state lines. At the same time, the Securities and Exchange Commission was given the authority to regulate issue of securities by holding companies, to order them to simplify their corporate structure, and to require service organizations to serve operating companies at cost. Most importantly, the law mandated outright dismemberment for holding companies that did not serve geographically unified areas.[105]

These initiatives inspired enormous controversy. Many of the specifics of these disputes differed from those associated with electric utility development in Boston, San Francisco, and Seattle during the late nineteenth and early twentieth centuries. Some broad themes, however, endured. At least in theory, for example, the Tennessee Valley Authority was an agency with "the prerogatives of government but the flexibility of a private corporation." To ensure public accountability, the authority's board of directors was appointed by the president with the advice and consent of the Senate. To avoid over-centralization and to promote local democracy, actual distribution of electricity was to be carried out through municipalities and rural electric cooperatives. Nevertheless, concerns over centralized and unaccountable political and economic power played a prominent role in attacks on the TVA, even as many of its defenders tarred privately owned service providers with a similar brush.

Despite all the changes wrought by the Roosevelt administration, outcomes of New Deal era disputes over ownership and regulation of electric utilities resembled those of past years in important respects. Now, as in the past, public ownership initiatives generally did not have even a chance of being adopted unless developmental concerns could be convincingly invoked as well. And for all of the Sturm und Drang associated with public power during the 1930s, the bulk of the electricity consumed in the United States at decade's end still came from privately owned utility firms. In other respects as well, development of the electric utility industry continued along more or less established paths. While demand for electricity did drop during the early years of the Depression, it soon became clear that the tide of electrification in both industry and households was still running extremely strong despite the general economic downturn. Indeed, unlike the case in almost every other sector of the economy, output of electricity in 1939 was substantially higher than it had been ten years earlier. Economic good times after World War II brought yet more growth, with consumption of electricity increasing at an average rate of almost 8 percent per annum over the years 1945 through 1965.

After World War II, simple familiarity had dimmed the gee-whiz aura of utopianism, mystery, and possible menace associated with electricity at the turn of the century.[106] As in the past, however, associations between growth in electricity consumption and visions of a democratic and affluent society continued to be vigorously expressed or simply taken for granted by partisans of both government and private ownership. Particularly during the 1940s and 1950s, these associations became embroiled with Cold War ideological and military rivalries. Ideologically, liberal use of electricity by the people of the United States as they went about their day-to-day lives represented a vital demonstration of the superiority of the American way of life over Communist collectivism and totalitarianism. Militarily, averting any threat of electricity shortage represented a necessary element of war preparedness.

After 1965, many of the technological, political, and economic factors that had underlain traditional growth paths in the electric utility industry began to shift. Consensus on the desirability of increasing consumption of electricity began to be challenged on environmental grounds. Previously effective approaches to increasing economies of scale in generation of electricity and in the operation of utility networks also began to reach the limits of their usefulness. As shall be discussed in chapter 5, much has changed in the electric utility industry as a consequence of these new challenges and constraints. Yet issues presented by reliance on fixed networks for transmission and distribution of electricity endure.

four

Cable Television and
Mass Communications

COMPARED TO EITHER WATERWORKS OR ELECTRIC utilities, cable television systems do not represent vital elements of urban and suburban infrastructures. An outage of either water or electricity in American cities is highly disruptive and can even be catastrophic to individuals and to the community as a whole. By contrast, a cable television system on the blink is merely inconvenient—the complaints of ESPN and MTV addicts notwithstanding. Unlike the case with either waterworks or electric utilities, the services furnished by cable television systems are almost completely irrelevant for use by businesses in the production of goods and services. From the beginnings of the industry to the present day, cable television has been developed primarily as an item of household consumption. And even in this domain, cable television has not risen to the status of an essential good to the same extent as waterworks or electric utilities. During the early 1990s, almost one out of three homes passed by cable television systems still did not take the service.[1]

But the cable television industry has grown enormously in recent years and an understanding of its history can shed light on issues associated with both networked and communications technologies. As shall be seen, the politics of cable television and the communications complex of which it forms a part have resembled that of both waterworks and electric utilities in certain respects. In cable television, as in waterworks and electric utilities, concerns have arisen that private firms will exploit monopoly control over networked facilities to charge overly high prices or to furnish poor-quality service. Here, too, the roles played by government have been shaped and limited by divisions of authority among different levels of jurisdiction and by court interventions. And, perhaps to an even greater extent than in waterworks or electric utilities, public policy itself has played highly significant roles in molding forms taken by cable television and communications technologies.

At the same time, forms taken by technology have also had consequences for public policy. Like both waterworks and electric utilities, cable television makes use of fixed and networked distribution facilities. As with the other systems, close attention to factors suggested by economic theory and transaction cost analysis can pay great dividends for understanding the public policy issues presented by reliance on fixed networks and the functioning of franchising and regulatory arrangements. In this regard, cable television is particularly interesting because municipal governments in some cities employed franchising arrangements far more sophisticated than those commonly found in either waterworks or electric utilities during the nineteenth and early twentieth centuries. Yet, as shall be seen, the arrangements still fell prey to severe transaction cost problems.

Because cable television is a communications technology, public policy issues have also differed in important respects from those presented by waterworks and electric utility systems. Communications are not just a commodity. The content, control, and flow of information, messages, and even entertainment over communications systems are matters of central importance to social and political as well as economic life and have long been recognized as such. As a consequence, concerns with concentrated political power in the hands of both privately owned service providers and government agencies have played even more important roles in shaping debate and decision making with respect to cable television and other communications systems than has been the case in either waterworks or electric utilities. The central role of communications in political life has also made for additional concerns. Particularly important in shaping discussion, if not always policy, have been notions of a sphere of public information and discourse deserving of a degree of autonomy not only from governments and political officeholders but from market forces.

In the next section of this chapter, I present a brief overview of major themes and tensions in American communications policy. This is followed by historical discussions of public policy and the development of broadcasting and cable television in the United States. I then present accounts of cable television franchising in Seattle, Pittsburgh, and Boston and discuss roles played by economic, transaction cost, and political factors in shaping the performance of cable television franchising in these and other cities.

A Brief Overview of Major Themes and Tensions in American Communications Policy

Communications' central role in political life has been recognized from the very first days of the United States. During the founding years of the American republic, lawmakers set forth a range of positive communications policies consciously designed to promote the wide diffusion of news and information. In particular, the Constitution, ratified over the years 1787 through 1790, provided specifically for protection of copyrights and patents and for the establishment of a postal service by the federal government. From the first, newspapers enjoyed a highly privileged position in the mails because of their perceived importance for binding together a widely dispersed republic, transmitting knowledge of public issues, and linking politicians with their constituents. Under the initial rate schedules set by Congress in 1792 and 1794, a newspaper could be mailed more than 450 miles for a price of one and one half cents. The post office also subsidized the collection and transmission of news by permitting printers throughout the country to exchange copies of their newspapers without charge for postage. This policy, too, was seen as promoting national cohesion by facilitating the exchange of news and information between citizens in different locales and between constituents and elected officials.[2] By contrast, the exchange of personal letters by individuals was not seen as being of nearly the same degree of vital public importance and rates for personal correspondence were high to underwrite the subsidies for newspapers.[3]

In many different contexts, public policy has also been shaped by beliefs that communications should be available to all and upon equal terms in remote as well as central locations. Forms of cross-subsidy have often been employed for this purpose. During the 1890s, for example, the establishment of free mail delivery in rural areas was promoted as extending a virtual right of citizenship to those barred by isolation from full participation in the country's political and economic life.[4] Similarly, during the 1930s and 1940s, the federal government and the privately owned American Telephone and Telegraph Company agreed to rate structures in which high long-distance and business charges subsidized cheap local and residential rates. It was partly because of this that the proportion of American households with telephones increased from about 39 percent to about 80 percent over the years 1941 to 1950.[5]

At the same time, however, the politics of communications have been characterized by tensions between hopes that national sources of news and information could serve as a unifying and homogenizing force in society, concerns that minority and local perspectives not be shut out, and beliefs that citizens should have access to diverse sources of information and entertainment. The lines of division have not been simply between advocates of nationalism and homogeneity and defenders of diversity and localism. During the 1830s, for example, many anti-Jacksonian politicians called for the reduction or elimination of all postage on newspapers. As is quite common in such cases, the campaign was motivated in part by narrow partisan considerations. Anti-Jacksonians believed (with some justification) that Democratic newspapers enjoyed privileged access to the mails and saw across-the-board rate cuts as a way to level the field. But this was not simply a partisan scramble for advantage. Broader beliefs about the role of communications in society drove the conflict as well. Lower rates for newspapers sent over long distances, advocates proclaimed, would help to bind the nation together and eliminate inequities in access to information. Jacksonians, by contrast, sought to retain or even increase the charges for sending publications long distances. Strengthening the position of local newspapers as the sole source of information in outlying locales, they maintained, would protect these virtuous elements of the country's political culture against the pernicious and immoral influences emanating from northeastern cities. At least in this case, a stand for localism derived not from a desire for citizens to have access to diverse perspectives and sources of information but from beliefs that such access could corrupt and destabilize local social and political orders—particularly in areas of the country in which such orders rested upon slavery.[6]

Free speech principles themselves have been a source of controversy in many different contexts. At least rhetorically, free speech has long been enshrined as a fundamental tenet of American democracy. Since ratification of the First Amendment to the Constitution in 1791, the Congress of the United States has been forbidden from making any law "abridging freedom of speech or of the press." But at no time has there been complete consensus as to the sorts of communication to which this guarantee should apply or even as to the specific public and private parties bound by its provisions. From the earliest days of the republic to the present day, there have been disagreements over the extent to which First Amendment protections apply to communications defined as seditious, libelous, false, or obscene.[7] Relatedly, the extent to which free-speech and free-press guarantees encompass access to channels of communication for materials regarded by authorities as undesirable has also been a matter of debate. Despite widely avowed commitments to free speech, pamphlets promoting the elimination of slavery, information about contraception, socialist and communist newspapers, sexually explicit pictures, and fraudulent advertisements have all been banned from the mails at one time or another as threats to public order or morality.

There have been debates as well as to whether the First Amendment applies to actions taken by state and local governments and as to whether and how forms of communication not in existence in 1791 should enjoy the protections afforded speech and the press. The law in these areas has shifted quite dramatically over time. It was only in 1924 in the case of *Gitlow v. New York* that the United States Supreme Court ruled that under the due process provisions of the Fourteenth Amendment, liberty of speech and of the press were safeguarded from interference by state and local governments as well as by federal authorities.[8] The extent to which different media enjoy First Amendment protections has also been limited and has shifted over time. Motion pictures, for example, did not receive federal freedom of speech protections under the First Amendment until 1952 and even then forms of censorship and government review that would have been struck down in the case of print as violating long-standing prohibitions against prior restraint were accepted by the Supreme Court.[9]

Even more deeply problematical in some respects have been relationships between democratic and free speech principles and the emergence of private-sector information monopolies. The issue first arose during the mid-nineteenth century in the context of telegraphic news gathering and transmission. A thirty-thousand-dollar congressional appropriation underwrote construction of Samuel Morse's first experimental telegraph line between Washington, D.C. and Baltimore in 1843 and 1844. But unlike the case with the mails, responsibility for subsequent development was left almost entirely to the initiative of private entrepreneurs. Many companies initially built lines but monopoly came quickly and with virtually no government intervention. In 1866, Western Union emerged as the country's largest corporation, virtually monopolizing carriage of telegraphs.[10]

As in waterworks and electricity, the emergence of monopoly attracted criticism on both economic and political grounds. Western Union, critics charged, failed to extend adequate service to rural residents, charged far higher rates than necessary, and bought off venal politicians with free message delivery as well as outright bribes.[11] At the same time, however, the nexus between information, communication, and democracy attracted more specific attention. By the 1860s the Associated Press, with the cooperation of Western Union, had gained a virtual monopoly on the dispatch of news throughout the United States. Newspapers that did not belong to the Associated Press could usually obtain dispatches only at prohibitive individual message rates or perhaps not at all. Through agreements between Western Union and the Associated Press, critics charged, news that might reflect badly on the telegraph system was not carried. Numerous credible allegations were also made that newspapers editorializing in favor of a postal telegraph were punished with higher rates than their competitors.[12]

From a free speech and First Amendment perspective, such issues presented a real quandary. Government intervention to prevent the alleged abuses perpetrated by the Associated Press and Western Union, or even to break up the combination altogether, could be viewed as justified on the basis of freedom of speech as well as economic concerns. At the same time, cogent arguments could be made that the First Amendment specifically prohibited such intervention, however valuable the purposes served. The issue came squarely before the United States Supreme Court in the context of a 1945 antitrust action against the Associated Press. In upholding a lower court's decision that members of the Associated Press should not be permitted to bar competing newspapers from joining the cooperative, Justice Hugo Black spoke for the majority: "[The First] Amendment rests on the assumption that the widest possible dissemination of information from diverse and antagonistic sources is essential to the welfare of the public, that a free press is a condition of a free society. Surely a command that the government itself shall not impede the free flow of ideas does not afford non-governmental combinations a refuge if they impose restraints upon that constitutionally guaranteed freedom. . . . Freedom to publish is guaranteed by the Constitution, but freedom to combine to keep others from publishing is not."[13] At the same time, however, Justice Roberts could plausibly cite free speech concerns in coming to a very different conclusion in his dissent: "The decree here approved may well be, and I think threatens to be, but a first step in the shackling of the press, which will subvert the constitutional freedom to print or to withhold, to print as and how one's reason or one's interest dictates. When that time comes, the state will be supreme and freedom of the state will have superseded freedom of the individual to print."[14]

All of the themes noted above can be seen in the field of cable television. As has been the case with the mails and with both telephone and telegraph networks in the United States, beliefs that news and information should be widely diffused and that access to channels of communication should be made available to all on equitable terms played major roles in shaping public policy toward cable television systems. And as with both the mails and the telegraph, some of the most intractable controversies arose over the delivery of news and entertainment from relatively small numbers of producers to relatively large numbers of consumers. The forms of the issues in cable television have also partaken of elements from both domains. As with the mails, decision making has been shaped by complex tensions among nationalism, localism, and beliefs in the value of diversity. As with the telegraph, relationships between democratic and free speech principles and private-sector monopoly have been particularly problematical.

But there are differences as well. In the case of the mails and the telegraph, the issues emerged in connection with newspapers. In cable television, the conjunction has been primarily with broadcast media. Unlike newspapers, broadcast media in the United States have themselves been subject to forms of regulation by federal agencies. Cable television itself developed in close association with its broadcast counterpart and the history of federal policy toward cable can be understood only in the context of this relationship.

Private Business, Public Policy, and the Shaping of Broadcasting in the United States

Use of the electromagnetic spectrum for wireless communications can be viewed as a defining phenomenon of the twentieth century. Its scientific and technological origins lay in Maxwell's equations, published in 1865, postulating that electromagnetic fields could be propagated through space, Henrich Hertz's brilliantly simple experiments, announced in 1888, in which he demonstrated the generation and detection of such waves, and Oliver Lodge's discovery of the technology of tuning during the 1890s.[15] Both Hertz and Lodge, however, were primarily concerned with electromagnetic waves as scientific phenomena. It was Italian-British entrepreneur and inventor Guglielmo Marconi who led the way in developing and refining practical methods of using radio waves for signaling and communication during the late 1890s.[16] Soon after he arrived in England in 1896, Marconi filed for his first patent on a device to receive wireless transmissions. To support further research and develop a market for wireless, Marconi and the wealthy relatives who backed him organized a Wireless Telegraph and Signal Company in 1897.

Marconi and other wireless pioneers envisaged uses for the new technology primarily in terms of functions already performed by existing telegraph and telephone networks. Even from the first, however, problems and possibilities of using an easily accessed electromagnetic commons for communication differed greatly from those of using the fixed wires of telephone and telegraph networks. For commercial and military organizations seeking to use radio to exchange information between specific parties and coordinate activities, preserving secrecy presented far greater difficulties than on conventional telephone and telegraph networks. Communications could be overheard or even jammed by individuals using modestly priced or homemade equipment. For the radio amateurs and hobbyists who began to take to the air in 1907 and 1908, by contrast, it was the very publicness of communication on the radio frequency spectrum that gave the hobby much of its appeal, both as a social activity and as a way to vicariously enter far-off and exotic worlds.

In its use of these public attributes of the radio frequency spectrum, amateur radio pioneered into terrain that would later be exploited by commercial broadcasters in the United States. Indeed, amateur radio could itself be viewed as a form of broadcasting, in that relatively few people undertook transmissions while large numbers listened in. Even before the United States entered World War I in 1917, a few amateurs regularly transmitted voice and music programs over the air for the entertainment of their fellow hobbyists. As a popular mass medium, broadcast radio exploded into prominence over the years 1922 through 1925. By the middle of the 1920s, hundreds of stations broadcast programs to members of the public and millions of Americans used their newly acquired radio sets to listen in to voices and music from near and far.[17] A wide variety of individuals and groups set up stations. Some colleges, churches, and nonprofit organizations took up broadcasting as a means to educate the public or propagate specific religious or political messages. Business enterprises such as department stores and newspapers also experimented with broadcasting for vaguely defined public relations purposes.

For broadcasting to be viable over the long term, however, the activity would have to be subsidized, supported by charity, or somehow made to pay its own way. In economic terms, broadcasting presented the problems and possibilities of a public good in virtually pure form. For a given transmission by a broadcast station, costs were the same no matter how many people tuned in. For one seeking to reach large numbers of people with a program or message, this attribute of broadcasting could be highly advantageous. By the same token, however, charging members of the audience for entertainment or information received over the air was highly problematical because of the difficulty and expense of excluding nonpayers. The publicness of broadcasting had a political face as well. From 1912 to the present day, the radio frequency spectrum has officially been a public domain, with the federal government making decisions as to access and setting rules as to use. From the first, views of the radio frequency spectrum as a public space that should be developed for public benefit played a major role in shaping debate and discussion as to how this power should be exercised, as did traditional concerns over both private monopoly and aggrandizements of governmental power.

The issues first arose in 1910 and 1911, when the navy called for amateurs to be barred from interfering with official communications and for the Secretary of Commerce to be given complete discretion as to who would be licensed to use the spectrum. The proposals failed to win congressional approval. No single official or organization, influential critics maintained, should have the power to limit access by ordinary Americans to a common space that belonged to all. Worse yet, in the view of some newspaper editorialists, granting such power to a federal official might ultimately lead to governmental control over the content of news dispatches transmitted by wireless.[18] Congress addressed these criticisms when it finally enacted a radio law in 1912 by specifying in the statute itself broad zones of the frequency spectrum to be used by the commercial, amateur, and military wireless operators of the day.[19] The arrangement proved workable at first. Growth of broadcasting during the 1920s, however, rendered obsolete the law's simple division of the spectrum.

Over the years 1922 through 1926, Secretary of Commerce Herbert Hoover responded to difficulties in allocating the frequency spectrum by calling together selected stakeholders for a series of radio conferences. In radio, as in other domains of the economy, Hoover believed, problems could best be resolved through collaboration between public-spirited businessmen and government officials.[20] In a 1924 address, Hoover encapsulated his vision as follows: "radio activities are largely free. We will maintain them free—free of monopoly, free in program, and free in speech—but we must also maintain them free of malice and unwholesomeness."[21]

Realizing these goals and reconciling the obvious tensions among them did not prove easy. Indeed, the legal framework furnished by the 1912 Radio Act did not provide the Secretary of Commerce the power and discretion needed to enforce the even minimal "control of the channels through the ether" envisioned by Hoover. Even if signals by broadcasters interfered with one another, a federal court ruled in 1923, the Secretary of Commerce had no authority under the Radio Act to deny broadcast licenses. The authority of the Secretary of Commerce broke down altogether in 1926 with findings by an Illinois federal court and the United States Attorney General that the increasingly elaborate frequency allocations worked out by the radio conferences could not be enforced at all.[22] Pandemonium ensued as broadcasters scrambled for the most desirable frequencies and boosted the power of their transmissions to increase listening areas and drown out rivals.

Questions of how broadcasting should be underwritten and structured aroused contention as well. After World War I, such leading firms in the radio industry as AT&T, RCA, and Westinghouse had allied themselves in a patent pool and agreed to market-sharing arrangements. Relationships between AT&T and RCA, however, were far from amicable. Particularly at first, leaders of the two firms viewed broadcasting through quite different analytical lenses. Not surprisingly, executives of AT&T initially defined broadcasting as a sort of one-way telephone system that could be used to send a single message to a large number of listeners. By linking radio transmitters to AT&T's wired communication network, a program, message, or event could be picked up from any locale and broadcast wherever desired.[23] Those seeking to communicate with the public by means of radio broadcasts, AT&T executives believed, should pay the telephone company to transmit the message just as individuals paid for telephone calls to other individuals.[24] As with ordinary telephony, the executives envisioned the primary role of AT&T as one of a common carrier furnishing facilities for use by others.[25]

Thus, when AT&T established its first experimental "toll broadcasting station" in New York City during the summer of 1922, virtually no plans were made for provision of programming. Unfortunately, finding commercial sponsors willing to take a chance on the new medium proved difficult and AT&T had to scramble to fill the void for the first broadcasts by its new station with such material as vocal selections by Miss Edith F. Mills of the Long Lines Traffic Department and violin music by AT&T draftsman Mr. Joseph Koznick.[26] By the end of 1923, AT&T had succeeded in finding buyers for the most popular listening hours. It was evident by this point, however, that for the foreseeable future the telephone company itself was going to have to furnish programming of its own in order to fill up the entire broadcast day.[27]

Although driven by exigencies of circumstance, AT&T's increasing involvement with production of programming during the early 1920s raised the specter of broadcast monopoly in sharp terms. A world in which ownership of broadcasting equipment was split from provision of programming and access to facilities could be purchased on a nondiscriminatory or common carrier basis was one thing. A world in which AT&T controlled content of all broadcasts was something else altogether. Other measures taken by AT&T, such as denying telephone lines for use in broadcasting by independent stations and attempting to assert patent control over transmitting equipment, contributed to fears that the company sought total control.[28] Furthermore, some manufactures and broadcasters feared that if uncontrolled advertising caused listeners to abandon their newfound interest in radio, the entire industry might be destroyed.[29]

At least initially, executives of Westinghouse and RCA took a different tack, one more consistent with notions of broadcasting as a public service. Leaders of these firms viewed the setting up of radio stations and production of attractive programming not as potentially profitable activities in their own right but as means of creating a consumer market for radio sets.[30] From this perspective, it made as little sense for radio manufacturers to be relied upon to support broadcasting as it would make for automobile manufactures to be relied upon to furnish roads. In keeping with such views, tentative attempts were made by David Sarnoff and other leading radio executives to interest philanthropic organizations in supporting broadcasting as a public service. Sarnoff also proposed at one point that radio manufacturers self-impose a voluntary levy to support a nonprofit broadcasting corporation. But responses to these proposals were limited and halfhearted at best. Nor was there solid support from any politically significant quarter for proposals to tax either radio listeners or radio manufacturers to support the broadcast of programs to the public. The public ownership that might follow from such taxation was opposed by large and small broadcast interests alike and raised obvious free speech and free press concerns.

Responses to these combined economic and political problems formulated during the late 1920s and early 1930s shaped broadcasting development in the United States for years to come. In 1927, President Coolidge signed into law emergency legislation establishing a five-member Federal Radio Commission with broad discretion to license and regulate users of the radio frequency spectrum based upon judgments of the "public inter-est, convenience, and necessity." Reflecting prevailing antimonopolistic sentiment and concerns by smaller entrepreneurs over efforts by AT&T and RCA to dominate broadcasting, the act prohibited the granting of a license to any firm adjudged guilty by a federal court of antitrust viola-tions. The legislation addressed free speech concerns by prohibiting the commission from censoring radio communications.[31]

Long-standing tensions between beliefs in the value of media as a unifying and nationalizing force and concerns over cultural dominance by major urban centers also shaped legislation adopted during these years. As with newspapers and the mails during the nineteenth century, many people envisioned the value of broadcasting as a means to increase cultural and political unity.[32] With the development of broadcast radio as a public forum encompassing the entire nation, local and sectional prejudices would breakdown. Americans, in the words of a breathless 1924 magazine article, would learn to "feel together, think together, live together."[33] At the same time, however, in radio as in newspapers dom-inance of communication by a few big centers aroused opposition, par-ticularly in the South and West. High-powered radio stations based in New York City and Chicago and networks linking stations together came under attack on these grounds. Reflecting such concerns, Congress added provisions to the Radio Act in 1928 designed to ensure that all parts of the country were served by equal numbers of broadcast stations.[34] The Communications Act of 1934 brought broadcasting under the jurisdic-tion of a newly created Federal Communications Commission but other-wise left intact the legal and regulatory framework established in 1927 and 1928.

The late 1920s and early 1930s also saw a sorting-out of the industry's economic and business arrangements. Stations and networks settled on sale of time to advertisers as the best means to profit from public attri-butes of the medium. From about four million dollars in 1927, annual sales of broadcast advertising increased to over fifty million dollars in 1936 and to about three hundred million dollars in 1945.[35] In some respects, the arrangements that emerged resembled those pioneered by AT&T for its early experiments in toll broadcasting. In particular, the role played by advertisers was not confined to that of paying radio stations and net-works for the airing of avowedly commercial announcements. Rather, advertising agencies purchased large blocks of time for corporate clients, produced the bulk of network programs heard during the choicest listening hours, and determined content.[36]

The telephone company itself, however, chose to escape the political entanglements and business complications of owning radio stations and producing programs. In 1926 AT&T sold its broadcast properties to RCA. Along with other stations owned by Westinghouse and General Electric, RCA grouped the former AT&T properties into a newly formed National Broadcasting Company. Over the years 1927 through 1930, NBC used the set of broadcast properties under its direct control as a nucleus for two networks of stations reaching throughout the country. The Columbia Broadcasting Company put together a third nationwide network during the same period. Partly because of regulatory requirements, ownership of most stations remained in independent hands. Nevertheless, a form of national broadcasting emerged. About half of all stations and almost all of the high-powered ones that could be heard over large areas during the 1930s were affiliated with either the National Broadcasting Company or the Columbia Broadcasting Company.[37] Playing to its particular strengths as owner of the country's telephone system, AT&T furnished the wired communication links used to simultaneously broadcast programs over these networks of stations.

During the late 1940s and early 1950s, the great radio networks succeeded in transferring this structure of technological and business organization virtually intact to the new field of broadcast television. Like radio, television too developed as a hybrid of wired and wireless communications technologies. Here, too, a system emerged in which locally owned and managed stations obtained the bulk of their programming from the national networks with which they were affiliated. Indeed, dominance of programming by national networks during the 1950s, 1960s, and 1970s was even greater in television than it had been in radio. Nine out of ten people watching television during the evening prime-time hours during the late 1970s viewed network programming.[38]

The rise to dominance of commercial network broadcasting did not go unchallenged. From the first, radio advertising came under attack from conservative as well as liberal quarters as far more intrusive than its print counterparts and as a usurpation for crassly mercenary purposes of a resource that supposedly belonged to all of the people. No fire-breathing radical, Secretary of Commerce Herbert Hoover criticized radio advertising in a 1924 address: "I believe that the quickest way to kill broadcasting would be to use it for direct advertising. The reader of the newspaper has an option whether he will read an ad or not but if a speech by the President is to be used as the meat in a sandwich of two patent medicine advertisements there will be no radio left."[39]

Domination of prime listening hours by advertiser-produced entertainment programs also conflicted with more high-minded notions of the public role of broadcasting. For good or for bad, the national consciousness created by broadcasting during the late 1920s and early 1930s was less one of confronting the great issues of the day than of listening to "Amos 'n' Andy." Sponsor control of programming content raised questions about the character of such discussion of public events as did occur over radio because large corporations had access to the medium that others did not. The "Ford Sunday Evening Hour" broadcast over CBS during the mid-1930s, for example, was an avowedly "entertainment" program but contained intermission talks attacking labor unions and the New Deal. Labor groups, by contrast, did not enjoy a similar degree of access to the airwaves.

During the early 1930s, a number of proposals came before Congress to restrict broadcast advertising and to reserve a portion of radio frequencies for use by educational institutions and nonprofit organizations. A 1932 Senate resolution even called for the Federal Radio Commission to investigate the feasibility of government ownership and operation of radio stations.[40] All of these proposals, however, came to naught. Indeed, the rise to dominance of commercial network broadcasting in the United States during the late 1920s and early 1930s came with the blessings and support of federal regulators. Because support by commercial sponsors represented the only viable means to support provision of broadcast programs to all members of the public, free of charge and without government subsidy or direct government control over content, the Federal Radio Commission ruled, advertising had to be excepted from general prohibitions on use of broadcast wavelengths for narrow and private purposes. Furthermore, the commission maintained, profit-seeking private firms represented more reliable trustees of the public airwaves than nonprofit political, religious, or even educational organizations. Even if frequencies could be allocated fairly between exponents of different religious, political, and economic points of view, according to commission documents, a world of "propaganda stations" shouting their creeds and prejudices into the ether would not be consistent "with the most beneficial sort of discussion of public questions."[41]

While federal regulators looked with equanimity toward the rise of commercial network broadcasting during this period, they also called upon owners of stations to take their responsibilities as public trustees seriously and to hold advertising within bounds. In terms that would change little in coming years, the commission put forth its ideals as follows in a ruling from the late 1920s. Broadcasters, the ruling maintained, should strive to serve "the tastes, needs, and desires of all substantial groups among the listening public . . . by a well-rounded program in which entertainment . . . , religion, education and instruction, important public events, discussions of public questions, weather, market reports, and news, and matters of interest to all members of the family find a place."[42] At least in theory, hopes of reaching large audiences, reaping lush advertising revenues, and maintaining a good reputation would all act as inducements for privately owned broadcasters to fulfill their public responsibilities, with federal authority to choose and renew licensees functioning as a protection against egregious abuses.[43] In accord with this view, the Federal Radio Commission denied a license renewal to station WCRW in 1928 on the grounds that the enterprise existed "chiefly for the purpose of deriving an income from the sale of advertising of a character which must be objectionable to the listening public and without making much, if any, endeavor to render any real service to the public."[44]

From the first, however, such efforts as the FRC and the FCC made to enforce limits on advertising and to take programming into account in awarding and renewing licenses faced informational and administrative problems of a kind familiar from previous discussions of waterworks and electric utilities. Required questionnaires provided only limited information concerning the character of what was broadcast and even less basis for judgment concerning quality.[45] In addition, neither the Federal Radio Commission nor the Federal Communications Commission maintained sufficient staff to seriously scrutinize the hundreds of applications for new licenses and renewals that came up each year.

Tensions between freedom of speech concerns and the demands of selecting and overseeing private parties in their use of a public resource also plagued broadcast regulation. On the one hand, selecting among many applicants for broadcast licenses and deciding whether licenses should be renewed required some consideration of the character of programming promised and the character of the programming actually provided. On the other hand, federal regulators were forbidden by statute to censor radio communications or to promulgate regulations that interfered with a broadcaster's freedom of speech. At the same time, however, failure to scrutinize the character or fairness of programming furnished by a broadcaster could also be criticized on freedom of speech grounds because under such conditions one party enjoys unfettered use of a scarce public resource to propagate its views while other parties do not.[46]

Federal regulators sidestepped these problems to a degree when they used their licensing authority not to dictate programming per se but to influence ownership and structure of the broadcast industry. Thus, during the late 1920s and early 1930s, the Federal Radio Commission used its licensing authority to award the most favorable frequency allocations to commercial stations and to force their nonprofit counterparts to share time on marginal channels or to cease broadcasting altogether. During the 1940s and 1950s, the commission partially reversed this course and reserved portions of the frequency spectrum for noncommercial radio and television broadcasting. Such noncommercial public broadcasting as there is in the United States could not have been established without these niches.

Federal regulators also attempted at times to use their licensing authority to increase competition and consumer choice in the world of commercial broadcasting. In 1941, for example, the Federal Communications Commission issued a ruling barring any single corporate entity from owning more than one broadcast network. Ownership by RCA-controlled NBC of two out of three of the country's major national broadcast networks, the ruling maintained, represented an undue concentration of economic and political power in the hands of a single firm.[47] Upheld by the Supreme Court in 1943, the decision led to NBC selling off of its Blue Network and the creation of the American Broadcasting Company.

The FCC also took steps to increase the number of independent broadcast stations serving radio listeners. During the 1940s and 1950s, the commission opened up bands of the frequency spectrum for FM radio and awarded a large number of licenses for use by low-powered AM stations. Such measures made it possible for the number of radio stations in the United States to rise from fewer than one thousand to more than four thousand from 1945 to 1960.[48] By 1988, there were about ten thousand radio stations in the United States.[49] Listeners in major urban centers could tune into more than sixty stations.

Unfortunately, arranging for availability of large numbers of stations and for extension of service throughout the country presented considerably greater technical difficulties in television than in radio. Unlike the case in AM radio, signals broadcast by television stations could not be received beyond a line of sight distance from the transmitter. While this attribute of the technology meant that many different communities could each have their own television station without interference, it also made for greater difficulties in furnishing service to rural areas. Arranging for availability of more than a few stations in any given locale was also more difficult in television than in radio because television signals occupied far more space on the spectrum than did their radio counterparts. The FCC's initial scheme for the allocation of television frequencies dealt with these problems very poorly and in 1948 the commission froze the granting of television licenses to gain time to work out a better arrangement.

Under its new plan released in 1952, the commission placed its main hope for better realizing localism and diversity goals in opening up the experimental UHF spectrum for television broadcasting. The new allocation increased the number of channels available for television broadcasting more than sixfold. Use of the new frequencies, the FCC hoped, would make it possible for viewers in larger centers to have available a reasonably large selection of both local and national network outlets and for even very small communities to have their own stations. At least initially, the plan failed. To avoid rendering useless large numbers of existing television sets, the commission awarded a mix of VHF and UHF frequencies in each city. But since most sets could not receive UHF, stations on this band soon went out of business. Commercial UHF stations began to succeed only during the 1960s after passage of a law requiring all new sets sold to consumers to carry their signals. Even then, however, their contribution to diversity and localism was doubtful, as their programming consisted largely of network reruns and other standardized fare.

Private Business, Public Policy, and the Shaping of Cable Television in the United States

Like its broadcast counterpart, cable television can be viewed as a shifting ensemble of technologies put together by entrepreneurs seeking to reap profit through the delivery of news, entertainment, information, and advertisements from a relatively small number of producers to a relatively large numbers of receivers. It is only a modest over-simplification to characterize the mix of wired and wireless technologies employed by cable television to carry out this function as the inverse of that used in network broadcasting. In broadcasting, wires and cables have been used primarily to link stations while messages and programs were delivered to consumers free of charge over the air. In the case of cable television, by contrast, operators of systems have plucked programs from over the air by means of antennas, microwave relays, or satellite earth stations and delivered them to paying consumers through fixed networks of coaxial cable manifesting the sorts of natural monopoly attributes found in waterworks and to a lesser degree in electric utilities.

The first cable television systems consisted of a master antenna to receive over-the-air broadcast television signals, equipment to amplify the signals, and coaxial cable to distribute them house-to-house. Interestingly, the coaxial cable used by these systems for local distribution had been originally developed by AT&T during the 1930s for the purpose of connecting over-the-air television stations for network broadcasting. As was the case with broadcast radio during its early years, some of the first entrepreneurs to set up cable systems did so primarily as a means to sell receiving sets to consumers. In Mahoney City, Pennsylvania, for example, a local appliance dealer named John Walsonovich is reported to have set up one of the first systems during the late 1940s as an inducement for residents to purchase television sets. Mahoney City is located in a valley in eastern Pennsylvania; its residents could not receive over-the-air television with their rooftop antennas. By linking the televisions of valley residents to a single master antenna located on a hill over looking the town, Walsonovich improvised a solution to the problem.[50] The solution was adopted elsewhere as well and by 1960, there were about 640 cable systems in the United States serving about 650,000 subscribers.[51]

Cable television enjoyed its greatest success during this period in moderate to densely populated locales with poor or nonexistent broadcast reception. Economical to build and almost completely without competition, cable television systems located in such places could be very profitable indeed. Where population was thinly spread, however, the capital costs of extending cable were usually too high for service to be economic. Where reception of broadcast signals was good, cable had little to offer that could not be obtained by owners of television sets free of charge. As a consequence, cable television occupied a secure but limited market niche. For all of the growth enjoyed by the industry during the 1950s, cable subscribers still represented but a small proportion of the country's fifty-two million television households as of 1960.

Matters began to change during the years that followed. Improvements in microwave transmission technology made it possible for cable systems to more economically obtain television signals from longer distances. At the same time, cable television vendors and operators began to refine amplifier and cable technology to increase the number of channels furnished by cable. In 1961, a pioneering venture in San Diego demonstrated that even in a medium-sized city already served by a number of broadcast stations, a cable system could attract subscribers and turn a profit by bringing in distant signals. Cable television also proved able to compete in Manhattan during the 1960s by offering sports and other programming unavailable over the air and by furnishing customers with a higher-quality picture than could be obtained otherwise, due to ghosting problems arising from the presence of large buildings.

But the really big breakthrough for cable television came in the late 1970s and early 1980s with the development and elaboration of a new technological ensemble. The launching of domestic communications satellites during the mid-1970s meant that programs could be transmitted to any number of cable television systems nationwide over the air and at minimal marginal cost. At the same time, local distribution through cable made for high channel capacities and relatively easy exclusion of non-paying customers. Entrepreneurs quickly seized the opportunity and by the mid-1980s, twenty-four hour news and weather channels, movie channels, music channels, sports channels, children's channels, religious channels, home shopping channels, and ethnic channels had been established. In even the largest of urban areas, cable television now had a unique product to offer and growth proceeded rapidly.[52]

As has been the case in broadcasting, notions that communications systems should in some sense play a public role and serve all members of society have played prominent roles in debate and discussion over government policy. The issues first arose in the context of cable television's close relationship with its broadcast counterpart. As cable systems began to invade markets already served by local stations during the 1960s, complaints by broadcasting interests grew increasingly vociferous. Local broadcasters feared competition from distant stations and the potential for reduced audience shares and advertising revenues. Networks and producers of programs feared disruption of payment schedules and royalty arrangements predicated on the basis of individual stations serving individual markets. Such complaints were, of course, motivated by economic self-interest. But to the extent that broadcasters were viewed as public trustees responsible for serving public as well as private ends, regulators, citizens, and even industry critics had reason to be concerned about these issues as well.

For all of advertising-supported television's defects and faults, the medium did function as a sort of public use of a public space. Rich or poor, all households in a community received entertainment, information, and coverage of public issues on equal terms and without charge. A world in which many or all programs could be obtained only by paying a cable company would not share these public attributes. The result, some feared, would be a diminution of the public realm and a society divided between communications haves and have-nots.[53] Cable television was also portrayed as a threat to FCC initiatives to carve out a secure niche for local broadcasting and to bring more diverse and responsive programming to the public airwaves. Indeed, there were even fears that local television broadcasting might disappear altogether in smaller markets if stations lost too much of their audience to cable systems importing distant signals. Under such circumstances, residents of built-up areas where cable was available would have no choice but to pay to receive distant stations furnishing but a parody of local service and residents of rural areas beyond the reach of cable lines would be left with no television at all.[54]

Over the course of the 1960s, the Federal Communications Commission took increasingly aggressive steps to protect broadcasters against these threats. The first major decision came in 1962, with a ruling denying cable operators in Wyoming permission to construct a microwave communications system to be used to import distant signals.[55] The economic base for over-the-air broadcasting in the area was already fragile, the FCC reasoned, and importation of distant signals could easily lead to the complete demise of local stations. In larger markets, the situation differed in that development of cable television clearly did not present an immediate and mortal threat to the viability of advertiser-supported over-the-air broadcasting. It was at least possible, however, that import of distant signals by cable systems could further fragment the already limited audiences available to infant UHF stations.[56] If this occurred, prospects for increased diversity in over-the-air television would be lost. Citing uncertainties with respect to these dangers, the FCC issued regulations in 1966 and 1968 greatly restricting the import of distant signals into the nation's top one hundred television markets.

The FCC also acted during the late 1960s to address concerns that the quality of commercially supported television might be threatened by the growth of arrangements to send popular sports events and movies to paying customers over the air by means of scrambled signals or through cable systems. To prevent good programming from being "siphoned off" in this way, the FCC issued rules in 1968 prohibiting over-the-air pay television services from carrying regularly broadcast sports events, series programs, advertising, and movies less than two years old or more than ten years old. The commission extended these prohibitions to cable television in 1970 and tightened them further in 1975.[57]

Already by the late 1960s and early 1970s, however, cable television had come to be viewed in influential quarters not just as a threat to public attributes of existing broadcasting arrangements but as an exciting new technology that could be structured and deployed to enhance consumer choice, increase opportunities for self-expression, and enrich the public realm. An influential Sloan Commission report published in 1971 coined the term "television of abundance" to describe the range of information, entertainment, and perspectives that could potentially be made available over cable systems. Advantages of cable over broadcast distribution, according to the report, included potentially unlimited channel capacity and flexibility in furnishing programming to small areas and distinctive and specialized audiences.[58] From a counterculture perspective, advocates and practitioners of public access and guerrilla television saw cable as a tool that could be used to liberate the making of programs from large corporations and "deliver it into the hands of 'the people' so that a Whitmanesque democracy of ideas and opinions could be 'narrowcast' on cable television."[59] Individuals and local communities, access advocates believed, should not only be able to use cable to passively receive programs more closely tailored to their needs but should also have opportunities to actively create programs for distribution over dedicated channels.

The rise of these perspectives represented something of a mixed blessing for cable television firms. Particularly during the 1970s, beliefs that development of cable television could help to revitalize the public sphere unquestionably aided the industry in its efforts to gain more favorable regulatory treatment. At the same time, however, furnishing the channel capacity and local production facilities believed necessary to fulfill these dreams could prove burdensome and costly. For cable television firms to afford access to their systems by alternate program suppliers could also run counter to their self-interest. In an astute analysis written during the early 1980s, Ithiel de Sola Pool summed up the tension: "From a social point of view the promise of cable lies in the pluralism made possible by its unlimited number of channels. From the programmer-cablecaster's point of view, this may be its horror. A program producer gains from limitations on competition that compel vast audiences, because of the lack of alternatives, to watch programs of moderate interest."[60]

As in broadcasting, the burden of protecting public interests in cable television has rested largely upon licenses or franchises awarded to private firms based upon avowed commitments to serve consumer and public needs. In broadcasting, the Federal Communications Commission in essence functioned as the franchising authority. In cable television, by contrast, this role has been played primarily by local governments. At first, municipalities did not seek to play a major role in shaping cable television development. Typically, city officials granted franchises on request and imposed few if any requirements with respect to price or service provision.[61] While cities increasingly specified minimum channel requirements and standards for quality of service when they issued cable television franchises over the years 1965 through 1970, the role played by municipal authorities in shaping cable television development remained of minor importance in most locales.[62]

Matters changed during the late 1970s and early 1980s. With cable companies themselves now eager to develop systems in major urban centers, some municipal governments began to systematically employ franchise bidding for the avowed purposes of shaping attributes of technologies deployed, obtaining specifically public services, and protecting consumers. Case studies follow of how franchising for cable television actually played out in different cities. This will be followed by a more complete discussion of factors that affected outcomes, the history of cable television since 1984, and implications for public policy.

Cable Television Franchising in Seattle

Unlike the case in many other major cities, the beginnings of cable television in Seattle date from the first days of the industry. The reason for cable television's early start in Seattle was primarily topographical. The city is very hilly and in some locales reception of over-the-air television is virtually impossible. To sell televisions in one such locale, a local television dealer called Holert Electric is reported to have set up the city's first cable television system as early as 1949.[63] Within two years, a second television dealer called Master Television was operating a small system as well. Formal recognition by the city came in 1951 with the awarding of twenty-five-year franchises to the two firms.

The turn to municipal franchise contracting represented little more than a formality. Although the contracts provided for the municipal government to regulate consumer charges and services on a rate-of-return basis, city officials did not choose to exercise this authority. Nor did franchising have much effect—either positive or negative—upon the extent to which cable operators faced market discipline. As was the case in waterworks and electric utilities during the late nineteenth century, Seattle granted nonexclusive cable franchises virtually on request. But while the franchises did not afford legal sanction to monopoly provision, duplicative competition between cable television firms did not occur.

The late 1960s saw change and growth in Seattle's cable television industry. New companies entered the market, followed by a complex series of ownership shifts and consolidations. The process culminated during the early 1970s with the city's cable television systems coming under the control of two national multisystem operators—TelePrompTer and Viacom. The new operators brought in signals from the nearby cities of Tacoma and Vancouver, British Columbia; upgraded distribution to be able to furnish subscribers a selection of twelve to fourteen channels; and extended service even in some neighborhoods where one or more local stations could be received over the air. At the same time, the new operators exercised considerable caution in making new investments. As a consequence, more than half of the households Seattle, as of 1976, still could not get cable.

In Seattle, as elsewhere, visions of cable television as an important public communications resource also arose during this period. As in broadcasting and other communications and networked systems, the ideal of publicness incorporated notions that service should be available to all citizens on equal terms no matter where they were located. For the avowed purpose of enhancing and revitalizing local democracy, funding of noncommercial community programming and the setting up of public access channels were also advocated. In its populism and opposition to control of local resources by outside corporations, the movement for cable access in Seattle bore at least a superficial resemblance to the crusades for a municipal electric utility that shook the city during the late nineteenth and early twentieth centuries. And in 1972, Seattle City Light did propose that the city set up its own cable system on the model of its electric utility. But unlike the case in electric utilities, not even the most strenuous advocates of cable access viewed provision as vitally important for economic development. In part for this reason, neither influential public officials nor major local newspapers seriously took up the cause.

Citing freedom of press concerns, high costs of buying up or condemning the existing cable systems, and the likely need for taxpayer subsidies in order to extend service to uncabled neighborhoods, a 1972 report to the city council came out against the City Light municipal ownership proposal.[64] With little fanfare, the plan went down to defeat. In 1974, the city council also turned back a far more modest proposal to set aside for the support of access programming a portion of the 6 percent franchise fee levied on Seattle's cable television firms.[65] At least during the early and middle years of the 1970s, elected officials in Seattle simply did not view goals to be fulfilled through cable television development as worthy of the expenditure of taxpayer funds.

Having cable companies themselves pay for extension of service throughout the city and provision of public access and local programming, however, was quite another matter. In March of 1976, the city council passed a master cable television ordinance requiring the companies to furnish at their own expense facilities for the production and distribution of public access, educational, and government programming. The new law also called upon TelePrompTer and Viacom to extend their systems so that all residents of Seattle would have cable television available within five years.[66] TelePrompTer and Viacom executives vigorously protested. Demand for cable television in areas of Seattle with unimpeded broadcast reception was simply insufficient, company officials maintained, to support the immediate and massive extension of service required by the ordinance. The companies refused to sign franchises containing the new requirements. The Citizens Cable Communications Advisory Board, appointed by the mayor, studied the matter and found justice in the companies' claims; in December of 1977, the city council enacted a new ordinance greatly relaxing the mandates.

Given municipal reluctance to spend taxpayer funds on cable television, the city may have had little choice but to retreat. If the municipal government had attempted to enforce the ordinance, expensive litigation would almost certainly have ensued. Even if the ordinance did survive a court challenge, the only real recourse possessed by the city in the face of continued refusal by the cable companies to make investments they regarded as unprofitable would be to acquire the systems and take on the costs itself. A tangled legal situation further weakened the city's bargaining position. The original Holert and Masters franchises that TelePrompTer and Viacom had acquired both expired in 1976. But other companies acquired by the firms operated under franchises that still had ten years to run. Like the Holert and Masters franchises, these too were nonexclusive and gave firms the right to furnish service anywhere in the city.

With the introduction of satellite programming services during the late 1970s, however, matters changed. Viacom and TelePrompTer suddenly found it to be in their own interests to lay cable at a rate far in excess of that specified in the cable ordinance they had so recently fought against. By 1982, residents in all but a few neighborhoods of Seattle could obtain cable if they so desired. Newfound interest in system extension on the part of cable television firms also gave the municipal government a chance to use franchise bidding for as yet unserved areas to obtain public services and shape system attributes. Seattle put two areas of the city out for bid in separate competitions. In both, bidders competed along a range of dimensions, including price and number of channels offered subscribers and provision of educational and public access programming. Deciding considerations, however, were rather different.

In the Northwest Franchise District, a middle-income area of about ten thousand households, access advocates succeeded in using the franchising process to realize some of their goals. While the city was evaluating the bids during the spring of 1980, an ad hoc Citizens Cable Committee began a campaign to have the city reopen the competition and call upon the bidders to offer more elaborate production facilities for community access programming. After public hearings in June and July, the city acceded to the request and reopened the bidding. All three competitors upped their offers, with TelePrompTer making the most ambitious proposal. TelePrompTer promised to produce its own local interest programming, to furnish three access channels for educational, governmental, and public use, studio facilities for production of access programming, provision of equipment to the city for production of its own programming, and construction of a small institutional network linking major public buildings. These commitments far exceeded the original requirements specified by Seattle in its original request for proposals. On March 31, 1981, Seattle awarded TelePrompTer the franchise.

In the Central Franchise District, a set of African American and Asian American neighborhoods located to the east of downtown Seattle, minority and local ownership represented deciding considerations in the competition to serve the area. Back in 1973, a local African American firm called Vahnu Incorporated had obtained a franchise to furnish service in the district. Unfortunately, the company proved unable to gain financial backing to actually build a system. After granting four extensions to construction deadlines over the course of the 1970s, Seattle finally revoked the franchise in April of 1981 and issued a new request for proposals in November of the same year. This time seven local and national cable operators submitted bids. In the spring of 1982, the Seattle Office of Cable Communications and the Citizens Cable Communications Advisory Board both recommended that a firm called Seattle Community Cablevision be awarded the franchise.

Reasons for preferring Seattle Community cited by the Office of Cable Communications included control and ownership of the firm by an African American businessman (William T. Johnson of Columbus, Ohio), Johnson's donation of a 15 percent ownership share to local and community groups, Seattle Community's offer to place community and local origination channels under the control of a coalition of community-based nonprofit organizations, and Seattle Community's promise to devote higher levels of staff and financial resources to the production of such programming.[67] Other applicants vocally criticized the award on the grounds that their own proposals were superior with respect to channel capacity and prices to consumers.

A city council staff report prepared during the summer of 1982 found some merit in these objections. In particular, the report concluded that in the Central District, as in the Northwest, TelePrompTer had put together the best proposal in terms of number of channels for consumers, support of local programming, and provision of a network for institutional use. Nevertheless, the staff report concluded that Seattle Community's offer was at least adequate along most dimensions and that obtaining minority and local ownership was of sufficient importance to justify award of the franchise to the firm.[68] The city council agreed and in March of 1983 awarded the franchise to Seattle Community.

Whether minority ownership actually made for more programming of minority and local concern actually being furnished is unclear. In 1986, the Community Program Board charged with administering public access and community programming in the area claimed that the cable company was not fulfilling promises of support made during the franchising process. In any case, minority ownership proved short-lived. In

1987, William Johnson sold Seattle Community to Summit Communications, a firm not owned by a minority. Ownership changed as well in the Northwest Franchise District. Soon after TelePrompTer won the bidding competition, the firm was taken over by Group W, owned by Westinghouse. Under its new owners, the firm did not market access programming as vigorously as it had implied in its franchise bid.[69] Otherwise, the company's operation inspired few complaints.

Overall, franchise bidding in Seattle simply did not play a major role in shaping the character of services furnished consumers. In particular, decisions as to channel capacity remained in the hands of the city's privately owned service providers, who continued to pursue a conservative investment strategy. In newly built portions of their systems during the late 1970s and early 1980s, Viacom, TelePrompTer, and Group W furnished twenty-channel service. This barely represented the minimum industry standard for the time. Such systems could offer a few popular satellite programming services such as HBO to attract customers but had insufficient capacity to afford subscribers the increasingly wide range of channels becoming available. In order to add the USA Network (largely a purveyor of old sitcoms) to its programming lineup in 1982, for example, Viacom dropped the Nickelodeon channel for children over the vehement protests of parents.[70] Quite rationally, companies also lagged in upgrading older, twelve-channel portions of their systems. Because such systems were located predominantly in areas of the city with poor broadcast reception, such upgrading was not needed in order to attract and retain subscribers. As late as 1994, residents of Seattle still had available to them a smaller selection of cable channels than did residents of most other cities and urban regions of comparable size.

Cable Television Franchising in Pittsburgh

Unlike Seattle, Pittsburgh turned to franchise bidding at the outset. Groundwork included the holding of a series of public hearings during the late 1970s on roles to be fulfilled by a cable television system, formal and informal meetings between city officials and local community and educational organizations, the commissioning of a report by an outside consulting firm, and the establishment of a city bureau of cable communications. Based upon this effort, Pittsburgh issued its request for proposals on October 11, 1979. The call for bids invited firms to compete along a range of dimensions, including price to consumers, channel capacity, investment in community access facilities, and willingness to furnish locally originated programming and to provide local residents an ownership share in the system.[71] The winner would receive a fifteen-year nonexclusive franchise to wire the entire city for cable. To ensure that promises would be kept, Pittsburgh required bidders to furnish detailed information concerning their financial wherewithal and expected revenues. As a protection to consumers and a check on opportunistic bidding, the city specified that no rate increases would be permitted for the first two and one-half years of the franchise period. For the period subsequent, the city council reserved the right to regulate charges for basic services.

Four companies bid for the franchise. The Pittsburgh Bureau of Cable Communications evaluated each proposal against a set of ten criteria that included rates, construction schedule, ownership and control, community access, and minority involvement. Competition among the bidders centered principally on issues of price, minority ownership, and community access programming. Two of the four applicants were eliminated fairly easily on the basis of this screen. TCI subsidiary Allegheny Cablevision was rejected because of high prices and limited minority and community involvement. Community Cable (51 percent owned by TelePrompTer) was dropped from consideration because of uncertainties about its ownership structure and inconsistencies in proposed rates.

Choosing between the two remaining bidders, however, proved more controversial. With respect to access programming, Three Rivers proposed to support an independent nonprofit organization to operate studio facilities and channels rather than to retain control in its own hands as did Warner. More distinctively, Three Rivers promised to furnish a limited cable service free of charge to every household in Pittsburgh. From a business point of view, this offer may have been risky but it was not insane. The hope was that by offering a free basic service, the market would be expanded for premium services upon which a profit could be made. To those who viewed cable as a public resource that should be available to all members of the community, a promise of universal service held obvious attractions as well. On the grounds of both superior provision of access facilities and the universal service promise, Pittsburgh's

Bureau of Cable Communications called for selection of Three Rivers. The city council's Cable Communications Advisory Committee also voted for acceptance of the Three Rivers proposal by a margin of six to four. In his recommendation to the city council, however, Mayor Richard Caliguiri put forth Warner as well as Three Rivers for consideration.

When it came time for the final vote in the council, the Warner bid won out by an eight to one margin. Three Rivers's loss before the council could be accounted for in part by its failure to promise an interactive capability comparable to that furnished by Warner's QUBE service. QUBE was inaugurated in Columbus, Ohio, in December of 1977, its technology hyped by its promoters as marking the end of television's "age of passive viewing."[72] With QUBE, viewers could "talk back" to television programs through use of a handheld keypad on which numbers could be punched in response to on-screen prompts. Consumer applications included quiz shows in which home viewers could participate, voting on which topics should be taken up on the "Home Book Club" program, ordering of pay-per-view programming, and home shopping. Experiments were also made using the technology to facilitate citizen involvement in public issues: instant (albeit nonscientific) polling of subscribers during televised discussions of public issues represented one application. In experiments with forms of call-in participation, QUBE subscribers could also use their keypads to indicate that they wished to ask a question of local government officials appearing on public affairs programs.[73]

The political sophistication of Warner's minority ownership provisions also played an important role in motivating the council's action. Three Rivers providing for the required 20 percent of local and minority ownership through issue of shares of stock for purchase by individuals. Warner, by contrast, donated 20 percent of its shares to seventeen local minority and African American organizations through a voting trust arrangement. In turn, these organizations lobbied the city council for acceptance of the Warner proposal.[74] Warner also employed several influential local leaders and compensated them well for their support.[75]

Initially, all appeared to go according to plan. Warner met construction deadlines mandated by its franchise and maintained reasonably satisfactory customer relations. Unfortunately, Warner was also hemorrhaging money. Nationally, Warner-Amex Cable reported losses of about forty-seven million dollars over the course of 1982. In Pittsburgh itself, revenues equaled or exceeded projections made by the company when it bid for the franchise but actually building the system proved far more expensive than expected. Warner had projected the costs of wiring Pittsburgh for cable at about forty-eight million dollars. By the end of 1982, construction had been mostly completed but expenditures had reached more than eighty million dollars. As reasons for the cost over-runs, Warner executives cited unexpectedly high inflation and interest rates, greater than expected complexity in building the system, high labor costs, and the costs of meeting the city's franchise requirements. Interestingly, the very popularity of the QUBE service itself created difficulties because of the high cost of installing the equipment needed.[76]

In order to recover a portion of these costs, Warner requested a rate hike of about 20 percent for its three highest tiers of service in January of 1983. In early May, Father Richard Emenecker, head of the Pittsburgh cable office, recommended that the request be approved. According to Emenecker, Warner figures for high capital costs were credible and no economies in operation could make up for this.[77] In mid-June, the city council approved the rate increase by a narrow five to four vote. Supporters cited the good quality of Warner's system and the company's need for an adequate return on its investments. Opponents asserted that the increase simply served to reward Warner for its own miscalculations.[78]

The rate hike did not end the crisis. In January of 1984, Warner asked for franchise revisions, proposing that it not be required to build a special institutional network to serve schools and governmental institutions. Before any decisions were made by the city in response to the request, Warner announced in March that it was selling its Pittsburgh system to TCI. As part of the transaction, Warner would buy back the 20 percent ownership share held by local organizations, on which no profits had yet been realized in any case.

TCI told the city that it would not purchase the Warner system unless major changes were made in the franchise. These included a further rate increase, a reduction in channel offerings, elimination of QUBE, and reductions in community access channels and studio facilities. TCI further proposed that community access service be paid for out of the franchise fee rather than out of the firm's revenue, as provided for by the original franchise. After months of negotiation, the city acceded to most of the demands. On October 17, 1984, the city council voted eight to zero, with one abstention, to approve the transfer.

The prevailing view among officials and city council members was that they had no real choice. If TCI did not purchase the system, they believed, Warner might disinvest in its Pittsburgh system—reducing service quality—or even declare the operation bankrupt. Enforcement provisions of Pittsburgh cable television franchise appeared to give the city a number of options if Warner did act in these ways. In the event of a violation of sufficient seriousness to warrant termination, the city retained the right to foreclose on the franchisee's performance bond, purchase the system at book value (original cost minus depreciation), order the franchise dismantled, and sue for damage. But at the least, attempting to activate such provisions could result in service disruptions. Nor was there any appetite among public officials for outright government ownership. Negotiations with TCI may also have been affected by the fact that during the time in which they were underway, Congress was considering legislation that would have almost completely foreclosed the ability of the city to regulate provision of cable television in any case.

In many other big cities that put out cable franchises for bid during the late 1970s and early 1980s, the results were broadly similar to those in Pittsburgh. In Dallas, Texas, for example, the franchising process included a study by a city council task force during 1979, numerous public hearings to ascertain community needs, and the issuance of a request for proposals specifying minimum requirements regarding the number of channels and access facilities. The request for proposals also suggested that bidders should consider offering other services, such as a dedicated network for use by public institutions. To prevent appearances that political favoritism might sway the award process, the request for proposals specifically noted that local ownership would not be considered in deciding among the bidders. The city hired a nonprofit organization, the Cable Television Information Center, to evaluate the bids. Harold Horn of the CTIC recommended that Warner be selected. Reasons included Warner's promise of QUBE interactive capabilities and eighty channels of service to consumers, a fifty-two channel institutional loop, and thirty channels and extensive production facilities for locally originated and community access programming.[79]

As in Pittsburgh, however, pursuit of a model franchise bidding process was not in itself sufficient to prevent subsequent problems from emerging. In 1984, Warner came to the city and demanded modification of its franchise on the grounds of financial hardship. In some respects, the problems experienced by Warner in Dallas were even greater than those in Pittsburgh. Here, too, construction costs were greater than expected and the carrying through of construction amid the record high-interest rates of the early 1980s did not help matters. In addition, Warner attracted far fewer subscribers to its system than expected. The main problem was that many owners of apartment complexes contracted to have their own satellite master antenna systems built and denied Warner access to their residents. A business network constructed by Warner at great expense in downtown Dallas also failed to attract the number of customers expected.

Concessions demanded by the firm included the deferral of requirements that Warner construct three public access studios and an institutional network. The city did not concede to all of Warner's demands but did agree to a substantial relaxation of initial franchise terms. The basis for funding the access corporation was shifted to a formula based upon number of subscribers rather than the $680,000 budget originally agreed to. The result was that Warner ended up having to furnish services less generous than those originally promised by any of the six original bids for the franchise.[80] Despite gaining many concessions, Warner sold the Dallas system to Heritage Cable during the summer of 1985 at a price sixty million dollars less than its initial investment. In turn, Heritage was bought by TCI in 1986.

Over the years 1983 through 1985, Warner also sold off cable systems in Atlanta and Tucson and gained franchise concessions in many of the other cities in which the firm continued to operate.[81] In Milwaukee, Warner succeeded in gaining elimination of many franchise requirements in response to claims of financial difficulty. Milwaukee cable television administrator Robert Welch justified granting the concessions on the grounds that "throwing them out didn't seem practical."[82] In 1984, Warner also abandoned the QUBE interactive technology that had played such a major role in winning some of these franchises in the first place. Warner ran into greater difficulties and lost more money than most other firms that competed for big-city franchises during the late 1970s and early 1980s. But as shall be seen in the discussion of events in Boston, problems in gauging consumer demand and accounting for changing conditions were limited neither to Pittsburgh nor to Warner-owned systems.

Cable Television Franchising in Boston

If anything, Boston carried through an even more elaborate and well-thought-out franchising process than did Pittsburgh. The first step taken by the municipality for determining what sort of cable television development would best serve Boston's needs took place in 1973, when Mayor White commissioned a report by the Boston Consumers' Council to look into the potentialities of the medium. On the grounds that too little was yet known about future cable television markets and technologies, the report recommended that the city put off franchising or acquiring a system until more became clear. Boston again took up the matter six years later.

In October of 1979, the Mayor's Cable Television Review Commission issued a report finding that many of the earlier uncertainties had been resolved and advocating that the city franchise a private firm to construct and operate a system. The report showed considerable sophistication about potential difficulties in franchise enforcement, noting that "franchise agreements . . . written for 10-15 year periods are . . . virtually impossible to revoke." Prior to award of a franchise, therefore, "careful and thorough investigation in the good faith, reputation, and past performance of each applicant" was essential.[83] Nevertheless, the report recommended against municipal ownership. Grounds cited included more pressing needs for public funds, inadequate management skills on the part of the municipal government, and potential First Amendment complications.

Instead, the report called for the city to put in place a municipal cable office to oversee the franchising process and to monitor compliance with contract terms. To reduce uncertainties and contingencies that might result in the winning bidder not being able to perform as promised, the report also called for the city itself to undertake a construction survey. Boston followed these recommendations, pursuing a series of consultations among city officials, public and private groups, and cable television firms over the next year and a half to formulate a more detailed set of requirements about what could be realistically demanded from a cable television system. On the basis of this process, Boston issued a request for proposals on February 7, 1981, putting forth a detailed description of the municipal government's goals.

The request for proposals called for the franchisee to extend service throughout the city and to furnish the widest possible variety of "high quality entertainment, cultural and educational, public affairs, and sports programming at the lowest possible cost to consumers." In addition, the winning bidder would be expected to support local nonprofit and access programming, to develop and market advanced interactive cable service to household and business customers, and to contribute to municipal initiatives designed to attract a video-production industry to the city.[84] While specifying minimum requirements about such attributes as channel capacity, the request for proposals left bidders free to offer more. The hope was to elicit competition among bidders concerning system configuration and provision of public services as well as prices to consumers. To gain the best possible knowledge regarding the ability of bidders to fulfill their promises, the request for proposals required revenue projections and documentation about financing.

Two large multisystem operators submitted bids—Cablevision Systems and Warner Amex Cable Communications. In many ways, the choice between the two contenders resembled that faced by Pittsburgh officials. As in Pittsburgh, both Cablevision and Warner promised to generously provide for public needs as defined by the municipal government and to build elaborate, state-of-the-art cable systems extending throughout the city. Cablevision did not offer a free universal package, as did Warner's competitor in Pittsburgh. But for the unprecedentedly low price of two dollars per month, Cablevision promised to offer Boston residents a fifty-two channel basic service. Warner, by contrast, offered to furnish a less generous thirty-four channel basic service for $5.95 per month. Concerning interactive capabilities, on the other hand, Warner appeared to have the advantage with its innovative QUBE system, unavailable from other vendors. Options for local ownership provision and provision of public access programming also resembled those in Pittsburgh. As in

Pittsburgh, Warner offered ownership shares to well-connected local organizations. By contrast, Cablevision proposed to meet the city's local ownership goals by offering high-interest one-thousand-dollar bonds to individuals.

As was the case elsewhere, deciding between the two bids involved far more than simply a matter of comparing prices. While the mayor was ultimately responsible for making the decision, Boston followed a process that included a consultant's report analyzing each bid in terms of a number of set criteria, evaluation by municipal officials, and two public hearings. On August 12, 1981, Mayor White announced that Cablevision had been selected. As justification, the mayor cited Cablevision's offer of basic service for two dollars, its promise of more funding and greater independence for community access programming, better local ownership provisions, and greater "imagination and innovation in its entire approach."

In its final state, the franchise contained detailed provisions concerning configuration of the system, construction of local access studios, technical performance, construction schedule, services and programming, subscriber rights, and affirmative action employment. The franchise ran for a period of fifteen years and was legally nonexclusive. Enforcement provisions included a schedule of fines for failure to complete construction on time and the posting of a two-million-dollar performance bond. In the event of a major breach of franchise terms, the city could revoke the franchise entirely and either purchase the system at a price to be determined by arbitration or order it dismantled. The city also retained the right to sue for damages.[85]

In important respects, Cablevision did initially live up to franchise requirements. As promised, Cablevision offered subscribers a fifty-two channel basic service for two dollars per month. The Boston Community Access and Programming Foundation also received the level of payment promised. Construction proceeded even more quickly than required under the franchise and by the end of 1984 more than 85 percent of the network had been completed. With some exceptions, system design and performance generally met technical specifications laid out in the franchise.

From the first, however, there were problems. Probably the most important lay in the area of customer relations. Although the franchise contained a number of requirements concerning the provision of adequate service, enforcement proved difficult in the face of simple incompetence and insufficient investment by the company in such resources as telephone lines to take consumer inquiries and complaints. Cablevision consistently failed to activate service within fourteen days of solicitation as required by the franchise, installers frequently missed appointments, billing complaints were rampant, and the company failed to respond to complaints about property damage. Those seeking to make contact with the company by telephone faced busy signals and interminable waits on "hold." In addition, Cablevision gave a low priority to those public obligations for which it received no remuneration. The firm lagged in connecting municipal offices and the Community Access and Programming Foundation to its institutional network, built only one of the three local origination studios required by the franchise, and failed to meet requirements to interconnect service hubs by cable as well as microwave links. According to the city Cable Office, the absence of cable links between hubs precluded "effective use of the Public Institutional Network by municipal agencies and other local institutions for city wide communications."[86]

Cablevision also delayed in furnishing promised two-way interactive services, despite the fact that the city appeared to enjoy a high degree of bargaining power in this domain. The franchise provided for a fine of one thousand dollars for each day after June 1, 1983 in which such services were not provided.[87] Citing technological and market uncertainties, however, Cablevision requested a delay in imposition of the requirement. Late in 1983, city officials agreed. Over the next two years, however, Cablevision did not make even the minimal efforts to offer such services called for under its modified agreement with the city. Although the city Cable Office repeatedly expressed frustration with this failure and pointedly noted Cablevision's franchise obligations, municipal officials did not choose to actually activate the penalty clause.[88]

Within a relatively short time (three and a half years) after Boston granted its cable television franchise, claims of financial incapacity on the part of Cablevision brought about further difficulties in enforcement. From the first, both the number of consumers who chose to subscribe to cable television and the revenue per subscriber fell seriously short of

Cablevision's projections. Cablevision initially projected that at least 56 percent of households with access to cable television would choose to purchase its more expensive "Omnibus" tier of services. By the end of 1984, however, only 43 percent of households chose to purchase any cable television at all. Among those who did subscribe, Cablevision had projected that average revenues would exceed fifty dollars per month due to the purchase of pay service. By the end of 1984, however, Cablevision revenues averaged $32.30 per month per subscriber.

In December of 1984, Cablevision announced that the revenue shortfall had reached critical proportions and that its banks had cut off the lines of credit needed to complete system construction. In response, the company halted further system construction, put in place a dramatic rate increase on all service tiers except for the basic level controlled by the city, and demanded that burdensome franchise requirements be reduced or eliminated. Revisions demanded by Cablevision included a cut in the franchise fee to 3 percent per year, a reduction in property tax bills, and modification of the contract with the Community Access and Programming Foundation. In a September 1985 newspaper interview, the president of Cablevision's parent company, Charles Dolan, called as well for a rise in the price of basic service to "self sustaining" levels comparable to those of other cities and for a franchise amendment "to make the company the judge of the need for additional capital facilities which will require further capital investments."[89] The parent firm, Dolan announced, would not commit the additional twenty million dollars in equity needed to complete construction of the Boston system until the firm gained the concessions demanded. In addition, Cablevision unilaterally cut its funding of the Boston Community Access and Programming Foundation from 5 percent of gross revenues to three hundred thousand dollars per month. This represented a direct defiance of franchise provisions.

At first, both Boston and foundation officials took a hard line against Cablevision's demands, publicly expressing suspicions that the firm had deliberately put in a deceptively low bid to obtain its franchise and that the financial crisis might be a setup. In a December 1984 interview, Mayor Flynn stated the city's determination to hold the firm to contract terms: "I remain determined to see to that the Boston public will not bear the burden for the problems Cablevision may be encountering whether due to internal management or marketplace circumstances. There are obligations we expect Cablevision to live up to." [90] By May of 1985, however, city officials were conceding their willingness to renegotiate some terms.

Given municipal goals of maintaining the best possible service, officials may have had little choice but to make some concessions. Boston did have the ability to harm Cablevision by imposing fines for certain forms of franchise noncompliance or even moving to have the franchise revoked entirely. But the city could not force Cablevision to invest in its system. In reality, the very severity of the penalty clauses in the original franchise may have actually reduced their usefulness. While threatening to apply severe penalties might have been valuable as a negotiating tool, actually following through on the threat would have increased the financial drain on Cablevision and thereby made the provision of good service even less likely. Given the city government's own straitened financial condition, its dependence on state aid, and doubts as to its ability to manage a cable system, municipal takeover held little attraction for city officials either. Nor would other companies purchase the Boston system, municipal officials believed, without demanding even more franchise concessions than those sought by Cablevision.[91]

Despite these weaknesses in their negotiating position, city officials sought to maintain as many of the original franchise requirements as they could by calling for the deferral of obligations rather than conceding their elimination altogether. Largely on this basis, the Boston Community Access and Programming Foundation and Cablevision did manage to reach an agreement during 1986. The agreement deferred some obligations and tied others more closely to the level of Cablevision's financial success. The stalemate between Boston and Cablevision, however, proved more difficult to resolve. In October of 1985, the city proposed an arrangement whereby in return for Cablevision resuming construction, the 3 percent franchise fee would be deferred until the number of cable subscribers reached half the level projected by Cablevision, a cap of four dollars would be placed on basic service through 1988 and five dollars thereafter, Cablevision and the city would hold regular meetings to resolve customer complaints, and the firm would donate $250,000 over a five-year period for job training. Cablevision rejected the proposal.

In the meantime, however, federal preemption of municipal regulatory authority gave Cablevision the opportunity it sought to eliminate the two-dollar basic rate mandated in the franchise. In November of 1985, Cablevision cut the number of channels on the two-dollar basic tier from fifty-two to twenty-nine and moved many of the more attractive satellite programming services to a new metro tier priced at $6.25 per month for existing subscribers and $12.50 per month for new ones. City officials tacitly agreed to the shift. In January of 1987, however, Cablevision took advantage of its rights under federal law to raise charges on basic service to $6.25 per month, one year earlier than the five-year commitment specified in the franchise. City officials disapproved of the shift but could do nothing to prevent it.

Cablevision and the city finally reached an agreement on franchise revision during the summer of 1988. The city used about the only source of bargaining leverage it now possessed, control over franchise fees, to gain lower cable prices for low-income residents. In return for the city cutting the franchise fee from 3 percent to 1 percent for a four-year period beginning January 1, 1988, Cablevision agreed to offer a half-price basic cable television service to residents of the city with Medicare cards. Cablevision also agreed to spend $250,000 over five years for job training for city residents and to pump more than $750,000 into the access organization.[92]

Transaction Costs, Legal and Political Contests, and the Performance of Cable Television Franchising

A great deal concerning the location, attributes, and timing of cable television investment in Seattle, Pittsburgh, and other cities can be understood in terms of economic and transaction cost factors. As would be expected based upon the discussion of natural monopoly in chapter 1, direct head-to-head competition between cable television firms has been very rare, irrespective of whether this has been legally prohibited or encouraged. While not as great as that possessed by waterworks in major cities, the resulting market power of cable television firms could be quite substantial—particularly in locales remote from urban centers or poorly situated to receive over-the-air signals. In Seattle and elsewhere, cable television systems enjoyed their earliest and most secure market niches in such locales.

In major urban centers with good broadcast reception, however, markets more closely resembled those found in electric utilities during the first years of that industry. Reaping profits here depended upon the ability of cable television firms to furnish a service with sufficiently attractive price and quality attributes to entice consumers in the face of substantial demand elasticities and competition for at least some of the kinds of programming offered. Unwillingness on the part of Seattle's cable television firms during the early 1970s to extend service to neighborhoods with good broadcast reception can be understood in terms of these factors, as can eagerness on the part of firms just a few years later to compete for franchises to build systems in these very same kinds of neighborhoods in Seattle, Pittsburgh, and elsewhere.

But while cable television development has been carried out by private firms engaged in the business of delivering media content to consumers, municipal governments have attempted to use franchise bidding for a wider range of purposes. Goals have included involvement of local citizens and organizations in system ownership, control over prices, the eliciting of specifically public services, and the shaping of system attributes. Because the bulk of development had already taken place by the time bidding procedures were put in place, franchise bidding played a comparatively limited role in Seattle. But even under these circumstances, the ability of Seattle to gain construction of an access studio and institutional network through the use of franchise bidding stands out in sharp relief against the previous inability of the municipal government to exercise virtually any influence at all on cable investment. Through use of franchise bidding from the outset, Pittsburgh and Boston obtained promises of far more elaborate system development.

These promises did not go completely unfulfilled. As of 1994, residents of both Pittsburgh and Boston had access to a far broader range of cable channels than did people in Seattle. At the same time, however, the leverage gained through franchise bidding also had its limits. As in both waterworks and electric utilities, municipalities have found themselves bound together in long-term relationships with privately owned service providers once initial franchises have been awarded and significant investments made. In the context of such relationships, any effort to hold franchisees to original contract terms or to sanction them for violations have had be weighed against the countervailing ability of the service provider to withhold needed capital investments for system development and the disruptions that would result if the firm actually did go bankrupt. Such bargaining leverage that municipal governments gained through their power to deny franchise renewals could also be quite costly in this respect.

As would be expected given the transaction-specific attributes of cable television distribution systems, very few municipal governments in the United States have even attempted to revoke cable television franchises once significant investments have been made. And incumbent firms that have sought to renew franchise contracts have almost always succeeded in doing so.[93] Cable television firms, however, enjoyed greater freedom of action than municipalities and have been rather more nimble. The buying and selling of cable systems and mergers and acquisitions of one firm by another have been very common and remain so. The result has been to introduce a certain asymmetry into relationships between municipalities and cable firms, which has generally redounded to the advantage of the latter.

For a cable television firm seeking to win new franchises, a reputation for amicability, faithfulness to franchise terms, and responsiveness to consumer and public demands could prove a vital competitive asset.[94] For a firm such as TCI, which grew largely by acquiring other systems, on the other hand, a good reputation in these domains was far less necessary. Indeed, for such a firm, a reputation for hard and even ruthless bargaining with municipal governments and other companies could even prove advantageous. More directly, at least in Seattle and Pittsburgh, minority and local ownership goals became immediate and direct casualties of the passing of cable systems into new hands. In Pittsburgh, calls for concessions that municipal officials were too weak to resist also accompanied the sale of Warner's cable system to TCI.

As in other utilities, the workings of relationships between municipalities and franchisees have also been shaped by the extent to which specifically public services have been demanded by governments and the degree to which changing public and private demands could be accommodated without the need to renegotiate contracts. In waterworks, the most severe strains on franchises and contracts arose from a combination of rapid urban growth, uncertainty as to investments needed for public goods such as fire protection, and lack of an easily observed measure of output that could be tied to investment and performance in a meaningful and incremental way. In cable television too, contracts typically had to be renegotiated under difficult circumstances in major cities. The exact sources of strain, however, differed. During the late 1970s and early 1980s, Pittsburgh and other major cities evaluated bidders for cable franchises based upon highly specific promises concerning prices, system attributes, service to consumers, and provision of public services. This approach had much to recommend it. Such specificity aided in fair comparison of bidders and enhanced accountability to the electorate of the government officials making these choices. Nor did measurement of whether terms were being fulfilled generally raise insuperable difficulties. Unfortunately, the very detail and specificity of cable franchise requirements also made for difficulties in a world of rapid technological change and uncertainty concerning consumer demands.

Cable television franchising and its vicissitudes did not play out in a legal and institutional vacuum. Since World War II, in most public utilities, judicial intervention into the details of economic regulation declined in importance as courts became reluctant to use constitutional property rights and due process protections as a warrant for overturning legislative and regulatory decisions. In cable television, however, matters have been rather different because of increased judicial solicitude for the First Amendment during this period and cable's role as a communications medium. Here, contests in the courts have at times played significant, albeit idiosyncratic, parts in constraining both federal regulation and municipal franchising.

In the case of federal regulation over cable television during the 1970s and early 1980s, the FCC claimed jurisdiction as an extension of its authority to regulate broadcasting under the Communications Act of 1934. While the courts did accept that the FCC could make some rules on this basis, they did not regard the statutory footing as sufficient to justify any and all interventions. Largely on the basis of limited jurisdiction, a United States Appeals court in the District of Columbia in 1977 overturned FCC regulations banning the showing of recently released movies and current sports events over cable systems.[95] In a 1979 ruling, the Supreme Court overturned FCC regulations imposed three years earlier requiring that some cable systems furnish public access channels.[96]

With passage of the Cable Communications Act of 1984, the FCC finally gained a more secure statutory footing for rule making concerning cable television. This did not, however, mean the end of legal challenge to either federal, state, or local initiatives to regulate cable. Increasingly, during the 1970s and 1980s, the focus of legal battles shifted to questions of constitutional interpretation. Debate hinged largely on the meaning of the First Amendment. From one perspective, the First Amendment could be viewed as presenting no bar to imposition of obligations about the minimum number of channels furnished, provision of access facilities, or extension of service throughout a community. Indeed, because cable television firms typically enjoyed local monopolies and numerous public privileges, the First Amendment could be understood as strengthening the case for such interventions as a means of preventing a private monopoly from abusing its privileged position to choke off the "widest possible dissemination of information from diverse and antagonistic sources."[97]

Precedents did exist for this line of interpretation. In its 1945 ruling in *Associated Press*, a divided Supreme Court rejected claims that First Amendment protections to freedom of the press precluded the application of antitrust law to overturn practices on the part of the news gathering association deemed monopolistic. Similarly, in the Red Lion case, decided in 1969, the Supreme Court refused to overturn on First Amendment grounds FCC requirements that those attacked by a radio or television station be given time over the air to respond. The FCC's right of reply regulations, the Court opined, advanced First Amendment ends by preserving "an uninhibited marketplace of ideas" from monopolization by private as well as governmental interests.[98]

At the same time, however, willingness on the part of the Supreme Court to uphold governmental interventions designed to promote access and diversity has been far from unlimited. In *Red Lion*, the Supreme Court classified the FCC's right of reply requirement not as a content-based governmental interference in editorial decision making but as a modest opening up of a public resource to citizens not fortunate enough to possess the privileges afforded by a government license to operate their own broadcast station.[99] Insofar as First Amendment rights are concerned, the decision maintained, those who have been favored with FCC licenses "stand no better than those to whom licenses are refused."[100] Even in the case of the most monopolistic of newspapers, however, a right of reply statute could not be plausibly viewed in these terms. And in the 1974 case of *Miami Herald* v. *Tornillo,* a unanimous Supreme Court held that even if economic circumstances did result in newspaper monopolies emerging, the First Amendment foreclosed the sort of governmental intrusion into content and editorial discretion represented by a right of reply statute.[101]

In the context of these decisions, even the most benignly motivated and fairly executed of bidding competitions for cable television franchises could be attacked as just as unconstitutional under the First Amendment as if a municipal government attempted to choose which daily newspaper should be distributed in a community. Initiatives by any level of government to impose requirements about provision of local programming or access facilities could also be vulnerable on First Amendment grounds. This line of argument began to be taken up with increasing vigor during the 1970s and 1980s by some cable operators seeking to avoid imposition or enforcement of franchise obligations and by conservative public interest law groups such as the Mountain States Legal Foundation.[102]

While scarcity of channels might serve as a basis for recognizing government licensing of broadcast stations as consistent with the First Amendment, advocates of this position maintained, such logic could not be applied to cable. Here, no insuperable technological barrier lay in the way of the furnishing of a virtually unlimited number of channels. It might be unfortunate, some advocates of this position conceded, that control over these channels typically rested in the hands of a single proprietor. But, without franchising, they maintained, cable television probably would not be a local monopoly. And even if economic forces did result in cable television being a monopoly, this did not affect the First Amendment rights of system operators. Just as the Supreme Court in *Tornillo* gave monopolistic local newspapers complete discretion as to what to publish, cable operators should enjoy the same rights under the First Amendment.

As of 1992, the United States Supreme Court had yet to issue a decisive ruling regarding these arguments. In its 1986 ruling in the case of *Los Angeles* v. *Preferred Communications,* the Supreme Court did affirm that a company might be able to claim a First Amendment right to build a cable television system even if denied a municipal franchise. Cable television operators, the opinion stated, do engage in some communication activities similar to those of newspaper editors. But while such activities "plainly implicate First Amendment interests," the context may be one in which "speech and action are joined in a single course of action," and in which "First Amendment values must be balanced against competing societal interests."[103] Rather than itself ruling on the constitutional standing of municipal franchising, the Supreme Court remanded the case back down to the district court in which it had arisen for further examination in light of these considerations.

In essence, the Supreme Court decision in *Preferred* affirmed that First Amendment challenges to franchising and regulatory decisions should be taken seriously by the courts but refrained from elucidating definitive criteria for decision making.[104] Not surprisingly, therefore, lower court rulings have varied. Some federal circuit courts during the late 1980s accepted that natural monopoly attributes of cable television systems represented a constitutionally permissible justification for both municipal franchising and imposition of access requirements.[105] In a 1989 case, a federal district court in Chicago even upheld enforcement of a requirement that a cable television system furnish locally originated programming as consistent with First Amendment prohibitions on abridgment of freedom of the press.[106] During this same period, however, other federal circuits took the position that "economic scarcity or natural monopoly, even if factually supported, do not warrant a First Amendment exception for cable television."[107]

In line with this latter perspective, a federal district court ruled in a franchise renewal case in Santa Cruz, California, that exclusive franchising of a cable television system violated the First Amendment, as did the imposition of requirements about public access, channel capacity, and extension of service throughout a community. Based upon promises of superior performance in these domains, Santa Cruz had awarded its cable franchise to a new firm and denied renewal to the incumbent. But the incumbent, too, the court ruled, had a First Amendment right to be granted a new franchise subject only to requirements relating to payment of a franchise fee and disruption of the streets.[108] Similarly, in a less sweeping 1991 decision, a Georgia federal court judge held that under the First Amendment, a cable company had the right to continue to operate on an air force base even though its franchise had expired and the government was seeking a new company to develop a system.[109]

In most cases, court decisions did not go so far in undercutting the governmental authority needed to elicit franchise competition and to enforce contracts. But even so, delays and the costs of litigation in and of themselves tended to favor incumbent firms. A case in Florida is illustrative. In 1985, the town of Niceville, Florida, began to put in place plans to build its own cable system. The existing privately owned system, some town residents complained, furnished poor service and charged high prices. Warner fought the case in the courts, suing the town on a number of grounds, including the claim that construction of a municipal system would violate its own free speech rights and alleging "unlawful municipal competition." As of 1992, the town had spent about three hundred thousand dollars on legal fees and had won every case in the courts—but because bond agencies were unwilling to rate the project's bond issues due to the litigation, Niceville had yet to even begin construction on its system.[110]

Municipal franchising faced even greater difficulties in the political arena. As did their electric utility counterparts, cable companies succeeded at times in outflanking restraints and impositions put in place by one level of governmental authority by appealing to another. In the case of electric utilities during the late nineteenth and early twentieth centuries, privately owned service providers generally gained increased security against both economic and political threats with the supplanting of municipal franchising by state regulation. In cable television during the late 1960s and early 1970s, by contrast, municipalities generally imposed few requirements or restraints on franchisees, while state utility commissions developed far more elaborate apparatuses of control over rates and service than anything electric utilities had faced at the turn of the century.

In consequence, the cable television industry quite sensibly took a different tack and strongly opposed proposals to supplant municipal franchising with regulation by state utility commissions. Utility-style regulation, proprietors of cable companies worried, would constrain profits, intrude on decision making, and impose burdensome reporting requirements. Worse yet, some in the industry feared, state utility commissions might choose to treat cable companies as a common carrier and attempt to set terms on which signals would be carried. With cable operators opposing state regulation outright and few well-organized constituencies pushing very hard for it, proposals for state regulation over cable generally went down to defeat.

During the early 1980s, however, matters shifted. With municipal governments now playing a more active role in overseeing the development of cable systems and regulating consumer charges, the industry turned to the federal government for relief. The time seemed ripe. With Ronald Reagan just elected to the White House on an "anti-big government" platform and Republicans in control of the Senate, the prospects of receiving a favorable hearing appeared far greater in Washington, D.C. than in either state capitals or local city halls. Interestingly, some of the arguments put forth to justify federally mandated deregulation of cable television resembled those used to justify imposition of state regulation over public utilities at the turn of the century.

In particular, allegations of municipal ineptitude, knavery, and corruption represented a major theme in turn-of-the-century calls for imposition of utility regulation. In Dallas, Boston, and many of the other major cities in which franchise requirements created the most difficulty for cable television firms, however, franchising had clearly been clean. Nevertheless, allegations of municipal corruption were sometimes brought forth by advocates of federal preemption. Advocates of deregulation also mounted a more fundamental attack on the legitimacy of municipal governments exercising control over attributes of cable television systems under virtually any circumstances. In 1983 Senate testimony, National Cable Television Association president Thomas Wheeler made the case as follows: "First, cable is the only telecommunications business which cannot reach its potential customers without first receiving approval from the local government. Moreover, this approval or lack thereof, can be completely arbitrary and varies from city to city. . . . Second, there is a basic misconception that the relationship between a city and a cable operator is that of buyer-seller. . . . Nothing could be further from the truth. . . . The city is a barrier standing between a cable operator and his potential customers. . . . Third, I don't know of any other private enterprise where a city can demand free services as the price of doing business." [111]

Mainly, however, advocates of federal preemption of municipal authority and deregulation of cable television rested their case on economic grounds. Even when cable television firms possessed distribution monopolies, deregulation advocates maintained, demand elasticities made for market discipline because the service was not essential and because at least a few television stations could be obtained over the air. Furthermore, they contended, inter-product competition for cable television was beginning to emerge, with the development of video discs and cassettes, low-powered television stations, multi-point microwave distribution systems ("wireless cable"), and soon direct satellite-to-home communications systems.[112] Some advocates of federal preemption also made the case that head-to-head competition between cable television systems themselves could play an important role in enhancing consumer choice and in subjecting privately owned service providers to market discipline.[113] From this perspective, it was not natural monopoly but municipal franchising that represented the main barrier to the emergence of such competition.[114]

In 1983, an industry-supported bill reported out of the Senate Commerce Committee would have left municipal governments in most urban and suburban areas with no authority to either regulate basic charges to consumers or to enforce franchise requirements about channel capacity and provision of most public services. The bill also prohibited municipal governments from considering proposals from prospective competitors at the time of franchise renewal, creating in effect a renewal presumption.[115] Opponents of deregulation enjoyed sufficient clout in the House and Senate, however, to prevent passage. Instead, over the course of 1983 and 1984, a series of negotiations between the cable industry (represented by the National Cable Television Association) and municipal governments (represented by the National League of Cities) finally resulted in agreement on legislation that affirmed the ability of municipalities to impose and enforce franchise requirements regarding number of channels and provision of facilities. In return, the industry gained inclusion of a provision eliminating municipal authority to regulate charges to consumers in locales in which cable systems faced "effective competition."[116]

With the issuing of a ruling by the FCC in 1985 that cable systems faced "effective competition" in locales in which viewers could receive as few as three broadcast stations over the air, it became clear that the industry had gained the better of the bargain. Irrespective of franchise commitments, cable companies gained complete freedom to set rates in most urban and suburban regions throughout the country from 1987 onward on the basis of this standard. Cable companies quickly seized the opportunity. Before deregulation, prices for the basic bundle of channels to which all cable customers had to subscribe had increased at a rate slower than that of inflation. Over the years 1986 through 1992, by contrast, average monthly charges virtually doubled from $10.67 to $20.35.[117] In part as a consequence, annual industry revenues increased an average of more than six hundred million dollars faster during the three years following deregulation than they had during the three years preceding it.[118]

The technological and business structures built up around national satellite program networks and cable distribution came into full flower during the late 1980s and early 1990s. By the spring of 1994, almost the entire country had been wired for cable and about six out of ten households took at least a basic service.[119] The numbers of cable subscribers, which stood at about eighteen million in 1980, reached more than fifty-seven million twelve years later. Average channel capacities increased as well, as new big-city systems came on-line and cable firms began to invest in new amplifiers and other equipment to enable systems built in earlier years to serve as outlets for at least some of the new satellite services. As a consequence of these trends, the proportion of cable subscribers connected to systems with fifty-four or more channels increased from less than 10 percent in 1985 to just under 38 percent in 1993.[120] Other avenues of video distribution opened up during this period as well. Over the course of the 1980s, the number of VCRs in use in American households increased from fewer than two million to almost eighty million. By 1990, almost eight out of nine of the country's television households owned the equipment.

Unquestionably, these developments reduced the dominance of the big three broadcast networks and increased viewer choice. They did not, however, represent a major departure from long-standing patterns in the evolution of mass media in the United States. The range of choice of video programming furnished by even the richest of the urban cable systems built during the 1980s is not all that much greater than that present in broadcast radio almost from the first.[121] Similarly, the VCR's role in relation to television can be viewed as analogous in many respects to that played by record players and tape recorders in relation to radio. Viewed in broad historical perspective, it is the continuities that are remarkable, the degree to which quite different communications and media technologies in the United States have been molded and structured in quite similar ways over the past one hundred years. This theme will be explored further in chapter 5.

five

Thinking about Fixed Networks in Historical Context

COMMENTATORS ON THE CONTEMPORARY WORLD OFTEN assert that we live in a time of unprecedentedly rapid change. And it is true that many aspects of today's world are in flux. But the antithesis, with an ostensibly slow-paced and predictable past, posited by such statements is incorrect. As can be seen in the preceding accounts, the histories of waterworks, electric utilities, and cable television have been rich in change from the very start. Franchising and contracting arrangements have been upended by the unexpected in settings as disparate as waterworks in San Francisco during the 1850s and cable television in Boston during the 1980s. At the same time, technological and political legacies of the past endure. Similarities in issues presented by change itself in many settings can also be discerned.

Brief discussions follow of continuities and change in the character of public policy issues that have arisen—and that continue to arise—in waterworks, electric utilities, and the telecommunications and media complex of which cable television forms a part. Each of the systems is taken up in turn. The discussions make no pretense of being completely up-to-date in every detail. The contemporary world *is* moving too quickly for that. Rather, the aim is to furnish examples of how the kind of history and analysis presented here can be used to understand new conditions and problems as they arise. The discussions are intended to be suggestive—to serve as invitations for further thought.

In waterworks, the oldest of the three networked systems discussed in this book, technological and institutional legacies of the nineteenth and early twentieth centuries can easily still be discerned. The world of waterworks in major American cities is arguably more rather than less stable and conservative than was the case 100 or 150 years ago. In some older American cities, water is still supplied and distributed through pipes that are more than a century in age. Nor has waterworks technology itself changed radically in many respects. If engineer John B. Jervis returned to life and was taken on a tour of the water supply and distribution systems of New York or Boston, he would doubtless be impressed by the scale of the facilities developed. But he would have little difficulty in understanding the fundamental workings of the systems of reservoirs, aqueducts, and pipes used to supply water to these cities. Government-owned systems also continue to supply water to most of the urban and suburban areas in which the bulk of America's population lives. As of 1989, about three-quarters of the people in the United States served by waterworks obtained their supplies from government-owned systems.

But although changes in technology and institutions have been relatively undramatic, there have been significant alterations in political and ideological contexts. During the nineteenth and early twentieth centuries, a range of both practical and idealistic concerns with public health, fire protection, property values, and urban growth all played roles in driving municipal governments to build large-scale waterworks. Government-owned waterworks themselves served as focal points of civic patriotism at times in Boston and other major American cities. Increasingly, however, government-owned waterworks have come under attack, not for poorly serving developmental goals and demands but for doing so all too well without taking competing interests and notions of the public good sufficiently into account.

One stream of attack has been essentially political. Even during the nineteenth and early twentieth centuries, identification between large-scale waterworks development and consensually accepted definitions of the public interest did not always hold up. Malign associations between government-owned waterworks, interest group manipulation by wealthy elites, and unaccountable power date to the nineteenth century and have continued to arise in different settings. An 1845 broadside in Boston, for example, criticized plans for government ownership on the grounds that they would result in the creation of a "closed Corporation of Water Commissioners with high salaries, offices for life, and despotic powers."[1] In 1911, Socialist mayoral candidate Job Harriman gained considerable popular support through his use of the Los Angeles Aqueduct then being built "as a symbol of all that was wrong and corrupt in the existing order."[2] Unneeded by Los Angeles itself, Harriman maintained, the aqueduct was being built primarily to benefit wealthy land speculators in the San Fernando Valley.[3]

Large water supply and distribution projects have also come under increasing attack on environmental grounds. The preservationist attack on San Francisco's plans to dam up the Hetch Hetchy for use as a municipal water supply was highly unusual for its time. As unspoiled wild environments have grown more scarce and ecological relationships have come to be increasingly appreciated, however, concerns over environmental damage from damming rivers and diverting water flows have swelled in political importance and potency. During the 1960s, for example, preservationists and environmentalists played a major role in blocking a plan by the United States Bureau of Reclamation to dam the Colorado River below the Grand Canyon for water and power development. More recently, environmentalists in a complex alliance with other interest groups managed to defeat a California plan to build a peripheral canal around the San Joquain Delta designed to increase water supplies for urban and agricultural uses in southern California.

Increasingly, over the past half century, economists have also criticized eagerness on the part of municipalities and other governmental entities to invest in large-scale water supply facilities. In particular, some economists criticize as highly unrealistic assumptions that water demand is price-insensitive and that supplies must keep pace with population and economic growth to avoid crisis. Rigid adherence to these assumptions, economists complain, results in inefficiency and waste as water supply facilities are constructed at a marginal cost far in excess of any marginal benefits. In a stinging critique of the California's State Water project written during the late 1950s, economist Jack Hirshleifer made the case as follows: "The water supply planners of California, and of the South Coastal Area in particular, find themselves faced with a great conundrum.

On the one hand, with rapidly expanding population and industry, it seems obvious that more water is 'needed'; on the other hand, it is equally obvious that customers are going to be hard to find at prices based on the unit costs for the Feather River supply, so that subsidy in one form or another seems the only way out. . . . The answer, of course, is that these 'requirements' and historic trends are largely based upon a low, heavily subsidized price for water. There is a shortage of water at $20 per acre-foot in just the same sense that there is a shortage of new Cadillacs at a price of $500."[4]

Critics of large-scale waterworks development have not always agreed with one another. Even as many economists call for more extensive use of market mechanisms in the allocation of water resources, for example, some preservationists find it highly objectionable in principle to assign a cash price to the value of a wild river. Other lines of disagreement can also be cited. To protect the purity of their water supplies and reduce the need for filtering, for example, cities such as New York, Boston, Seattle, and Newark have attempted to preserve large areas of watershed lands in a more or less natural condition. From a preservationist perspective, such efforts are obviously worthy of applause. With improvements in water filtration technology, however, these efforts have come under attack in some cases on the grounds that they cost too much and restrict the ability of citizens who live in watershed areas to develop their land as they see fit or require the taking of their property altogether. In the case of Los Angeles's water supply, historian William Kahrl makes the case that the city's actions in preventing economic development in the Owens Valley contributed to preservation of the natural environment but also disenfranchised valley residents and kept them in what has been an essentially colonial relationship.[5]

Frequently, however, the critiques have been mutually supportive of one another. In and of themselves, for example, issues of central control and allegations of unaccountable power in the hands of government-owned waterworks have not generally sufficed to halt development of large-scale water supply and distribution facilities. In the absence of environmental and economic concerns, claims of professional expertise on the parts of those running waterworks have historically been highly respected and fears of abuse have centered at least as much on political interference and corruption as on any loss of accountability that might result from loosening the bonds of control held by elected officials. At times, however, both environmentalists and critics concerned with economic efficiency have effectively drawn upon concerns with concentrated political power to bolster their own arguments against what they regard as damaging or wasteful projects. Despite suspicion of market mechanisms on the part of some environmentalists, those opposing large-scale water projects have also not hesitated to draw upon critiques based on economic and efficiency considerations.

Similar shifts in political and ideological contexts have taken place in electric utilities. As in waterworks, the rise of the environmental movement during the 1960s and 1970s meant the breakdown of consensus concerning the desirability of unlimited system growth and expansion. Instead, increasing numbers of people came to believe that sustainable improvements in living standards could best be realized not by increasing use of electricity but by tapping such renewable and nonpolluting resources as the sun and the wind and by enhancing the efficiency with which all forms of energy were utilized.[6] The result was a political and regulatory climate very different from that faced by either private or government-owned electric utilities in the past. No longer would utility managements be free to site and operate generating plants and transmission lines without public controversy or review by government agencies.

To a greater extent than in waterworks, changes in technology, regulation, and industry organization have also taken place. Starting in the mid-1960s, private and government-owned electric utility enterprises alike found themselves facing new constraints and difficulties arising from technical and organizational problems within the industry itself. In the case of the coal- and oil-fired generating plants that supplied the bulk of the nation's power, the sort of incremental increases in steam temperatures and pressures and improvements in generator and turbine design that had brought about steady reductions in fuel consumption per kilowatt hour for more than fifty years finally began to be played out after 1965.[7] Efforts to lower cost through exploitation of scale economies also began to run into trouble, with many large units furnishing power far less reliably than expected.[8] The effects of these difficulties would be exacerbated during the 1970s by inflationary pressures and a souring economic climate.[9] Utilities that relied upon imported oil to generate electricity faced particular difficulties. Concentrated in the northeastern

United States, such utilities found themselves in severe straits during the 1973 Arab oil embargo. While the embargo soon passed, price increases and a newfound sense of vulnerability persisted.[10] During the Iranian Revolution of 1978 and 1979, petroleum prices again soared. The cumulative result was that the oil burned in electric generating plants cost more than ten times as much in 1980 as it had a decade earlier.[11]

Nor could relief be obtained by turning to nuclear power. As with conventional thermal plants, rapid scaling-up made for unexpected difficulties in ensuring reliable operation of nuclear facilities.[12] More importantly, increasing the size of nuclear power plants raised a host of safety and environmental concerns that proved difficult to address. As plants became larger, containment structures could no longer be relied upon to prevent core melts and other serious accidents from exposing the public to heavy doses of radiation. To avoid catastrophe, therefore, nuclear plants would have to be developed and overseen in such a way that "errors in design, construction, and operation *never* triggered significant releases of fission products from the core."[13] Year after year, theoretical analyses as well as untoward experiences with existing plants revealed new possibilities for disaster, which in turn inspired new regulations and new disputes.[14] Inflation and high real interest rates during the 1970s magnified both the costs of meeting new standards and the financial consequences of delays in construction.[15]

Hard-pressed by rising costs and interest rates and with demand for electricity growing more slowly than expected, private and government-owned utilities alike found that they had little choice but to sharply cut back on investment in new plants during the late 1970s. During the years which followed, rates of growth in consumption of electricity remained modest by historical standards.[16] As pursuit of traditional growth paths came to seem increasingly problematical, some private and government-owned utilities even began to cooperate with environmental groups in the forging of conservation and renewable energy initiatives.[17] In part as a result of such collaborations, some states in recent years have adopted regulations under which utilities can profit as much or more by underwriting conservation reduction investments on the part of their customers as by building new plant.[18]

But for all the changes that have occurred and are occurring in the electric utility industry, striking continuities can also be discerned. As has been the case throughout the history of the electric utility industry in the United States, thermal plants burning fossil fuels still accounted for the bulk of output during the early 1990s. While development of large conventional as well as nuclear power plants has almost completely ceased in recent years, efforts to site transmission lines and newer types of cogeneration and waste to energy plants continue to inspire controversy. Nuclear power continues to cause contention as well. Citing the threat of global warming and the promise of new and purportedly safer designs, some in the electric utility industry look toward a new round of development. Many environmentalists remain opposed because of concerns about weapons proliferation and waste disposal as well as plant safety.

Older sorts of disputes over government versus private ownership of electric utilities also show no signs of disappearing completely. Particularly during the 1970s, public and private power interests faced similar political and economic challenges and staked out common positions with respect to much proposed energy and environmental regulation. Collaboration in research and development was institutionalized in 1971 with the formation of the Electric Power Research Institute. As generating plants became more expensive and siting more difficult during the 1970s, government- and privately-owned electric utilities increasingly began to take ownership interests in each other's facilities as a means of spreading the financial burdens and risks.[19] Even shifts from private to government ownership represented examples of cooperation in some instances. In 1974, for example, Consolidated Edison voluntarily sold one of its nuclear generating plants at Indian Point to the Power Authority of the State of New York as an expedient to raise cash, avert bankruptcy, and get the plant up and running.

As in earlier years, however, beliefs that overly high utility charges threaten local economic and business development can still inspire broad-based political coalitions to rally in support of government-ownership initiatives. Indeed, it is possible that conflicts of this sort may become even more prevalent in the future as transmission networks are opened up to independent buyers and sellers of electricity. During the early 1990s, an old-fashioned donnybrook of this sort took place in Brook Park, Ohio, a small industrial city located about thirty miles from Cleveland. Despite such new ingredients as nuclear generating stations and bulk power markets, the conflict in Brook Park played out along lines that would have held few surprises to an observer from early twentieth-century Seattle or San Francisco. Due to utility investment in expensive nuclear capacity and lower-than-expected demand, charges for electricity in northern Ohio during the early 1990s were among the highest in the country. A government-owned distributing system in Brook Park was seen by advocates as a means for consumers in the city to gain access to relatively low-cost coal-generated power available on the wholesale bulk power market. Support for the municipal-ownership initiative came not only from local unions and populist community organizations, but from the Ford Motor Company, which owned an engine plant in the city. Indeed, Ford went so far as to underwrite a four-hundred-thousand-dollar consulting report on the feasibility of municipal ownership. The local utility, Cleveland Electric Illuminated, also responded in traditional ways, threatening litigation and challenging claims that municipal ownership would really bring lower rates.[20]

Continuities can also be discerned in issues associated with the structuring and functioning of transactions and contracts. In some situations, such as street light contracting during the late nineteenth century, declining costs of production and the presence of inter-product competition coupled with ease of measuring output and monitoring quality rendered the task of deriving workable contractual relationships fairly undemanding. But in electric utilities, as in waterworks, situations have also arisen in which parties have faced greater difficulties in structuring viable long-term relationships. As early as 1944, for example, a report published by the Twentieth Century Fund cited informational and transactional difficulties as major factors preventing privately owned utilities from cooperating with each other: "The coordination of generating facilities through intersystem contracts is not perfect largely because of the absence of full competition. The 'market' often consists of only one seller and one buyer. The accounting between companies, checking of costs, and the difficulties and delays in negotiations may involve heavy expenses and even duplicate efforts. The clash of divergent interests may entail costly negotiations over the division of the savings. . . . Differences of opinion may arise concerning the economies from a given interchange, and each of the parties may be ignorant of the factors in the other's operations that make economies possible." [21]

Thirty years later, Stephen G. Breyer and Paul W. Macavoy made a virtually identical set of points concerning the difficulties in arranging for inter-system power sales and coordination between independent electric utilities. According to Breyer and Macavoy, "bargaining over how to divide the potential gains from coordination among partially competitive, partially regulated companies has not worked well." As a consequence, they maintained, coordination and power pooling were not developing as needed.[22]

Problems of two-party bargaining and long-term contracting arose during the 1980s as the independent power production industry began to emerge. Signed into law by President Carter in 1978, the Public Utility Regulatory Policy Act required electric utilities to buy power from independent "qualifying facilities" at a price equal to the cost that would be borne by the utility to generate the power itself. Qualifying facilities could be co-generators of any size or plants of under eighty megawatts' capacity that ran on waste products, wind, solar energy, hydropower, or other renewable resources.[23] Court challenges during the early 1980s stymied federal enforcement of these provisions and many states were slow to stipulate prices for power purchases. Nevertheless, independent power producers accounted for about 5 percent of the country's electricity production during the early 1990s and for about half of the new generating capacity added each year.

While independent power producers relied upon long-term contracts to ensure that their investments would be recompensed, many utilities claimed that the arrangements reduced flexibility and harmed consumers. In practice, it proved no straightforward matter to set prices for independently generated electricity on the basis of costs avoided by utilities in not generating the power themselves. Such avoided cost determinations under the Public Utility Regulatory Policy Act involved judgments concerning hypothetical future events and could be highly controversial.[24] Even if the independents had an initial cost advantage, critics charged, changing conditions sometimes resulted in utilities being forced to buy power at higher costs than if they had generated it themselves. Some regulators and utility executives during the late 1980s and early 1990s advocated addressing such problems by writing off competition in the supply of electricity as a failure and returning to a world of regulated, vertically integrated electric utility firms. Legislation signed into law by President Bush in October of 1992, however, took a different course.

The law reduced restrictions on independent power producers even as it enhanced the authority of federal regulators to order access to transmission lines. The results, drafters of the legislation promised, will be the emergence of full-fledged markets for electricity and the disappearance of the rigidities and distortions described above. The extent to which this hope will be realized remains uncertain. Even if true markets for electricity do develop, however, long-term contracting of one sort or another may continue to play a prominent role in structuring relationships between buyers and sellers. For risk-averse consumers, such contracts represent a means of obtaining reliable supplies of electricity at predictable prices. For investors, long-term contracts can be a form of security for capital sunk into fixed and large-scale generating and transmission facilities. Now, as in the past, issues of measurement and change are likely to be of crucial importance in determining the success of such relationships. Such issues may also play a role in driving more vertical integration than might otherwise be expected, given theoretical possibilities for competition.

An even more tangled web of contracting and transaction issues can be found associated with utility-sponsored conservation and demand-management programs. The rationale for such programs is straightforward. Particularly if environmental costs and harms are taken into account, it can be more expensive for a utility to produce a given quantity of electricity than for consumers to invest in conservation and efficiency measures that would result in the energy not being needed. But why then do consumers not make the investments themselves? Responses to this question by advocates of such programs generally rest on two points. The first is that electricity pricing often does not reflect marginal, let alone social, costs. While pricing electricity to reflect these costs may be the most economically efficient way to elicit appropriate behavior by consumers, less perfect approaches can be better than doing nothing. The second response is that consumers and utilities have different time frames. Residential consumers are often unwilling to invest in conservation if the payback in lower energy costs is more than two or three years away. Utilities, by contrast, are satisfied with far longer payback periods.[25]

Much of this difference in time frames, advocates of conservation programs maintain, can be attributed to imperfect capital markets, incomplete information, and transaction costs. Particularly for consumers with limited access to capital, investing in conservation can be quite risky. Exact payback periods depend not only upon the effectiveness of the measures in saving energy but upon future energy prices. Benefits also depend upon the quality of work performed by contractors, which can be difficult for a consumer to evaluate. In addition, recourse can be difficult to obtain even if poor workmanship is detected. Compounding the difficulties are "uncertainties about the performance of some technologies, and about the optimal techniques to design or retrofit heating, cooling, lighting, motor, and ventilation systems."[26] Other measurement and transactional issues can constrain economically advantageous investment as well. Builders may be reluctant to make energy efficiency a priority in design, for example, if they are not assured of recompense in the sale price. Similarly, landlords may be reluctant to invest in energy efficiency if utility bills are paid by tenants and there is no recompense in higher rents.

Moreover, utility subsidies for consumers to invest in conservation measures themselves raise contracting and transactions issues. In particular, projecting and evaluating the performance of such programs presents a number of difficulties. Consumers, for example, may demand and even obtain subsidies for conservation investments that they would have been willing to make in any case. If this occurs, utility expenditures will be greater than needed to achieve demand-reduction goals, and the performance of the programs themselves will be overstated. Regulatory formulas under which utilities profit from investment in conservation programs may also lead to performance being overstated. On the other hand, the performance of such programs may be better than projected because of consumers being inspired to make additional conservation investments not paid for by the utility. This sort of effect, too, can be difficult to measure.[27]

The issues have a political face as well. Utility programs to subsidize or finance conservation investments on the part of homeowners and businesspeople can be viewed as increasing corporate and governmental control over consumer decision making. Measures to reduce peak demand, such as utility-controlled operation of customer hot-water heaters, can also be viewed in these terms. Not surprisingly, familiar sorts of arguments against concentrated economic and political power are already being invoked in opposition to such programs. According to one opponent, demand-side management programs are objectionable in principle because they "directly increase the scope of government control over private decisions."[28] Similarly, 1991 congressional testimony submitted by an association of small energy service contractors and fuel oil dealers decried utility provision of conservation services on the grounds that it would result in a "reduction in options available to consumers, a substantial decline in competition in the energy sales and services field, and a further explosion in the monopoly market power of utilities."[29]

Concerns with concentrated economic and political power in the hands of those who control electric utilities continue to crop up in other contexts as well. Even before the 1970s, the politics of nuclear energy had been characterized by concerns that radioactive materials could be mishandled, with catastrophic consequences, and awareness that this presented problems for democratic governance. As early as 1953, Yale political scientist Robert Dahl wrote that because of the secrecy believed necessary to prevent knowledge of atomic weapons and strategy from falling into the wrong hands, decision making with respect to atomic energy issues was confined to an unusually small elite, public accountability was limited, and democratic political processes operated far less effectively than in other domains of high importance.[30] In more recent years, some prominent critics of civilian nuclear power have contended that measures needed to protect against sabotage and accident are likely to prove incompatible with civil liberties and democratic decision making.[31]

Many alternative energy advocates have called for the development of small-scale solar and wind technologies not only on environmental grounds but as a means to strengthen individual and community control over important resources. With such systems in place, bureaucratic and unaccountable utility enterprises would no longer have a stranglehold over necessities of day-to-day life. With a tightly insulated house, a wood stove in the den, and a solar collector on the roof, one could tell large, overbearing, and uncaring electric utilities and oil companies alike to go to hell. Or a small group of people could get together and develop a local energy system to strike back against the impersonality of both markets and bureaucracies, build community, and gain economic empowerment.

Published in 1981, a book entitled *Resettling America* describes a wide range of such community initiatives. A group of families gathers to build the environmentally sustainable village community of Cerro Gordo twenty-five miles south of Eugene, Oregon. The New Alchemy Institute in Woods Hole, Massachusetts, studies intensive environmentally sustainable agriculture and aquiculture alternatives. Low-income residents of the Lower East Side in Manhattan work together to rehabilitate tenements on East 11th Street. For electricity, they build a windmill on the roof, pictured mocking a hulking Consolidated Edison generating station in the background.[32]

Even in the case of some of these initiatives, however, the major thrust was not to cut ties to networks of electricity supply and distribution but to change terms of access to them. The windmill developers on East 11th Street, for example, can be viewed as acting in this way as they sought to bankroll the machine by selling electricity to Consolidated Edison. More broadly, the Public Utility Regulatory Policy Act of 1978 and the Comprehensive National Energy Policy Act of 1992 both struck against concentrated economic and political power in the hands of vertically integrated electric utility firms not by reducing the role of transmission and distribution networks but by increasing access to them by a diverse array of buyers and sellers of energy.

The future of electric utilities in the United States is, of course, uncertain. Decentralized and renewable methods of furnishing energy may become substantially more important in coming years. Or they may not. Vertically integrated electric utilities may be supplanted by markets. Or they may not. But whatever happens, networks of some sort are likely to remain indispensable. Even if the visions of alternative energy advocates are realized, it is likely that a network will continue to remain valuable as a means for consumers to obtain reliable supplies of power from a multitude of diverse providers. A well-elaborated network of transmission and distribution facilities is likewise indispensable if markets for electricity are to function reasonably efficiently. Contracting difficulties and conflicts over the exercise of power will undoubtedly take different forms in the future than they do at present. But they will not go away.

The same can be said for cable television and for the telecommunications and media complex of which it forms a part. Although dystopian shadows can be discerned, the sense of optimism, the hype, and (not coincidentally), the smell of really big money surrounding new communications technologies are almost palpable. Far more than in waterworks or even electric utilities, what historian John Staudenmaier has defined and decried as technological whiggery—the sense that technological change is both good and unstoppable—is now afoot in this domain. Nor is enthusiasm concerning potential benefits of these technologies necessarily unjustified. Even clichés, after all, can contain within them elements of truth. But the realm of media and communications has long been very dynamic and characterized by great change and flux. And amid the changes of both past and present, continuities can be discerned in patterns of development and in the kinds of public policy issues that continue to arise.

For all of the many differences that can be cited in technology, public policy, and industry organization, development of both cable television and broadcasting in the United States proceeded in large part along grooves carved out during the nineteenth century for production and mass distribution of newspapers and periodicals. As with older forms of print media, ownership of both over-the-air broadcast stations and cable systems has been predominantly private. Here, too, firms have derived their revenues from advertisers vying to purchase the attention and goodwill of audience members, purchase of outputs by audience members themselves, or combinations of the two. As did their counterparts in newspapers, broadcasting and cable television entrepreneurs made use of a variety of long-distance communications technologies to link local outlets with national production centers and gain economies of scale and agglomeration in gathering information and in producing and promoting programs.

From the beginning of the nineteenth century to the present day, the rise of these assemblages has been accompanied by geographical clustering of a large share of media production in a few major urban centers. Such centers have long furnished the most fertile spawning grounds for diverse cultural and communications enterprises. They are the home of the new, the hip, and the different—the raw materials of culture. In the case of some media, such as book publishing, such geographical clustering has not historically been accompanied by concentration of production and distribution in the hands of a few major firms. In other mediums, however, this has occurred.

Probably the epitome of such concentrated corporate control over a dominant medium came in broadcast television during the decades after World War II. Reasons included the extraordinarily limited number of broadcast outlets in each locale, the great expense of connecting stations through telephone company land lines and microwave links, and the high costs of producing and promoting polished programs. In cable television too, however, distribution and production of the most-watched programs is dominated by a few major firms. By the end of 1994, industry leader TCI had more than eleven million subscribers and accounted for about a quarter of the industry total. TCI and other large cable companies also employed their leverage over distribution to engage in substantial vertical integration back into the national networks that supplied programs.

At least in their present form, these particular arrangements may not survive long into the future. The technological as well as the political ground is shifting and possibilities for more radical change may be in the offing as digital communications increasingly supplant their analog counterparts. The technologies themselves are not entirely new. As early as 1948, Claude Shannon's mathematical theory of communication conceptualized information not as meaningful data but as the reduction of uncertainty. From this perspective, the process of communication could be usefully viewed as a sort of game of "Twenty Questions," in which content is represented as the minimum number of binary yes/no questions required to arrive at a given data.[33] This perspective underlies the sampling, compression, and error-checking techniques that make possible digital communications and render them more flexible and reliable than their analog counterparts. Practical stored-program, general purpose digital computers also date from the mid-1940s. Even today, most computers work more or less according to principles sketched out by John von Neumann in a paper written in 1945.[34]

But computing and communications technology has only recently become powerful and cheap enough to make digital processing of sounds and moving images commercially viable in consumer products. And in this sense, we are only at the beginning. Abilities to store, manipulate, and transmit data in digital form have been increasing at exponential rates since the late 1950s. Costs have declined commensurably. In some respects, the dynamism and sense of ever-expanding possibility associated with these developments recall those surrounding the conquest of scale frontiers in electric utilities during the early years of the twentieth century. But unlike the case in electric utilities, in which traditional growth paths stalled during the 1960s and 1970s, there is no end in sight to these trends—no limits or constraints arising from lack of natural resources, pollution, or even the laws of thermodynamics.

Already, the technologies have reached the point in which they can be used to increase by orders of magnitude the range of video content that can be delivered through coaxial cable and by a variety of other means as well. In the case of cable, for example, equipment-makers did manage to eke out increases in the number of conventional analog television channels that could be carried over a single line from about twenty in 1970 to about fifty in 1985 through improvements in amplifiers and other system elements. But the gains were hard won, and increasingly complex problems of signal interference, degradation, and reliability arose as the number of channels was increased. Through use of digital compression, by contrast, the equivalent of five hundred or more television channels can be furnished over a single cable—and with improved picture quality and greater reliability than can be obtained from analog systems requiring far greater bandwidth.[35]

New digital technologies can also be configured in a variety of ways to deliver a wide range of video programming without use of either wires or coaxial cable at all The most polished entry thus far has been the Direct Broadcast Satellite system, introduced in 1994 by a consortium of large companies including Hughes Electronics, RCA, and Hubbard Broadcasting. Digitally compressed signals are broadcast over the high-powered Ku band by satellite. The signals are received using a small eighteen-inch dish antenna and decoded and converted back into analog form in order to be viewed over conventional analog television sets. Number of channels and the choice of pay-per-view movies are greater than those offered over conventional cable systems, picture and sound quality is superior, and monthly charges are comparable.[36]

And there are other possibilities as well. Digital compression technology and computer processing power can be used to substitute for bandwidth and deliver video or other kinds of programs in ways that do not quite represent broadcasting at all. For example, BellCore, the laboratory of the regional Bell companies, has even developed a digital compression technique called ADSL (asymmetrical digital subscriber line) through which video content can be delivered to households through existing twisted pair telephone lines.[37] Coupled with high-capacity video servers in central switching facilities, such a technology could give subscribers a choice of video programming superior to that furnished by many conventional cable systems. With fiber optics and coaxial cable rather than conventional telephone lines being combined with computers in this way, an even richer array of movies, television programs, electronic games, and other forms of information, entertainment, and communications services can be made available to subscribers on demand.

The regulatory and political ground is shifting as well. In essence, during the late 1980s and early 1990s, cable companies enjoyed the best of all worlds—de facto monopoly, cheap access to broadcast programming, and virtually complete freedom to make pricing, investment, and programming decisions as they saw fit. Politically, however, the regime proved unsustainable. By the early 1990s, an extraordinarily wide array of constituencies and interest groups, including consumer organizations, municipalities, broadcasters, satellite programming networks seeking access to cable systems, and backers of alternate delivery systems seeking access to programming, had lined up in support of legislation to rein in cable. In the one instance in which Congress overturned a presidential veto by George Bush, it passed into law a bill designed to do just that in 1992.

The 1992 Cable Act imposed a new "must carry" and copyright regime favorable to broadcasters and modified federal franchising requirements to make it less difficult for municipalities to deny renewal. Recognizing that cable television firms currently did enjoy a local distribution monopoly in most locales, the law established a complex federal-local regime to regulate consumer charges for basic services.[38] At the same time, the law created greater openings for competition by requiring that national program suppliers and satellite networks not give exclusive rights to local cable systems to distribute their offerings. Under the act, such programming would have to be offered to distributors on equal terms.[39] Since passage of the 1992 Cable Act, legal openings for competition have increased further as a consequence of FCC "video dial tone" rulings, and an assortment of court decisions eliminating long-standing prohibitions on telephone company provision of video content.

What does the future hold? One kind of vision is embodied in Warner's "full service network" experiment of the mid-1990s in Orlando, Florida. Through a remote control that turned a virtual carousel on the television screen, subscribers could instantly order up movies and television programs for viewing at any time, play electronic games, and examine and compare merchandise in virtual stores.[40] By past standards the system represented a technological tour de force. The processing power in the set top converter located in each subscriber's home, for example, exceeded that of the central computers originally used in Warner's QUBE cable systems of the late 1970s and early 1980s. For all of the Orlando demonstration's razzmatazz, however, its architecture and design deeply reflected the traditional commercial media orientation of its builders. In the words of Silicon Graphics head Ed McCracken, whose company designed the system's set top controller, the new television, like the old, will be "about entertainment" and "in the entertainment world the television does things and you react to it."[41]

Other people beg to differ. As was the case with cable itself during the years in which it began to expand into urban markets, the rise of new technological possibilities has inspired hopes that more diverse and democratic media and communications systems can emerge. From this perspective, using computer processing power to increase distribution outlets for video content is not necessarily undesirable. On the whole, however, it is not five-hundred-channel cable systems, Direct Broadcast Satellite, or Warner's Orlando test bed that are viewed as embodying the most interesting of future possibilities, but computer bulletin boards and the Internet. The real civic, cultural, and even economic promise of the new technologies can best be realized, it is believed, through diffusion of powerful and flexible microcomputers controlled by their users and linked to one another through publicly accessible two-way communications networks.

Proponents of these kinds of views can be found across the political spectrum. Writing with Schumpterian bombast from the Right, George Gilder has described broadcast television as "at its heart a totalitarian medium."[42] By contrast, the spread of computing power to individuals, Gilder asserts, will lead to both a rebirth of high culture and greater political and economic freedom. So long as the entrepreneurial spirit of the best of American capitalism is given full play and meddling government regulators stay out of the way, Gilder writes, "the force of micro-electronics will blow apart all the monopolies, hierarchies, pyramids, and power grids of established industrial society. . . . All hierarchies will tend to become 'heterarchies'—systems in which each individual rules his own domain . . . a society of equals under the law." [43]

Albeit with less faith in the unfettered workings of the market or idealization of techno-visionaries and entrepreneurial empire-builders, many enthusiasts for small-scale and alternative energy development from the Communitarian and Libertarian Left have also turned their hopes in this direction. Probably the most well-known figure who has taken this path has been Stewart Brand, who played a leading role in founding both the *Whole Earth Catalogue* during the late 1960s and the WELL—the "Whole Earth Lectronic Link"—in 1985 as an electronic meeting place and communications link. Writing in this tradition, Howard Rheingold sees linkages between microcomputers and telecommunications networks as potentially bringing to ordinary citizens "intellectual leverage, social leverage, commercial leverage, and most important political leverage."[44] At least temporarily, Rheingold maintains, we "have access to a tool that could bring conviviality and understanding into our lives and might help revitalize the public sphere."[45]

Hopefulness concerning civic and political potentials of new computing and communications technologies may not be entirely out of place. Computers and networks are undoubtedly capable of being used in ways that enrich the public realm. Enhanced methods of furnishing a range of communications services over the air as well as through wires and cable may reduce chances that those who control any one set of channels will gain undue economic or political power. It could be that dramatic drops in the costs of furnishing video channels and distribution outlets made possible by new technologies will not only enhance viewer choice but open up opportunities for a wider range of voices to be heard in the political arena.

Possibility, however, is not the same as inevitability. A great variety of technologies have been taken up for use as mass media in the past and nothing has occurred yet to stop the process. Indeed, the very malleability and flexibility of emerging digital and communications technologies may work at times to the advantage of those who seek to profit by molding them into older patterns. Nor are contemporary concentrations in mass media and communications likely to be eliminated solely by increasing distribution outlets.[46] There are still products and causes to be sold by reaching large numbers of people and popular hunger for experiences, entertainments, and events shared with others. In a world in which there has never been any shortage of active and public-spirited things that need doing, passive entertainments are also likely to retain much of their attraction.

In the future, as in the past, vigorous and creative application of common carrier and antitrust principles may be needed to prevent abuses by those who control communications bottlenecks and to prevent situations from arising in which a few media enterprises enjoy total dominance. There may also be a role for public and nonprofit institutions in underwriting provision of certain kinds of programming and content and in shaping new communications infrastructures themselves. This idea is neither new nor particularly radical. Nonprofit and public institutions and organizations such as schools, universities, museums, and libraries have long been of vital importance in making and diffusing knowledge, nurturing culture, and serving as forums for discourse.

In parceling out the radio frequency spectrum and franchising cable television firms, however, policymakers chose a different approach to meeting avowedly public needs. A selection of private firms was given privileged access to a resource and mandated to act as if they were public trustees. Such policies appeared to afford a means of realizing public goals while avoiding either expenditure of taxpayer funds or the appearance of direct government control over media content. At best, this promise has been imperfectly fulfilled. After more than sixty years of experience with broadcast regulation, practical and constitutional difficulties in holding stations to public obligations while refraining from censorship have yet to be satisfactorily resolved. Problems with respect to First Amendment interpretation arose in cable television as well. In addition, changing conditions and unexpected developments strained even the best drawn up and most conscientiously adhered to of franchise contracts.

Given the difficulties presented by change and uncertainty to contract and franchising arrangements, nonprofit and public institutions directed from within toward the fulfillment of public goals may now be more important than ever. Such ventures as C-SPAN, as well as the public broadcasting system, represent contemporary examples of such organizations. The Net too is largely a product of the world of nonprofits and big government. The Net's "agreeable anarchy," as a thoughtful observer has pointed out, "rests on an efficient and unobtrusive (largely informal) bureaucracy, just as the individualism of the American suburb and the romance of the open road require billions in tax and public works subsidies."[47]

IT IS EASY to find irony in the set of histories presented in this volume. Physical networks of fixed facilities really can play a role in addressing economic, social, and political problems. Yet in turning to this kind of technological fix, we are at the same time led further away from a world in which another sort of mechanism—that of the market—can be counted upon to serve the overall interests of society. Indeed, as any given type of networked system comes to be successful and relied upon, the likelihood increases of situations arising in which conscious decision making concerning the shape and attributes of such systems affects not only individual consumers but society as a whole. As it is human beings with all of their flaws and limitations who ultimately have to make such decisions, this is not an entirely comfortable finding.

But so what? Is it really such a great indictment to say that networked systems—or any other set of technological artifacts, for that matter— cannot ultimately be counted upon to afford us escape from basic features of the human condition? And consider the alternative. A world in which either technology or markets did solve all problems without need for conscious human thought or scope for conscious human agency would be a cold, sterile, and mechanistic place indeed. Viewed from this perspective, it is not necessarily a bad thing that attributes of technologies throw us back into having to face one another and make decisions concerning the fate of society. Indeed, the very difficulties presented by provision of services through fixed networks for the functioning of market relationships may, at the same time, open up possibilities for the exercise of human moral and intellectual powers and for the development of skills in democratic self-governance. I hope the history presented in this volume will be of use for those seeking to grapple with these challenges.

Notes

Notes to Chapter 1

1. Mark H. Rose, *Cities of Light and Heat: Domesticating Gas and Electricity in Urban America* (University Park: Pennsylvania State University Press, 1995), 3, 4. For a richly textured history of electrification that places even greater emphasis on social and cultural themes, see David E. Nye, *Electrifying American: Social Meanings of a New Technology* (Cambridge: MIT Press, 1990).

2. Ronald C. Tobey, *Technology as Freedom: The New Deal and the Electrical Modernization of the American Home* (Berkeley: University of California Press, 1996), 6.

3. For a good overview of older views of technology and society and the reaction against them, see Rose, *Cities of Light and Heat,* 189–98. A similar shift has occurred in the literature on technology assessment. During the 1970s and early 1980s, the main focus was on anticipating technological "impacts" on society. By contrast, newer constructive technology assessment approaches focus not on "predicting the impacts of a given technology but on exerting leverage on its development and diffusion into practice." See Arie Rip, Thomas J. Misa, and Johan Schot, eds., *Managing Technology in Society* (New York: St. Martins, 1995), 15.

4. Langdon Winner, "Do Artifacts Have Politics?" in Michael E. Kraft and Norman J. Vig, eds., *Technology and Politics* (Durham: Duke University Press, 1988), 53.

5. Joanne Abel Goldman, *Building New York's Sewers: Developing Mechanisms of Urban Management* (West Lafayette: Purdue University Press, 1997), 71.

6. Alfred D. Chandler, Jr., *The Visible Hand: The Managerial Revolution in American Business* (Cambridge: Harvard University Press, 1977), 89.

7. Thomas P. Hughes, "The Evolution of Large Technological Systems," in Wiebe E. Bijker, Thomas P. Hughes, and Trevor Pinch, *The Social Construction of Technological Systems* (Cambridge: MIT Press, 1989), 77.

8. Hughes, "Evolution of Large Technological Systems," 76, 77.

9. Joel A. Tarr, "Water and Wastes: A Retrospective Assessment of Wastewater Technology in the United States, 1800–1932," in *The Search for the Ultimate Sink* (Akron: University of Akron Press, 1996), 210.

10. In that they incorporate economic theory into their explanations of historical

phenomena, economic historians can be viewed as an exception to this generalization. At least in universities in the United States, however, economic historians are more often found in economics rather than history departments. In a sense, therefore, they can be viewed as the kind of exception that proves the rule.

11. This is not to say that private firms can play no role at all in the provision of public goods. Under some conditions, private firms have been able to draw on revenue other than user fees to underwrite provision of goods with public attributes. The use of advertising to underwrite radio, television, and other forms of media is an example. Hopes to profit from increased property values have also induced entrepreneurs at times to build networks and other infrastructures. In the case of passenger rail and trolley service in Los Angeles during the late nineteenth and early twentieth centuries, entrepreneurs were able, at least at first, to draw upon appreciation of property values to finance facility development without any direct subsidies at all. In a pattern found in many other cities at the time as well, one entrepreneur (Henry Huntington) owned both the major transit company (the Pacific Electric Railway Company) and large tracts of suburban land. Fares alone, at least during the early years, would have been inadequate to finance extension of the Pacific Electric lines to Huntington's landholdings in the San Gabriel Valley. But profits in subdividing the land, made possible by access to the rail line, more than compensated Huntington for any losses in operating the facility.

This sort of approach to infrastructure finance, however, also has its limits. While a private firm could only "internalize" the positive externalities of furnishing infrastructure through a one-time sale of the property that benefited from its development, governmental entities have had a relatively free hand to assess taxes to invest in facilities defined as supporting public purposes and to support operation of such facilities in an ongoing way. Decision making by Huntington himself reflected this distinction. To support his land speculation activities, Huntington set up a water company in the San Gabriel Valley on a similar basis to that of the transit system. But although the potentially profitable rail company remained in private hands, Huntington deeded over the water company to the municipality at the earliest possible opportunity.

This pattern of private construction followed by governmental maintenance and operation has been commonly employed for streets and other infrastructure where there is free public access to the facilities and no user fees are charged at all. To take but one example, the extension of Connecticut Avenue in Washington, D.C. north into Maryland during the late nineteenth century took place on this basis. The Chevy Chase Land Company undertook construction of the thoroughfare as part of its land development activities. Upon completion, however, the company deeded over the street to the District of Columbia and the state of Maryland.

For a rich discussion of infrastructure development in Los Angeles, see Robert Fogelson, *The Fragmented Metropolis: Los Angeles, 1850–1930* (Cambridge: Harvard University Press, 1967). For the Connecticut Avenue example, see Elizabeth Jo Lampl and Kimberly Prothro Williams, *Chevy Chase: A Home Suburb for the Nation's Capital* (Crownsville: Maryland Historical Trust Press, 1998), 28–32.

12. The term natural monopoly refers not to the actual number of sellers in a given

market, but to the relationship between demand and the technology of supply. A strong believer in the efficacy of market forces under most circumstances, "Chicago School" economist Richard Posner defines this relationship as follows: "If the entire demand within a relevant market can be satisfied at lowest cost by one firm rather than by two or more, the market is a natural monopoly, whatever the actual number of firms in it. If such a market contains more than one firm, either the firms will quickly shake down to one through mergers or failures, or production will continue to consume more resources than necessary. In the first case competition is short-lived and in the second it produces inefficient results. Competition is thus not a viable regulatory mechanism under conditions of natural monopoly." See Richard Posner, "Theories of Economic Regulation," *Bell Journal of Economics* (autumn 1974): 548.

13. Whether or not it is in the public interest to even permit rival firms to engage in such competition is open to question. Any course of action involves trade-offs. On the one hand, leaving open even the possibility of such competition may help to check monopolistic exploitation on the part of the dominant firm and serve as a spur to technological dynamism and entrepreneurial vigor. If rivals choose to actually enter the market, consumers in areas served by the duplicate systems also may enjoy short-term gains. On the other hand, jousting among owners of rival systems and the systems' eventual consolidation may result in excess costs, inefficiencies, inequities, and uncertainties that outweigh any benefits to society realized by permitting competition in the first place.

14. R. H. Coase, "The Nature of the Firm," *Economica* (November 4, 1937): 386–405.

15. Oliver E. Williamson, *The Economic Institutions of Capitalism* (New York: Free Press, 1985), 61–63.

16. In a well-known 1968 paper, conservative economist Harold Demsetz made the case for franchise bidding: "Why must rivals share the market? Rival sellers can offer to enter into contracts with buyers. In this bidding competition, the rival who offers buyers the most favorable terms will obtain their patronage; there is no clear or necessary reason for *bidding rivals* to share in the production of the goods, and, therefore, there is no clear reason for competition in bidding to result in an increase in per-unit production costs." See Harold Demsetz, "Why Regulate Utilities?" *Journal of Law and Economics* 57, (April 1968): 63. For a discussion of how franchise bidding could be applied in the case of water works, see Steve H. Hanke and Stephen J. K. Walters, "Privatizing Waterworks," *Proceedings of the Academy of Political Science* 36, no. 3 (1986): 104–13. For a brief discussion advocating the sale of New York City subway lines one by one to the highest bidder, see James B. Ramsey, "Selling the New York City Subways: Wild Eyed Radicalism or the Only Feasible Solution?" in the same volume, 93–103.

17. Williamson, *Economic Institutions of Capitalism*, 61. For a detailed discussion of the issues in the context of franchise bidding for natural monopoly, see pp. 326–64. For an analysis built upon a principal-agent perspective that is in many respects parallel to that of Williamson, see David E. M. Sappington and Joseph E. Stiglitz, "Privatization, Information, and Incentives," *Journal of Policy Analysis and Management* 6 (1987): 567–82.

18. Particularly in the case of public goods such as water for fire protection, or electric street lighting, the situation is analogous to that of a private firm facing a "make or

buy" decision under conditions of asset specificity. In such situations, private firms often opt for vertical integration. To illustrate why this should be the case, economists Benjamin Klein, Robert Crawford, and Armen Alchian cite a hypothetical example of a newspaper publisher renting the services of a printing press at a cost of $5,500 per day. This rent covers both daily operating costs of $1,500 and amortized fixed costs of $4,000. Because of the specialized nature of the press, the highest rent the printing press owner can obtain elsewhere is $3,500 per day. The printing press owner therefore is vulnerable to the publisher finding some excuse for cutting the daily rent to just over $3,500 per day, even though this price would not even cover fixed costs. At the same time, the publisher may be vulnerable to the printing press operator seeking an even higher rent because of his own vulnerability to any disruption or slow down (legal or not) by the printing press operator in getting out the daily print run. In such a situation, common ownership serves as a simple and straightforward means of eliminating the risks faced by both parties. See Benjamin Klein, Robert Crawford, and Armen Alchian, "Vertical Integration, Appropriable Rents, and the Competitive Contracting Process," *Journal of Law and Economics* 21 (1978).

19. For discussions of transaction costs that highlight the importance of informational, measurement, and enforcement issues, see Douglass C. North, *Institutions, Institutional Change and Economic Performance* (Cambridge: Cambridge University Press, 1990), 27–35; Yoram Barzel, "Measurement Cost and the Organization of Markets," *Journal of Law and Economics* 25 (April 1982): 27–48; and Burton A. Weisbrod, "Rewarding Performance that Is Hard to Measure: The Private Nonprofit Sector," *Science* 244 (May 5, 1989): 541–45.

20. Steven Kelman, "Why Public Ideas Matter," in Robert B. Reich, ed., *The Power of Public Ideas* (Cambridge: Harvard University Press, 1988), 31–53.

21. David E. Nye, *Electrifying America*, 147. As evidence, Nye cites utopian novels of the period and widely publicized predictions by Edison and other inventors and scientists of future progress as electricity was employed for more and more uses. More than 160 utopian books appeared in the United States, according to Nye, during the two decades following publication of Edward Bellamy's wildly popular *Looking Backward*. Electricity was one of the most commonly discussed marvels of the future heralded in these books, with automated factories, elimination of smoke, disinfection of germs, and liberation from darkness among the benefits to be realized.

22. A fine account of the transformative and utopian possibilities associated with electricity can be found in David Nye's *Electrifying America*. As Nye notes, arc lights, when first introduced, burned and illuminated with an unprecedented intensity, making the night seem as day, while Edison's incandescents—even more amazingly—seemed to illuminate without the presence of heat or fire at all. "The Edison light was unlike all previous lights, whether candles, oil lamps, torches, fires, or gas mantles. Light by definition had always implied consumption of oxygen, smoke, flickering, heat, and danger of fire. . . . But inside the clear glass of an Edison lamp was a glowing orange filament, throwing off a light at once mild and intense, smokeless, fireless, steady, seemingly inexhaustible." See Nye, *Electrifying America*, 2.

23. Ralph Lee Smith, *The Wired Nation: Cable TV; The Electronic Communications Highway* (New York: Harper & Row, 1972), 8.

24. Bernard Bailyn, *The Origins of American Politics* (Vintage: New York, 1968), 43. See also Edmund Morgan, *Inventing the People: The Rise of Popular Sovereignty in England and America* (New York: W.W. Norton, 1988), 144.

25. For a good discussion, see Harry N. Scheiber, "Federalism and the American Economic Order," *Law and Society Review* 10, no. 1 (fall 1975): 116. "Forum shopping" of various sorts continues to be a widespread phenomenon with respect to many different kinds of economic and environmental regulation. A 1991 *New York Times* article, for example, describes a lobbying effort by large manufacturers of packaged consumer goods to have the Federal Trade Commission issue guidelines regulating the use of environmental claims on labels and in advertising. The manufacturers hoped by this means to preempt the emergence of different (and likely more stringent) requirements in different states. See John Holusha, "Some Corporations Plead for the Firm Hand of Uncle Sam," *New York Times*, February 24, 1991.

26. Legal historian Harry Scheiber describes the dynamics in the case of state governments before the Civil War: "Scrambling to compete with other states to attract enterprise and encourage growth, each state was impelled to adopt liberal policies for distribution of largesse or privilege. And at the same time, rivalistic state mercantilism tended to militate against effective regulatory policies that would have placed firm controls for well considered and defined 'public interest' objectives upon private enterprises. The balance between government power and private sector interests became even more unequal in the 1850s, when railroads emerged as America's first giant enterprises." See Scheiber, "Federalism and the American Economic Order," 99. Eric Monkkonen describes the dynamic in the case of cities during the middle and later years of the nineteenth century as follows: "beginning in the mid-nineteenth century, cities chose to intervene aggressively in the local economic setting, intentionally creating what they hoped would be the ideal environments for economic growth. . . . Success, defined as population growth, increased the wealth of all real property owners." See Eric Monkkonen, *America Becomes Urban: The Development of U.S. Cities and Towns, 1780–1980* (Berkeley: University of California Press, 1988), 4–5. For an interesting account of how this played out in one case, and some of the political tensions that resulted, see Robert J. Kolesar, "The Politics of Development: Worcester, Massachusetts in the Late Nineteenth Century," *Journal of Urban History* 16, no. 1 (1989): 3–27.

27. In some respects, the approach taken here resembles that of well-known economic historian Douglass North. Like North, I place great importance on relationships between transaction costs and institutions for understanding aspects of historical experience. I also concur with North that analysis of incentives and the assumption that all actors seek to maximize wealth do not suffice to explain outcomes. As North points out, legal and institutional arrangements and informal constraints, attitudes, and ideology all have profound effects on the cost of executing different transactions. Furthermore, these vary over place and over time.

Although I share these perspectives with North, the questions I address are rather different. North's primary interest is in the puzzle of why economic growth has been so much more rapid in some societies than in others. The main concern here, by contrast, is in public policy issues associated with particular kinds of technological systems. For an exposition of North's approach, see North, *Institutions, Institutional Change, and Economic Performance.*

Notes to Chapter 2

1. Ellis L. Armstrong, ed., *History of Public Works in the United States: 1776–1976* (Chicago: American Public Works Association, 1976), 217.

2. A. M. Hillhouse, *Municipal Bonds: A Century of Experience* (New York: Prentice Hall, 1936), 31.

3. At least in proportional terms, other major urban centers in the United States grew even faster than Chicago. To take but one example, the number of people living in Minneapolis-Saint Paul increased from about 1,100 in 1850 to about 302,000 in 1890. This represents an approximately 275-fold increase in population. See Adna Ferrin Weber, *The Growth of Cities in the Nineteenth Century: A Study in Statistics* (New York: Macmillan, 1899), 40–47.

To make an even more broadly telling—if slightly inexact—comparison, the number of people living in urban places with a population of 10,000 or more in England and Wales increased ninefold over the years 1801 through 1891: from 1,895,800 to 17,926,210. Over the course of approximately the same period, by contrast, the number of people living in places with a population of 8,000 or more in the United States increased from about 210,000 to about 18,300,000—an 87-fold increase. See Weber, *Growth of Cities,* 43–46.

4. Eric H. Monkkonen, *America Becomes Urban: The Development of U.S. Cities and Towns, 1780–1980* (Berkeley: University of California Press, 1988), 138–39.

5. Hillhouse, *Municipal Bonds,* 146.

6. Monkkonen, *America Becomes Urban,* 139.

7. Monkkonen, *America Becomes Urban,* 139.

8. Letty Anderson, "The Diffusion of Technology in the Nineteenth Century American City: Municipal Water Supply Investments" (Ph.D. diss., Northwestern University, 1980), 105.

9. Moses Baker, *Manual of American Water Works, 1897* (New York: Engineering News, 1897), E.

10. Stuart Bruchey, *Enterprise: The Dynamic Economy of a Free People* (Cambridge: Harvard University Press, 1990), 206.

11. Baker, *Manual of American Water Works, 1897,* K.

12. As of 1891, according to Moses Baker in the *Manual of American Water Works,* there were twenty-five cities in the United States served by more than one waterworks. However, Baker reported, "these duplicate works are so circumstanced that there is, with two or three exceptions, little or no real competition between them, or the works in

themselves are very small." See Baker, *Manual of American Water Works, 1891* (New York: Engineering News, 1892), xxxix.

13. Thus while the proportion of waterworks owned by private firms declined from 94 percent to 47 percent over the years 1800 through 1896, such systems increased in number from 15 in 1800 to 127 in 1870 and to 1,489 in 1896. See Anderson, "Diffusion of Technology," 105.

14. Historian William Cronon describes the advantages presented by balloon framing and resulting wide use of balloon-frame building: "Because the balloon frame consisted of light, milled wood, a small number of workers could erect it quickly; because it was held together with nails instead of intricate carved joints, it required less skill than earlier buildings; and because its components were easy to modify and repeat, it was wonderfully adaptable to buildings of different shapes and forms. . . . Even inexperienced carpenters could use it with reasonable success, and builders' manuals promoted it accordingly. By the second half of the nineteenth century, the vast majority of America's wooden buildings were using it." See William Cronon, *Nature's Metropolis: Chicago and the Great West* (New York: W.W. Norton, 1991), 179.

15. Nineteenth-century balloon-frame buildings burned quickly, according to historian William Cronon, because "the tall two-by-four studs supporting both the second-floor joists and the roof rafters formed continuous air spaces that ran from basement to roof. . . . In the event that any part of the structure started to burn, the walls quickly began to act as flues and the building became an inferno." See Cronon, *Nature's Metropolis,* 179. Construction practices in more recent years have improved but wooden balloon-frame buildings remain far more vulnerable to fire than their stone or brick counterparts.

16. E. H. Clarke, in the *North American Review* 73 (July 1851): 117–35, cited in Barbara Rosenkranz, *Public Health and the State* (Cambridge: Harvard University Press, 1972), 34.

17. In an extreme case, a 1914 conflagration in Salem, Massachusetts, required about 17,000 gallons per minute of water over a period of fourteen hours. The normal demand for a city of that size (about fifty thousand) would be in the range of 3,500 gallons per minute. See Harold E. Babbitt and James S. Doland, *Water Supply Engineering* (New York: McGraw Hill, 1939), 91.

18. A 1924 article in the *Journal of the American Water Works Association* described the problem as follows: "Let the character of the development change and the existing gridiron becomes inadequate, although this inadequacy may not be manifest for the gridiron may yet be delivering sufficient water consumption and the pressures may still remain unchanged by customary draught upon the system." See V. Bernard Siems and D. Benton Biser, "Fire Protection Requirements in Distribution System Design," *Journal of the American Water Works Association* 11 (January 24, 1924). According to the 1926 *Water Works Practices* manual, the water mains serving a section of a city "containing small buildings of low height occupying not more than one third block" would only be required to provide two streams of water of five hundred gallons per minute to put out any fire likely to arise. In a more densely built-up section, by contrast, the local distribution system might be called on to supply up to six thousand gallons per minute. See Ameri-

can Water Works Association, *Water Works Practices* (Baltimore: Williams & Wilkins, 1926), 301.

19. One engineering text described the problem this way: "The total amount of water used in a year for extinguishing fires is usually a negligible part of the total consumption, but during a fire the rate of demand is so great as to be the deciding factor in determining the capacities of pumps, reservoirs, and distribution mains in all but the largest cities." See Babbitt and Doland, *Water Supply Engineering*, 90. The 1926 *Water Works Practices* manual issued by the American Water Works Association estimated the cost of fire protection investments in American cities as "60 to 80 percent of the entire cost of the physical property in the case of communities having less than 10,000 population; 30 to 40 percent of the entire cost in communities of about 50,000 population; 20 to 30 percent in communities of about 100,000 population; and 10 to 20 percent in the case of our largest cities." See American Water Works Association, *Water Works Practices* (1926), 593.

20. The complexity and degree of professional judgment involved in evaluating the level of fire protection furnished by a waterworks is reflected in the schedules employed by the engineering staff of the National Board of Fire Underwriters to make these evaluations during the late nineteenth and early twentieth centuries. Among the many attributes of waterworks evaluated and ranked by the underwriters were reliability of source of supply, quality and condition of pipes, evidence of electrolytic action, condition of gate valves, proportion and placement of mains of four-inch diameter or less, and number and location of dead ends. The schedule can be found in full in the American Water Works Association, *Water Works Practice* (1925), 725–47.

21. Nelson Blake, *Water for the Cities* (Syracuse: Syracuse University Press, 1956), 258–61. See also Armstrong, *History of Public Works in the United States*, 235–38.

22. Blake, *Water for the Cities*, 257.

23. Mayor Wells, "Inaugural Address, 1833," in *The Inaugural Addresses of the Mayors of Boston*, vol. 1 (Boston: Rockwell & Churchill, 1894), 170.

24. *Letter from Lemuel Shattuck in Answer to Interrogatories of J. Preston in Relation to the Introduction of Water into the City of Boston* (Boston: Samual N. Dickinson, 1845), 10, 15, 16. See also John B. Blake, "Lemuel Shattuck and the Boston Water Supply," *Bulletin of the History of Medicine* 29, no. 6 (November-December 1955): 554–62.

25. Blake, *Water for the Cities*, 172.

26. Martin Brimmer testimony, *Massachusetts Legislature, Joint Special Committee on the Petition of the City of Boston for Leave to Introduce Pure Water into the City from Long Pond* (Boston: 1845), 64.

27. As of 1817, according to the historian Nelson Blake, the system consisted of four main logs that "led from the Pond to the town and thence through most of the principal streets. Two of these were of four inch bore, and the other two of three inch. The lateral pipes were of only one-and-one-half inch bore. Forty miles of logs had been laid and about eight hundred families were supplied. The smallness of the pipes was one deficiency of the system; another was the fact they had not been laid deep enough to prevent freezing in severe winter weather." See Blake, *Water for the Cities*, 67.

28. Allan Hinckley testimony, *Massachusetts Legislature, Joint Special Committee on the Petition of the City of Boston*, 36.

29. Blake, *Water for the Cities*, 175.

30. A few private ownership advocates suggested other schemes, such as use of the Charles River or the Middlesex Canal, but they did not have a major impact on the debate. None backed the more expensive Long Pond plan.

31. R. H. Eddy, *Report on the Introduction of Soft Water into the City of Boston* (Boston: John H. Eastburn, 1836), 4.

32. Eddy himself supported private development. Appended to his report was a charter for the Massachusetts Hydraulic Company, organized to bring in water from Spot Pond. The charter provided for free water for fire protection but contained no requirements concerning quality of service, nor for regulation of the price of water supplied to private consumers. The charter also envisioned a sort of mixed private-public enterprise giving the city of Boston the right to purchase one-third of the firm's stock. The city would be allowed to purchase the entire system at any time by paying a price that, together with the firm's revenues, would provide for reimbursement of all expenditures plus 10 percent annual interest. See Commonwealth of Massachusetts, *An Act to Incorporate the Boston Hydraulic Company* (April 16, 1836). For a brief description of some charter provisions, see Blake, *Water for the Cities*, 180.

33. Mayor Josiah Quincy made this point during an 1826 address : "it being an article of the first necessity and on its free use, so much of health, as well as of comfort depends, every city should reserve in its own power the means, unrestrained of encouraging its use, not only to the poor, but to all classes of the community. This can never be the case, when the right is in the hands of individuals, with any thing like the facility and speed as when it is under the entire control of the city." See Josiah Quincy, "Address," January 2, 1826, in *Inaugural Addresses of the Mayors of Boston*, 54.

34. Quincy, "Address," 54. Quincy also had an acute awareness of the dangers of negotiating contracts with limited information. In his 1824 address to the city council he described an experience in which the city put up for bid to private firms a contract to clean the city's streets. According to Quincy, "when it was found that the city was about to perform the operation on its own account, the same persons fell in their offers, from *eighteen* to *eight hundred dollars*; and when this was rejected, they offered to do it for *nothing*. And since the city operations have commenced, the inquiry now is, at what price they can enjoy the privilege." See Quincy, "Address," May 1, 1824, in *Inaugural Addresses of the Mayors of Boston*, 23.

35. Quincy, "Address," January 2, 1826, 54.

36. The Standing Committee on the Introduction of Pure and Soft Water into the City, *Report* (Boston: January 29, 1838), 2.

37. *Records of Boston*, vol. 16, 412–13.

38. According to Chapman: "It is an enterprise which, if undertaken by the City, must involve a very considerable outlay, and it cannot but be admitted that some doubts may reasonably be entertained as to its pecuniary results, for at least a considerable period of time. It seems to me, therefore, that no prudent government would enter upon

it, unless with the hearty concurrence of a large majority of its own members, and of the citizens generally." See Jonathan Chapman, cited in Blake, *Water for the Cities*, 187.

39. John B. Jervis and Walter Johnson, *Report to the Committee of the City Council, Having Charge of the Subject of Supplying the City of Boston with Pure Water* (Boston: November 18, 1845), 117.

40. Blake, *Water for the Cities*, 212–13.

41. Excerpt from "A Song for the Merry-Making on Water Day" (by a member of the Franklin Typographical Society), in *Celebration of the Introduction of the Water of Cochituate Lake into the City of Boston*, October 25, 1848 (Boston: 1848), 10–11.

42. *Report of the Water Registrar, Waste of Water by Hopper Closets* (1862), 8.

43. *Report of the Cochituate Water Board to the City Council of Boston for the Year Ending April 30, 1870*, 51.

44. Blake, *Water for the Cities*, 268.

45. *Report of the Cochituate Water Board to the City Council of Boston, 1864*, 8.

46. Consumption of water declined from a daily average of 16,681,000 wine gallons in 1864 to 12,662,200 wine gallons in 1865. By 1873, however, water consumption in Boston was back up to average levels of about 18,000,000 gallons per day. See *Report of the Cochituate Water Board to the City Council of Boston for the Year 1865–66*, 56–57 and *Report of the Cochituate Water Board to the City Council of Boston for the Year Ending April 30, 1870*, 5.

47. An 1862 report by water registrar William Davis diagnosed the situation as follows: "The increased consumption of water for seven years past, is about in proportion to the increased number of water fixtures, and very far exceeds the proportional increase of water-takers. . . . I know of no better method of reducing the daily consumption of water in this city, than to exercise more control than has hitherto been done to limit the number and style of water fixtures upon the premises of water-takers." *Report of the Water Registrar, Waste of Water by Hopper Closets*, 9.

48. *Report of the Cochituate Water Board to the City Council of Boston, 1864*, 8.

49. According to an 1862 report, for example, "some radical change in this enormous disparity between the amount of water used, and paid for, is desirable; and it is quite certain that the most just, satisfactory, and equitable method of charging for the water, would be by actual measurement, so that each citizen may pay for just the quantity he uses." See *Report of the Cochituate Water Board to the City Council of Boston, 1862*, 11.

50. *Report of the Cochituate Water Board to the City Council of Boston, 1864*, 9.

51. *Report of the Cochituate Water Board to the City Council of Boston for the Year 1865–66*, 9.

52. *Report of the Cochituate Water Board in Reply to an Order of the City Council . . . relating to the Available Quantity and Purity of the Mystic Water . . . 1874*, xi–xii.

53. *Report of the Cochituate Water Board to the City Council of Boston, 1864*, 17.

54. *Report of the Cochituate Water Board to the City Council of Boston, 1863*, 8.

55. The Cochituate Water Board report for 1865–66, for example, declared: "The present arrangements for a supply of water, particularly in case of fire, are somewhat more extensive than during the early days of the town. Mr. Quincy says 'In 1653 leave was granted to the inhabitants to sink a twelve-foot cistern at the pump which stands in

the highway, to be helpful against fire.' And in 1670, 'There has been found a great want of water in case of fire, every inhabitant was ordered to have a hogshead well.'"

56. *Report of the Cochituate Water Board to the City Council of Boston for the Year 1865–66*, 10.

57. Christine Rosen, *The Limits of Power* (New York: Cambridge University Press, 1986), 208, 209.

58. Rosen, *Limits of Power,* 177, 178.

59. *Report of the Cochituate Water Board to the City Council of Boston, Year Ending April 30, 1869,* 8–10. *Report of the Cochituate Water Board to the City Council of Boston, Year Ending April 30, 1870,* 7–10.

60. *Report of the Chochituate Water Board to the City Council of Boston, 1865–66,* 11. Fern Nesson, *Great Waters* (Hanover, NH: University Press of New England, 1983), 10, 11.

61. *Report of the Cochituate Water Board, . . . Mystic Water and . . . Other Matters Connected with an Additional Supply for Boston* (1874), xi, xii.

62. Nesson, *Great Waters,* 11.

63. Rosen, *Limits of Power,* 210.

64. Rosen, *Limits of Power,* 211.

65. Blake, *Water for the Cities,* 273.

66. For a detailed description of the water supply situation in San Francisco during the 1850s, see Barton Harvey Knowles, "The Early History of San Francisco's Water Supply, 1776–1858" (master's thesis, University of California at Berkeley, 1948) .

67. To ensure that the works would be completed, the franchise required the company to post a fifty-thousand-dollar bond. To protect consumers against monopolistic pricing, the franchise provided for rates to be set by a board of three commissioners, to be appointed by the city. Reflecting the contemporary lack of awareness about the extra capital investments needed to adequately provide for these purposes, the franchise specified that water for fighting fires and supplying the prison and hospital would be supplied free of charge. The franchise looked toward eventual municipal ownership by requiring the company to deed its works to the municipal government at the time of franchise expiration, although it did not specify whether the city would be required to pay for the works. For the complete text of the franchise, see Knowles, "Early History of San Francisco's Water Supply," 64–65.

68. The new franchise, awarded on July 14, 1852, extended the deadline for completion of the works, made the franchise exclusive, repealed the provision that the works be turned over to the city after twenty-five years, and gave the company the right to appoint two representatives to the rate setting board.

69. During the summer of 1853, for example, one of the tunnels under construction for the works became flooded out by underground springs. Both financing difficulties and unexpected construction obstacles continued to plague the venture during subsequent years, and at one point the firm even asked the city to purchase and complete the project in return for "equitable considerations." See Knowles, "Early History of San Francisco's Water Supply," 80.

70. The Mountain Lake promoters initially believed that by developing a supply

from Mountain Lake they could capture the water flowing into Lobos Creek as well. The coup de grâce to the project came during the summer of 1857, when it became clear, as construction proceeded, that the two bodies of water were not connected.

71. These returns reflect the extreme shortage of capital in San Francisco during the early years of the city.

72. Compared to a daily per capita water consumption of more than ninety gallons in Boston, for example (a figure that reflects both widespread use and considerable wastage due to lack of metering), average daily per capita water consumption in San Francisco amounted to only about eleven gallons as of 1860. With system development, this increased to about forty gallons in 1870 and about fifty-four gallons a decade later, but system performance remained problematical, particularly for fire protection and other public purposes. The fire chief described the situation at one major fire in 1865 as follows: "A scant supply of water in the hydrants was again experienced at this fire. Had not the tide in the bay been favorable at the time, a more serious loss might have occurred." See Ray W. Taylor, *Hetch Hetchy* (San Francisco: Ricardo J. Orozco, 1924), 11. In his reports for 1871 and 1875, the fire chief continued to complain that water mains were too small and water pressures inadequate in many parts of the city for necessary fire protection. Other needs suffered as well. On December 4, 1871, retiring Mayor Thomas H. Selby made note in his final address that the city's water supply was inadequate to flush the sewers for health purposes. See *San Francisco Municipal Reports, 1870–1871*, 615. In 1877, a drought nearly emptied the reservoirs of the company, resulting in bans on washing sidewalks, sprinkling gardens, and other optional uses of water. See *San Francisco Municipal Reports, 1896–97*, app., 67.

73. Under this law, water companies had to supply water free to the city for all governmental purposes. This decision also meant the elimination of the expiration provisions of the San Francisco city franchise as well. For an all-too-detailed account of the convoluted history of this litigation from the city's point of view, see the report by John E. Swift, "Water Litigation," in the *San Francisco Municipal Reports, 1876–1877* (San Francisco: 1877), 675–99. The city and the water company also entered litigation over the powers of the city to regulate water rates. On March 6, 1876, the California legislature passed an act permitting the city to appoint a Board of Water Commissioners to regulate the rates charged by the water company to private consumers. The water company challenged the law, maintaining that the only rate regulation to which it could be legally subjected was that provided in its act of incorporation. That act provided for rate regulation by a process in which city and company each had two representatives, those four to appoint a fifth. On July 5, 1877, the California Supreme Court ruled in favor of the company's position.

74. Thus, at a time when the Spring Valley system provided an average per capita water consumption of forty gallons per day, B. S. Alexander, the engineer involved in planning for a city-owned system, advocated that San Francisco "obtain for herself an abundant supply of good, wholesome, fresh water—one hundred gallons for each inhabitant daily—and the diminished rates of insurance, the increased comfort of living, the new demand for houses and lots, and the increased value of property, will be such,

that none of her citizens will be found willing to forgo its advantages for the relief it might afford from taxation." See *San Francisco Municipal Reports, 1871–1872*, app., 639. In desperation at the failure of negotiations to purchase the Spring Valley system, the mayor, in a letter written in 1875 to the Board of Supervisors, perceived some possibility of legislative compulsion as a means to obtain public goods, but saw municipal ownership as the only ultimate solution:

> We believe, however, that some restrictions should be, by legislative action, placed upon the private company, not only as to rates, as to proper pipes in all streets to properly supply us in case of fire; also to furnish necessary water for flushing sewers, watering streets, as well as to an extension of pipes to supply the whole population.
>
> We believe, however, in the principle that the city, in proper time, should own and have control of its own water works; that water should be provided to all; that to the poor, or those who cannot pay, it should be given free, if from sanitary motives only.

See *San Francisco Municipal Reports, 1874–1875*, app., 697.

. 75. On June 30, 1875, Spring Valley proposed a price of $14,500,000 for their works, plus an additional $1,000,000 for the Calaveras property. The city rejected the price as too expensive. During 1877, the city instead offered Spring Valley a price of $11,000,000. Spring Valley in turn rejected this offer as inadequate.

76. As early as 1892, San Francisco's fire chief complained of the inadequate size of older water mains to meet contemporary needs and of an inadequate supply of water in the Mission and Western Addition districts. See *San Francisco Municipal Reports, 1891–1892*, 417. The report of the fire chief for 1894–1895 called for the removal of "all three, four, and six inch water mains and replacing them with eight, twelve, sixteen, and twenty four inch mains in all portions of the city, not already supplied with mains of large and sufficient capacity." See *San Francisco Municipal Reports, 1894–1895*, 232.

77. On February 17, 1896, the Board of Supervisors Committee of the Whole considering water rates reported that a decision had been "tacitly agreed to, that if the Spring Valley Water Works carried out its proposed improvements, the rates then fixed were to be re-enacted and established during the coming year to enable the company to continue and carry out the substitution and laying of larger water mains in the business and thickly settled portions of our city, and in affording facilities in the outlying districts to supply water to the higher levels and other projected improvements. . . . Your committee are bound to acknowledge that the Spring Valley Water Works have kept faith with the city." See *San Francisco Municipal Reports, 1895–1896*, 21. On the basis of this finding, the Board of Supervisors reenacted the water rates set in place the previous year by a vote of eleven to one. Writing one year later, fire chief Sullivan described the results of the agreement (and the deficiencies of previous investments by the company) as follows: "Spring Valley . . . has . . . done more work in the last two years than I believe they did before in ten . . . if they continue for four or five years, as they have in the last two years, they would put this town in a safe condition, but today I don't consider that it is." See *San Francisco Municipal Reports, 1896–1897*, app., 76.

78. H. Schussler, *Estimate of the Value of the Spring Valley Water Works* (San Francisco: Spring Valley Water Company, 1901), 4–39. While the population of the city increased by

about a third over the period, rising from 233,959 in 1880 to 342,782 in 1900, the water company's yearly total receipts rose by about half, from $1,270,000 in 1880 to $1,926,707 in 1900. Total dividend payments fluctuated from a low of $213,333 in 1883 to a high of $778,000 in 1897. The company's debt burden followed a more steady path, annual interest payments increasing from $267,557 in 1880 to $532,405 in 1897.

79. Writing in 1901, chief engineer Schussler himself articulated and defended the company's gradual and risk-averse investment policy over the previous thirty-five years as follows:

> As the city gradually grew, and the demand for water increased, the company not only gradually acquired the necessary additional water rights and land, but it gradually and successively added to its works, thereby showing good judgment and proper economy. In 1865, when the city had about one hundred and twenty thousand inhabitants, when interest on money was from 15 to 20 per cent. per annum, when iron, cement, lumber, and machinery cost fully twice its present price, if the company had then built works capable of supplying say, from twenty-five to thirty million gallons daily (which would have sufficed for three times the population of 1865) this would have been improper extravagance then, aside from being unnecessary. It would have been entirely unremunerative, and the managers of the works would have then been justly and properly criticized for useless waste of money—particularly, as in those days, when mining was on a downgrade, most people believed that the growth of San Francisco was seriously checked, and would be very slow for many decades to come.

See Schussler, *Estimate of the Value of the Spring Valley Water Works*, 2–3.

80. Hermann Schussler, "Relating to Water Rates for the Fiscal Year 1904–1905," in *San Francisco Municipal Reports, 1904–1905*, 502. While this reflected a substantial increase, San Francisco's water supply remained less generous than that of other large American cities. New York City in 1900, for example, had a per capita water consumption of 114 gallons per day.

81. Writing in 1881, Spring Valley president Charles Howard, for example, maintained that "The political experience of the community during the past two years must convince any candid mind that so great a power over the property of the Spring Valley Water Works should not be exclusively exercised by the *purchasers of water* and their political representatives . . . the provision of the New Constitution, which gives the power entirely to the *purchasers themselves*, and their political representatives in the Board of Supervisors is unjust and oppressive." Communication from Charles Howard, in *San Francisco Municipal Reports, 1880–1881*, app., 5–6.

82. Howard, in *San Francisco Municipal Reports, 1880–1881*, app., 5–6.

83. Though some supervisors served more than one biennial term, the vast majority did not. Between 1860 and 1905, only 23.3 percent of those serving on the Board of Supervisors had been incumbents or other city officials at the time of their election. See Terrence J. McDonald, *The Parameters of Urban Fiscal Policy* (Berkeley: University of California Press, 1986), 140.

84. According to historian Terrence McDonald, "the San Francisco supervisors

combined executive and legislative functions in a list of responsibilities that must at times have overwhelmed some of these part-time officials. The supervisors were empowered by charter to pass ordinances, levy taxes, appropriate money, let contracts, and serve as a board of equalization for tax assessments, as well as to control the activities and audit the books of all city departments. In addition, each supervisor was required individually to inspect the activities of government in his own ward." See McDonald, *Parameters of Urban Fiscal Policy*, 23–24.

85. The board's decision making process reflected these limitations. In setting a valuation for the Spring Valley plant during 1880, for example, the supervisors failed to undertake an independent investigation. Instead, the board simply split the difference between the cost of $17,000,000 claimed by Spring Valley as the cost of its plant and the market value of the firm's securities of $11,500,000. See *San Francisco Municipal Reports, 1879–1880*, app., 938–42.

86. *San Francisco Municipal Reports, 1894–1895*, app., 10.

87. "Report of Committee on Water and Water Supply," May 20, 1897, in *San Francisco Municipal Reports, 1896–1897*, app., 91. For an argument for municipal ownership of all public utilities expressed in similar terms, see "Address of Retiring Mayor Adolf Sutro," January 4, 1897, in the same volume, 7.

88. On July 30, 1894, for example, the Board of Supervisors Committee on Water and Water Supply reported that because of cheaper financing, the cost of a municipally owned system over a period of forty years would be about $46,000,000 compared to the $66,000,000 that would be required by the water company if payments were held at the present level. See *San Francisco Municipal Reports, 1893–1894*, app., 184.

89. For an articulate expression of this argument, see "Report of Committee on Water," in *San Francisco Municipal Reports, 1891–1892*, app., 13.

90. For an articulate expression of the company's contention that these rate cuts represented a breach of trust, see Schussler, "Water Rates for the Fiscal Year 1904–1905," 507–9.

91. See Schussler, *Estimate of the Value of the Spring Valley Water Works*. The dispute largely hinged on the value of Spring Valley's partially developed Alameda Creek system. The city valued that portion of the system at $1,699,000 on the grounds that this constituted the value of the works and property in use for the city. The company, by contrast, claimed that system development thus far had already cost the company $3,209,463 and that the property had a value of over $17,000,000 because of its potential for future development. The potential of Alameda Creek to meet the future needs of San Francisco constituted a basic source of disagreement. The company maintained that development of Alameda resources could serve San Francisco's water needs into the distant future. The city argued that the resource had more limited potential for future development.

92. Marsden Manson, a member of the committee that selected the site (and later city engineer), maintained that the "unrivaled advantages" of the Hetch Hetchy site included its "absolute purity," "abundance far beyond possible future demands for all purposes," availability of superior reservoir sites, freedom from conflict with other private

water rights, and potential power possibilities. See Marsden Manson, "Struggle for Water in Great Cities," *Journal of the Association of Engineering Societies* 38, no. 3 (March 1907): 116.

93. The Board of Supervisors made the point explicitly in a 1901 letter to the company: "The Spring Valley Water Company is also requested to bear in mind that any over valuation of its water system will compel the people of San Francisco to look elsewhere for their water supply and the withdrawing of San Francisco as a market for the sale of the company's water will reduce the value of the company's lands to what they are worth for agricultural purposes only." See *San Francisco Municipal Reports, 1900–1901*, app., 400. In opposing Hetch Hetchy before Congress, company attorney E. J. McCutchen criticized the city's strategy as extortionate. "It does seem to me that it is going a long way for Congress to pass an act which will have the effect of dismembering a national park in order to supply a municipal corporation with a big stick as a trading asset to acquire the plant of a quasi-public corporation. . . . If they could get this grant from Congress they could go to Spring Valley and say: . . . We can proceed with the building of this system if we see fit. . . . If you are not willing to trade on a basis that is satisfactory to us we will build this plant, and will drive your company into bankruptcy." See Taylor, *Hetch Hetchy*, 94, from Hetch Hetchy hearings, 68–79.

Writing in 1902, city engineer Grunsky advised against bypassing the Spring Valley works on the grounds that the firm possessed the best available sites for storing large quantities of water near San Francisco (an important consideration in case of an accident to the aqueduct) and because of the waste that would be involved in duplicating the company's distribution system. Nevertheless, despite the obvious nature of these points, city officials had such little faith in the possibility of obtaining a good price for the Spring Valley system that they continued to pursue engineering plans to construct an independent system until after 1908.

94. In its suit before the United States Circuit Court, filed in 1903, Spring Valley asked for a ruling that its property, as of 1903, had a value of about $45,000,000 compared to Grunsky's $24,250,000 figure, and that the Board of Supervisors be required to set rates that would give the company 7 percent return on this valuation (plus subsequent improvements) as well as providing for operating costs, taxes, and depreciation. See Spring Valley Company, *Analysis of Brief and Argument*, 519–29. The title page is lost from my copy of the document, but by the context its date is probably 1908 or 1909.

95. A. H. Payson, "Report of the President of the Spring Valley Water Company, San Francisco, California, Made to the Stockholders at Their Annual Meeting, January 8, 1908," in *San Francisco Municipal Reports, 1907–1908*, 961.

96. Writing in 1904, fire chief Sullivan described the situation as follows: "I desire to assert in the most positive manner that a disaster such as has recently overtaken the city of Baltimore is, under existing conditions, quite possible in this city. . . . During the past few years many five and six story frame hotels have been erected in the most exposed positions on the hillsides, notably on Pine Street from Stockton to Jones. The main on Pine Street is only six inches in diameter, and the pressure is only thirty-five pounds— not enough to supply the companies that would respond on first alarm of fire. . . . At Sacramento and Mason Streets, where the Hotel Fairmont is rapidly approaching com-

pletion, the main is only four-inch, and on Powell Street it is only six-inch." See "Report of Chief Engineer, San Francisco Fire Department, On Fire Hydrants & Water Mains Urgently Required to Afford Adequate Protection from Fire," February 29, 1904, in *San Francisco Municipal Reports, 1903–1904*, 599–600.

97. The earthquake not only ruptured the Pilarcitos and Crystal Springs aqueducts leading to San Francisco, but broke water mains within the city. These breaks "rapidly wasted the water stored in the City reservoirs and cut off entirely the direct supply to the districts where the main fires originated." See Subcommittee on Water Supply and Fire Protection, "Report on Water Supply and Fire Protection" to Committee on Reconstruction of San Francisco, May 26, 1906, in *San Francisco Municipal Reports, 1905–1906 and 1906–1907* (combined report), 783.

98. Alfred Stillman, "Communication from Board of Underwriters, Calling Attention to Danger from Fire in Western Addition Owing to Lack of Water Pressure," May 19, 1910, in *San Francisco Municipal Reports, 1909–1910*, 1183, 1184.

99. The system, according to the report, was "efficiently managed, but lack of satisfactory agreement with city has caused a complete cessation of construction. Sources of supply ample, if properly developed . . . but the supply lines into the city are barely sufficient to deliver at a rate corresponding to that of maximum daily consumption and are not in duplicate. Distributing reservoirs within the city hold only two day's supply. . . . Pressures in the congested value and the manufacturing districts range from moderate to light, insufficient to operate sprinkler equipment; moderately well maintained during periods of maximum consumption, except at remote points at high elevations. Main arteries barely sufficient in carrying capacity and not sufficiently in duplicate; lacking in some sections. Minor distributors mainly small, generally poorly connected; pipes in fair condition but electrolytic action has been serious in several small areas." See National Board of Fire Underwriters, "Report on the City of San Francisco, Ca.," July 30, 1910 (New York: National Board of Fire Underwriters, 1910), 56. According to the report, "Since the inspection of the city in 1905 practically no improvements have been made on the works. . . . None of the recommendations contained in the previous report have been complied with" (p. 16).

100. For a more detailed descriptions of the system, see National Board of Fire Underwriters, Committee on Fire Protection, "Report on the City of San Francisco, California, July 1910" (New York: National Board of Fire Underwriters, 1910), 18.

101. "Does this Beautiful Lake Ruin this Beautiful Valley? The Real Facts about Hetch Hetchy," unsigned editorial, *San Francisco Examiner*, December 2, 1913, cited in Taylor, *Hetch Hetchy*, 126.

102. "The Real Facts about Hetch Hetchy," 126.

103. John Muir, *Yosemite* (1912), cited in Michael L. Smith, *Pacific Visions: California Scientists and the Environment: 1850–1915* (New Haven: Yale University Press, 1987), 177.

104. Marsden Manson, "Appraisement by City Engineer of Properties of Spring Valley Water Company," in *San Francisco Municipal Reports, 1908–1909*, 1223.

105. P. H. McCarthy, "Mayor's Inaugural Address," January 8, 1910, in *San Francisco Municipal Reports, 1909–1910*, 1145.

106. In 1914, for example, residents of the Richmond District of San Francisco com-

plained to the Railroad Commission that the "Spring Valley Water Company has refused to supply complainants with an adequate supply of water, that while the water supply in the homes of all the complainants is distressingly inadequate, some of the complainants have no water at all during certain hours of the day and must store water tanks each night for use on the succeeding day; that the cause of the inadequacy of the water supply is the insufficient size of the mains and pipes used by Spring Valley Water Company to supply that part of the Richmond District . . . and that the water company's revenue from this section is estimated at $20,000 annually." On the grounds of lack of jurisdiction, the Railroad Commission as well as the city refused to act on the complaint. See "Decision No. 1531, *Roy A. Pratt et al. v. Spring Valley Water Company*," in *California Railroad Commission Decisions, 1914,* 1077–85.

107. Taylor, *Hetch Hetchy,* 42.

108. According to a 1933 notice put out by the Board of Supervisors advocating passage of a waterworks bond issue, "distribution reservoirs within the City limits held only two days' supply as against the seven days' supply considered essential to guard against failure of the pipes leading from the peninsula reservoirs." The report maintained that "during the last ten years of its ownership, the Spring Valley Water Company made no extensions to the distributing system that could possibly be avoided. The distribution system is underbuilt. . . . Extensions to pipe system contemplate over 140 miles of supply and distributing pipes throughout all districts of the City to provide the necessary fire protection service and improve service to consumers. These pipe extensions are in line with recommendations of the Board of Fire Underwriters and will induce lower insurance rates." See San Francisco Board of Supervisors, *Arguments Favoring Bond Propositions* (San Francisco: 1933), 3–4.

109. According to an article in the *Daily Pacific Tribune,* the promoters agreed "to supply the city of Seattle with sufficient water for fire purposes, to keep filled all tanks the city may provide, and to put up and keep within the present fire limits twenty-five plugs at such points as may be designated by the City Council; agreeing also in the future to increase the number of plugs in proportion as the assessment of the fire district increases. . . . In consideration of these things proposed to be done . . . an assessment of three mills on the dollar is to be levied upon all property within the fire district; and the money arising from said tax paid to them." See "The Water Question," *Daily Pacific Tribune,* May 30, 1876.

110. Roger Sale, *Seattle: Past to Present* (Seattle: University of Washington, 1976), 12.

111. "The Water Question Again," *Daily Pacific Tribune,* May 31, 1876.

112. City of Seattle, Ordinance 566, approved June 25, 1884.

113. *Report Chief of Fire Department 1888, Annual Message of the Mayor of the City of Seattle . . . together with the Reports of City Officers, Fiscal Year Ending May 31, 1888* (Seattle: 1889), 70.

114. Sale, *Seattle,* 50.

115. *Seattle Daily Press,* June 7, 1889, cited by Margaret Louise Heyes, "The Seattle Municipal Water System," (master's thesis, University of Washington, 1907), 8.

116. According to 1913 reminiscences of ex-Mayor Moran, the Spring Hill company

claimed a value of $840,000 and offered to sell for $600,000. "It was due largely to the technical knowledge and advice" of the city's consulting engineer Benezette Williams, according to Moran, that enabled the city to bargain the company down to a price of $352,000 instead. See Heyes, "Seattle Municipal Water System," 26.

117. The report of the Board of Public Works for 1891 justified the purchase of the Union system on policy, health, and pecuniary grounds. According to the report, "the purchase of the Lake Union system at a cost of $27,500 was in line with the policy of the city to control the entire municipal water supply, and was rendered absolutely necessary by the just and pressing demands of the residents for relief from the impure water supplied by Lake Union. The price paid for the system was reasonable and the additional revenue derived from the system made the system from a business standpoint, a profitable one." *Report of the Board of Public Works, City of Seattle, Year Ending 1891* (Seattle: 1892), 99.

118. Committee on Fire and Water, Seattle Common Council, "Report," October 18, 1888, in John Lamb, *The Seattle Municipal Water Plant* (Seattle: 1914), 20.

119. Committee on Fire and Water, Seattle Common Council, "Report," Lamb, *Seattle Municipal Water Plant*, 20.

120. *Annual Message of the Mayor, City of Seattle, 1892 Report of Fire Department*, 37.

121. The quote can be found in Dick, "Genesis of Seattle City Light," 96.

122. Writing in 1913, chief clerk and auditor of the waterworks John Lamb summarized the financing of the system as follows: "Broadly speaking, the municipal water plant of the City of Seattle has been built and is maintained from two sources of revenue— the local improvement assessments, which amount to about one-third of the cost of the plant and receipts from water services from which are paid the interest on the bonded debt, and operating charges, together with a considerable item of new construction." See Lamb, *Seattle Municipal Water Plant*, 305.

123. Blake, *Water for the Cities*, 77.

124. Harold Platt, *City Building in the New South* (Philadelphia: Temple University Press, 1983), 135, 137, 149.

125. Platt, *City Building*, 210.

126. William Kahrl, *Water and Power* (Berkeley: University of California Press, 1982), 24–25.

127. An 1873 account described the state of building codes in American cities as follows: "The large cities in this country have grown up without any restrictions in regard to the construction of buildings; and it is within the last half-dozen years only that municipal governments have considered that they had any concern in the matter. . . . Previous to 1871 there was no attempt to regulate the construction of buildings in the city of Boston. . . . With the exception of New York, Washington, and Boston, scarcely any supervision is exercised over the construction of buildings in the larger cities of the United States, although most of them have been visited . . . by many destructive fires." See M. Bugbee, *North American Review* 165 (July 1873), excerpted in Ann Cook, Marilyn Gittell, and Herb Mack, eds., *City Life, 1865–1900: Views of Urban America* (New York: Praeger, 1973), 152. According to planning historian Anthony Sutcliffe, "From the late eighteenth

century American towns had introduced various regulations affecting the environment, including the inspection of lodging houses, the removal of dilapidated buildings, the control of fire hazards, and rudimentary public health regulations. However, codes of building regulations were slow to emerge, if we exclude the crude requirement to build in brick in the central areas which some municipalities imposed after disastrous fires. When, in 1867, the state of New York passed its first tenement house law, laying down rudimentary building regulations for tenement blocks in the cities of New York and Brooklyn, building codes were virtually unknown anywhere else in the United States." According to Sutcliffe, "the history of building regulation in New York reveals the underlying strength of the private land and building interests, for which the weak American municipalities and the spasmodic and divided efforts of the reformers were no match." See Anthony Sutcliffe, *Towards the Planned City: Germany, the United States and France, 1780–1914* (New York: St. Martin's, 1981), 99.

Writing during the early twentieth century, an insurance company executive and advocate of stricter building standards, Everett Crosby, described the overall result for American cities: "We do not possess Old World conditions, where buildings are comparatively small in area, low, generally of solid masonry construction, with small window openings, and frequently separated by wide avenues and parks. Our towns, with few exceptions, have been built hurriedly and cheaply, using vast quantities of wood in floor and roof construction, if not in walls, this material being the most available and least expensive. Consideration has been given only to the needs of the present and immediate future. . . . Where municipal building regulations exist they have been poorly drawn in respect to fire prevention, and sometimes peculiarly observed." See Everett U. Crosby, "Fire Prevention," in *Annals of the American Academy of Political and Social Science* 24, no. 2 (September 1905): 404. During the early decades of the twentieth century, building code provisions were still far more lenient in the United States than in France, Germany, England, and other western European nations. The 1926 *Water Works Practices Manual* issued by the American Water Works Association described European building codes as stricter than those in the United States, enforcement procedures as more systematic, and sanctions for those who may have caused fire by negligence more firm. In Frankfurt, Germany, for example, there was "strict enforcement of regulations which prohibit the erection of buildings over 72 feet in height, prescribe materials of construction, the storage of hazardous substances, and the construction of stairways, exits, and lighting installations. Neglect to conform to the building and fire regulations renders property owners subject to heavy penalties." See the American Water Works Association, *Water Works Practices* (1926), 586–87. By contrast, "In all our American cities," according to the manual, "the majority of buildings are of such character as to offer little resistance to the spread of fire." As a consequence, "cities in the United States and Canada find it necessary, in order to hold the annual fire loss within bounds, to provide water supplies and fire departments so greatly in excess of those found necessary in European cities." See American Water Works Association, *Water Works Practices* (1926), 583.

128. Sutcliffe, *Towards the Planned City*, 128.

129. Historian David Owen describes the situation in London until the last years of

the nineteenth century: "When the supply was intermittent and the pressure low, the work of the fire fighters was seriously handicapped . . . with intermittent pressure. Delay [in putting out a fire] was inevitable. If there was no water in the pipes, the Brigade would have to wait for the appearance of a company turncock to turn the water on to the point of delivery, and this could be a long and uncertain process." David Owen, *The Government of Victorian London, 1855–1889: The Metropolitan Board of Works, the Vestries, and the City Corporation* (Cambridge: Harvard University Press, 1982), 136.

130. In 1904, for example, per capita water consumption in London, England, and its environs ranged from thirty-three to about forty-nine (U.S.) gallons per day. During the same period, by contrast, per capita water consumption in the Bronx and Manhattan amounted to about 121 gallons per day. Hence, the municipal waterworks of New York City supplied about as much water to the two million people of Manhattan and the Bronx as London's water companies did to the over six and a half million people of that urban region. In some other American cities, levels of water consumption were even higher. In the industrial center of Chicago on Lake Michigan, for example, per capita consumption of water during the early years of the twentieth century amounted to over two hundred gallons per day. For the London consumption figures, see Percy Ashley, "The Water, Gas, and Electric Light Supply of London," *Annals of the American Academy of Political and Social Science* (January 1906): 20–31. For New York, see "New York's Water Supply—Present and Future Capacity," *Scientific American* (March 24, 1900): 178. For Chicago, see Frederic Rex, "Chicago," in "The Relation of the Municipality to the Water Supply," *Annals of the American Academy of Political and Social Science* 30, no. 3 (November 1907): 559. According to historian Nelson Blake, "The rate at which American cities consumed water had no parallel in foreign countries. Before World War II the average per capita use in ten European cities including London, Paris, and Berlin was only 39 gallons per day; while in ten American cities, including New York, Philadelphia, Baltimore, Chicago, and Detroit, the rate was 155 gallons per day." See Blake, *Water for the Cities*, 271–72.

Notes to Chapter 3

1. Article XII, *Charter of the City and County of San Francisco*, ratified May 26, 1898, approved by the state legislature January 26, 1899.

2. James D. Phelan, "Mayor's Message," January 3, 1899, *San Francisco Municipal Reports 1898–1899*, 8.

3. More detailed accounts of these events can be found in William Issel and Robert W. Cherny, *San Francisco, 1865–1932: Politics, Power, and Urban Development* (Berkeley: University of California Press, 1986) and Terrence McDonald, *The Parameters of Urban Fiscal Policy: Socioeconomic Change and Political Culture in San Francisco, 1860–1906* (Berkeley: University of California Press, 1986).

4. Section 6 of the Raker Act prohibited San Francisco from ever "selling or letting to any corporation or individual, except a municipality or a municipal water district or irrigation district, the right to sell or sublet the water or the electric energy sold or given

to it or him by the grantee . . . in case of any attempt to so sell, assign, transfer or convey, this grant shall revert to the Government of the United States." This excerpt of Section 6 of the Raker Act is taken from Ray W. Taylor, *Hetch Hetchy* (San Francisco: Ricardo J. Orozco, 1926), 195.

5. A 1948 Twentieth Century Fund report, for example, explained and justified regulation of electric utilities in these terms: "Government has participated in the electric power industry because technological and economic conditions make a local monopoly the most economical type of organization. In the absence of government intervention, a monopoly is under no pressure to charge prices covering only competitive costs and profits." See Twentieth Century Fund, *Electric Power and Government Policy* (New York: Twentieth Century Fund, 1948), 42. For a useful, if overly simplistic, typology defining this sort of explanation as an example of "the public interest theory of regulation," see Richard A. Posner, "Theories of Regulation," *Bell Journal of Economics* (autumn 1974): 335–38.

6. Arc lighting systems used high voltages and lamps wired in series. As a result, arc lighting systems could serve considerably larger geographical areas than could the low-voltage Edison plants. Limits on the voltage that could be generated by early dynamos (and as a result on the number of lamps that could be served by each one) constituted the most salient scale limitation on arc lighting plants.

7. In the case of street lighting, according to historian Harold Passer, electric utilities had to compete almost solely on the basis of quality because their price remained higher than that of gas for many years: "In most cities of the United States, the price of gas was sufficiently low so that the arc-lighting companies could not expect to light the streets more cheaply than the gas companies if there were to be no dark areas. . . . It was primarily on the basis of increased illumination that municipal authorities had to be convinced of the desirability of arc lighting. . . . It was a question of whether the extra light was worth the extra costs." See Harold C. Passer, *The Electrical Manufacturers* (Cambridge: Harvard University Press, 1953), 50–51.

8. These figures are taken from United States Department of Commerce, Bureau of the Census, *Census of Electrical Industries* for 1927 and 1937.

9. For a lucid contemporary description of technological developments in the electric utility industry for the period 1910–1927, see George Wittig, "Technical Developments," in Bureau of the Census, *Census of Electrical Industries 1927: Central Electric Light and Power Stations* (Washington, D.C.: GPO, 1930), 82–92.

10. Industry growth reflected the increasing success of electric lighting during these years. The number of arc lamps in service in the United States increased from 6,000 to 386,000 over the years 1881 to 1902. The number of incandescents increased even more quickly, from 250,000 in 1885 to 18,000,000 in 1902. See Passer, *Electrical Manufacturers*, 70–206. Not only increasing economies of scale but technological improvements in lamp efficiencies contributed to these trends. In the case of incandescent lamps, average efficiencies increased form 1.7 to 3.4 lumens per watt over the years 1880 to 1900. With the introduction of vacuum tungsten lamps during the first decades of the twentieth

century, efficiencies took a quantum leap. As of 1910, such lamps were rated at an efficiency of 8.3 lumens per watt. Improvements continued during subsequent years. See Jacob Martin Gould, *Output and Productivity in the Electric and Gas Utilities: 1899–1942* (New York: National Bureau of Economic Research, 1946), 31.

11. Storage batteries constitute an exception to this statement, but not a major one. Such batteries can store only small amounts of power. Except for a few of the early direct current systems, such batteries have not played a significant role in the technology used by electric utilities. More recently, pumped storage plants have been used to store the power needed to make electricity, but the capital costs of such plants are very high and the energy loss involved in pumping water uphill for future use is large. Under certain conditions, hydroelectric plants coupled with large reservoirs can also effectively store power by allowing water levels in the reservoir to rise. The extent to which such storage can be used, however, is highly dependent on natural conditions. Even after the capital investment for reservoirs and hydroelectric plants have been made, such facilities cannot always be counted upon to store power.

12. Historian David Sicilia describes the marketing efforts of electrical utilities during the first decades of the twentieth century:

First, they emphasized reliability, especially in trying to convert isolated plant users. But this strategy lost much of its impact over time: isolated plant users vanished, competition with gas became limited to heating and cooking markets, and more important, the success of the strategy contained the seeds of its own destruction because electric service came to be viewed as more of a right than a privilege. The second strategy was to create new uses for a uniform product. . . . When such markets seemed important enough, utilities were willing to enter new businesses to develop them such as the appliance business, the electric vehicle business, and, to promote house wiring, the finance business. . . . Utilities recognized that there were price sensitivities in some markets, and leading firms such as Boston Edison, adopted pricing schemes designed to appeal to consumers while taking into account their investment structures. Although utilities periodically battled with regulators and disgruntled citizens over their prices, they continued to benefit from the continuously and dramatically falling real cost of producing electricity.

See, David Sicilia, "Selling Power: Marketing and Monopoly at Boston Edison, 1888–1926" (paper presented at the annual meeting of the Organization of American Historians, 1986), 14–15.

13. An example of such an incremental penalty clause can be found in the 1890 Boston street lamp contract. See Boston Lamp Department, *Annual Report of the Lamp Department for the Year 1891* (Boston: 1892), 5. Of course, at least in theory, a contractor could try to bribe or otherwise influence public officials or regulators not to impose such sanctions for furnishing poor-quality service. But because quality of service could be so easily observed by members of the electorate, it would be politically far less costly for elected and appointed officials themselves to be "persuaded" to let prices remain high rather than to let quality of service slip.

14. "Acts of 1887: An Act Constituting a Board of Gas and Electric Light Commissioners," in *Third Annual Report of the Board of Gas Commissioners of the Commonwealth of Massachusetts* (January 1888), ch. 382, app. C: 121–25.

15. For a lengthy description of the history of financial regulation of railroads as well as gas and electric utilities in Massachusetts, see Irston R. Barnes, *Public Utility Control in Massachusetts* (New Haven: Yale University Press, 1930), 20–84.

16. The gas lighting contracts ran for periods of only three years, but were almost always renewed. The contracts provided for a fairly well-defined division of responsibility between the municipality and the privately owned service providers. The gas companies furnished gas at a set price per thousand cubic feet and were responsible for extending and maintaining service pipes with the city reimbursing them for all "actual and reasonable expenses." Lamp posts and lanterns were owned by the municipality and the municipality employed the lamp lighters as well. Prices paid by Boston for gas declined from a range of $2.00 to $2.50 per thousand cubic feet in 1875 to a range of $1.50 to $1.88 per thousand cubic feet in 1880. See City of Boston, *Report of the Superintendent of Lamps, 1880* (Boston: 1880), 5.

17. City of Boston, *Report of the Superintendent of Lamps for the Year 1883* (Boston: 1884), 7.

18. For typical examples of the points made by the board in arguing against duplicative competition, see Board of Gas and Electric Light Commissioners, *Seventh Annual Report* (Boston: Commonwealth of Massachusetts, 1892), 20–21.

19. See *American Gas Light Journal* 42: 117, cited by Leonard D. White, "The Origin of Utility Commissions in Massachusetts," *Journal of Political Economy* (March 1921): 190.

20. It is possible that this figure understates the role of the board. In a 1907 report, the board argued that its power "to order reductions in price and the publicity given the affairs of the companies have . . . been potent factors in bringing about many voluntary reductions in price." See Board of Gas and Electric Light Commissioners, *A Statement of Its Jurisdiction and Work since Its Establishment in 1885* (Boston: 1907). The empirical validity of this statement is difficult to determine. There is good reason for doubt, however, given declining price trends in states in which no regulation existed. Nor were charges for electricity and gas service notably lower in Massachusetts during this period than in states in which there was no regulation.

21. *Nineteenth Annual Report of the Massachusetts Board of Gas and Electric Light Commissioners*, public document 35 (Boston: 1904), 153.

22. See, for example, *Boston Electric Light Company v. A. W. Perry*, in *Fourth Annual Report of the Board of Gas Commissioners of the Commonwealth of Massachusetts* (January 1889), 81–82, and *Attorney General ex rel. Board of Gas and Electric Light Commissioners v. Walworth Light and Power Company*, in *Eighth Annual Report of the Board of Gas and Electric Light Commissioners* (January 1893), app. C: 257–59.

23. This sequence of events implies active or tacit collusion between the firms, but whether they actively conspired to rig the bids is unclear. There are, however, some interesting inconsistencies in the written record. Contemporary municipal documents portrayed the competition as one in which firms submitted sealed bids to discourage

collusion. Twenty years later, however, in an after-dinner address recalling the events, the attorney for one of the companies involved recounted that officers of his firm waited to learn of the prices to be charged by the other two firms before submitting their own bid. See Everett W. Burdett, "Address Delivered at the Twenty Fifth Anniversary Dinner of the Edison Electric Illuminating Company of Boston," February 20, 1911.

24. *Massachusetts Acts of 1891*, sec. 2, ch. 360. The act deprived a city of its most powerful source of negotiating leverage—the threat it could pose to the interests of an operating electrical utility firm, which would lose the value of its investments in fixed physical plant due to construction of duplicate facilities. In addition, depending on the unpredictable and inevitably time-consuming results of arbitration procedures and court appeals, the requirement meant that some or all of the monopoly price exploitation from which a city sought to escape through municipal ownership could well be incorporated into the valuation of the property that it had to purchase. For this expression of the problem posed by such buy-out requirements, the author is indebted to David Schap, *Municipal Ownership in the Electric Utility Industry* (New York: Praeger, 1986), 26–28.

25. City of Boston, *Annual Report of the Superintendent of Lamps for the Year 1900* (Boston: 1900). Boston finally ceased its use of gas and oil lamps for street lighting only in 1909. In some other major cities, gas street lamps continued in use well into the 1930s or even later.

26. Although the proportion of incandescent lamps capable of being supplied by isolated plants declined from almost half that of electric utilities in 1900 to about two-fifths in 1912, the total output of these facilities in Boston continued to increase during the first decade of the twentieth century.

27. L. L. Elden, *The Boston Edison System* (Boston: Edison Electric Illuminating Company, 1909), 15–17.

28. See *Electrical World* 80, no. 12 (September 16, 1922) and Sicilia, "Selling Power," 10–11.

29. A copy of the contract can be found in the *Annual Report of the Superintendent of Lamps for the Year 1882* (Boston: 1883), 15–16. Over the course of the year, Boston purchased fifty-nine lamps under the terms of the contract. Quality of service, according to the superintendent of lamps, was good.

30. Josiah Quincy, *Message of the Mayor Relative to Public Electric Lighting and Transmitting a Copy of an Agreement for the Extension of the Existing Contract between the Boston Electric Light Company and the City of Boston*, document 117 (Boston: 1898), 3.

31. *Mayor's Message Transmitting a Communication from the Superintendent of Streets Submitting Copies of Contracts with the Edison Electric Illuminating Company for Street Lighting in Boston together with Certain Other Information*, document 110–1909 (Boston: 1909), 1–11.

32. Massachusetts Board of Gas and Electric Light Commissioners, *Boston—Edison Street Lighting Arbitration* (Boston: 1918).

33. The 1918 figure should be considered only approximate, as both lamp types and compensation formulas changed over the course of the period.

34. One such case occurred in 1882, when the New England Weston Company ini-

tiated service. In his report for the year, Boston's superintendent of lamps described the service provided by New England Weston this way: "These lights, when burning in good order, give good satisfaction; but seemingly, for the want of proper care and management, the service rendered has at times been poor, and the complaints of citizens and of the police have been very frequent. A change of management has been recently made, and it is hoped that a more reliable and satisfactory service will be rendered in the future." See the *Annual Report of the Superintendent of Lamps for the Year 1882*. These hopes were realized and the service furnished by Weston did improve in subsequent years.

35. *Boston City Council Minutes* (Boston: 1925), 197.

36. See Charles M. Coleman, *P.G. & E. of California* (New York: McGraw-Hill, 1952), 59.

37. Coleman, *P.G. & E. of California*, 66.

38. Thomas P. Hughes, *Networks of Power: Electrification in Western Society* (Baltimore: Johns Hopkins University Press, 1983), 265–67.

39. Hughes, *Networks of Power*, 272–73.

40. Hughes, *Networks of Power*, 274–75.

41. Hughes, *Networks of Power*, 278.

42. As of 1910, the City Electric Company earned $774,372 from the sale of current compared to $2,546,865 earned by Pacific Gas and Electric in San Francisco. See "Gas and Electric Rates," in *San Francisco Municipal Reports* (1909–1910), 1194–1202.

43. For a more extensive account of this incident, the confessions of the supervisors, and the complexities of the graft trial as a whole, see Walton Bean, *Boss Ruef's San Francisco* (Berkeley: University of California Press, 1952), 89, 90, 193, 197.

44. Mansel Blackford, *The Politics of Business in California, 1890–1920* (Columbus: Ohio State University Press, 1977), 86.

45. During its early years, the California Commission explicitly characterized its policy as one of "regulated monopoly with potential competition." According to one official, the commission "has protected utilities against competition in their given fields, but has given this protection only in so far and for such time as the utility rendered proper service at proper rates. . . . In one of its most important cases, the commission found that a gas and electric company had not given adequate services and that its rates had been unduly high, and therefore when a second utility sought to enter, the commission granted the necessary certificate. In another case which assumed state-wide importance, the commission found that the gas and electric company serving the city of Stockton was rendering as complete service as the new applicant could offer and that the rates proposed in competition were not sufficiently different from those in force to warrant the substitution of the dual for the single agency." See Paul A. Sinsheimer, "Ten Rules for Service," *Annals of Political and Social Science* 53 (1914): 294–95. In practice, the latter case, in which the commission prohibited competition, was more typical than the former one, in which it did not.

46. "Gas and Electricity Rates," in *San Francisco Municipal Reports for the Year 1911–1912*, 1141–45.

47. Although the actual results do not seem to have been greatly different, the com-

missions did use somewhat different rate-setting methods. The Massachusetts Board of Gas and Electric followed a somewhat unusual policy in that it made no effort to base rate making on a physical valuation of utility properties. Instead, the Massachusetts Commission relied on its supervision over security issues to gain assurance that capitalizations were not inflated, and used capitalization as the basis for setting rates. For an all-too-detailed account of the workings of these procedures in Massachusetts, see Barnes, *Public Utility Control in Massachusetts*. The California Commission followed a more conventional practice, relying on physical valuations of utility properties to determine the "rate base" upon which a firm would be entitled to earn a fair return.

48. Paul A. Sinsheimer, "Public Utility Regulation in California," *Outlook* (September 6, 1916): 34.

49. For brief descriptions of these events, see "Pacific Gas and Electric Rates to Be Reduced," *Electrical World* (January 6, 1923) and "Six Month's Gain in Business Offsets Rate Decrease," *Electrical World* (August 4, 1923).

50. Section 6 of the Raker Act prohibited San Francisco from ever "selling or letting to any corporation or individual, except a municipality or a municipal water district or irrigation district, the right to sell or sublet the water or the electric energy sold or given to it or him by the grantee. . . in case of any attempt to so sell, assign, transfer or convey, this grant shall revert to the Government of the United States." This quote of Section 6 is taken from Taylor, *Hetch Hetchy*, 195.

51. James D. Phelan, "Address," in *Transactions of the Commonwealth Club of California* 18, no. 7 (December 1923): 311–12. For a more pointed contemporary critique of specific regulatory practices and procedures in California, see Franklin Hichborn, "Why the Corporations Win before the State Railroad Commission" (1926), Bancroft Library, University of California at Berkeley.

52. Testimony of supervisor McSheehy, U. S. House, *Committee on Public Lands: Hearings on Amending Section 6 of the Raker Act* (January 1942), 430.

53. In a 1933 proposal for the city to build a transmission line from Newark (forty miles away) into the city, and to construct a small distribution system, city manager of utilities E. G. Cahill maintained that the city would be able to cut electric rates by 10 percent to 12 percent in the area to be served and still make money on the project. In the more ambitious 1941 proposal to acquire the entire electric distribution system in San Francisco, the city Public Utilities Commission calculated that under municipal ownership, the city would earn a yearly surplus of more than $5,200,000 on the sale of electricity, even after paying operating costs, bond interest and redemption, depreciation, and replacement of taxes formerly paid by Pacific Gas and Electric. Such a surplus, Cahill maintained, would be sufficient to cut tax rates sixty-five cents on each one hundred dollars of assessed valuation, or to reduce electric rates to consumers by over 30 percent. See E. G. Cahill, *Plan Nine: Ownership and Operation of Entire San Francisco Electric Service* (San Francisco: Public Utilities Commission, 1941), 17.

54. For a brief statement of the point that the city could obtain cheaper financing than that available to a private firm, see Civic League of Improvement Clubs and Associations of San Francisco, "Hetch Hetchy Power Problem," (June 12, 1923), 6. According

to the report, the city could finance construction of a municipally owned plant at 5.5 percent interest per year compared to the 7 percent dividends of the preferred stock issued by the power companies. For an articulate statement of the argument that consumers in San Francisco unfairly subsidized those outside the city, see Cahill, *Plan Nine*, 19–20.

55. Phelan, "Address," 315. Writing eighteen years later, city utility manager Cahill, like Phelan, argued that high electric rates hindered San Francisco's economic development. According to Cahill: "San Francisco has always been at a disadvantage on account of the high rates charged by the Pacific Gas and Electric Company here for industrial power as compared with the rates charged by the Los Angeles Bureau of Power and Light and the Seattle Department of Lighting, both municipally owned. . . . The result of this, as well as other adverse factors, has been to greatly reduce the number of large industrial plants which located in San Francisco during the past fifteen years. Such plants have gone to our competitor cities, wherein industry could buy large blocks of power for approximately one-half what the Pacific Gas and Electric Company charges in San Francisco." See Cahill, *Plan Nine*, 18.

56. Over the summer of 1926, the newly elected Board of Supervisors (elected on a pro- municipal ownership slate) attempted to use the income from Hetch Hetchy power sales to extend the city's transmission lines forty miles further, from their termination at the Pacific Gas and Electric substation at Newark to San Francisco. Comparatively inexpensive, such an arrangement would permit San Francisco to supply its own municipal needs with Hetch Hetchy power, and to begin construction on a competitive distribution system or make contracts to serve large customers. Because of the threat of competition, such an extension would also have placed the city in a much better bargaining position to purchase the distribution systems of the privately owned companies. A taxpayer suit by Adolph Uhl blocked the effort. In a 1926 decision, the California Supreme Court ruled that the project constituted a capital expenditure rather than an ordinary operating or extension expense. Under the city's charter, bonds for capital expenditures to secure a public utility had to be submitted to the voters at referendum and required a two-thirds majority for passage.

57. *Statement of San Francisco Chamber of Commerce* (September 5, 1941), 3–4.

58. Louis Leurey, *Transaction of the Commonwealth Club of California*, 331. A 1939 editorial in the *San Francisco Chronicle* made a similar point: "It all comes down to this: A proposal to spend $55,000,000 for an electricity distribution system the city already has; a proposal that makes no new jobs—although it would put a lot of existing jobs under political control; a proposal that promises no advantage to either rate payers or tax payers, but does hold danger of raising both rates and taxes." See the *San Francisco Chronicle*, May 18, 1939.

59. See Harold Platt, *The Electric City: Energy and the Growth of the Chicago Area, 1880–1930* (Chicago: University of Chicago Press, 1991); Nicholas B. Wainwright, *History of the Philadelphia Electric Company* (Philadelphia: Philadelphia Electric Company, 1961), 31; Forrest McDonald, *Let There Be Light* (Madison: American History Research Center, 1957), 50–51.

60. Wainwright, *Philadelphia Electric Company*, 119.

61. According to Douglas Anderson: "The National Civic Federation had advocated regulation by the states because state regulation promised to rectify the unfair treatment given different classes of customers by the utilities and because it would ensure evenhandedness in the setting of rates and the authorizing of stock issues. Best of all, a state commission that was scientific and expert would take public utilities out of politics thereby removing one of the chief obstacles to good government. . . . In the electric power industry, the heads of many—though not all—of the leading utility systems supported the movement for commissions because they believed commissions would protect them from political bosses, from competition, and most of all from municipal ownership." See Douglas Anderson, *Regulatory Politics and Electric Utilities* (Boston: Auburn House, 1981), 56. Samuel Insull's support of regulation dated from as early as 1898, a year after a group of corrupt aldermen had sought to extort money from him by granting themselves a competitive electric utility franchise on such favorable terms that Insull felt compelled to buy them out to protect his monopoly. Not surprisingly, Insull's support for regulation emphasized legal protection against competition as an important attribute. Perhaps because they felt secure in their monopoly position in any case, many utility executives were not initially convinced by Insull's position. As movements for municipal utility ownership grew in strength, however, increasing numbers of private utility executives became convinced of the logic of Insull's arguments.

62. T. Eugene Jordan, "Cedar River System," *Seattle Idea* (1895).

63. Seattle obtained a direct rail connection to the east only when James Hill's Great Northern line was completed in 1893. Accounts of the near-legendary tribulations experienced by Seattle in obtaining rail links can be found in Robert C. Nesbit, *"He Built Seattle": A Biography of Judge Thomas Burke* (Seattle: University of Washington Press, 1961) and in Murray Morgan, *Skid Road: An Informal Portrait of Seattle* (New York: The Viking Press, 1951). In his account, Morgan argued that these events left many in Seattle "with a deep hatred for high finance. The realization of the degree to which their destinies could be controlled by the decisions—even the whims—of a Philadelphia banker and a few of his economic henchmen had shocked them deeply. Hostility to Eastern capital became a persistent strain in the community consciousness" (p. 74).

64. John W. Pratt, comp., *Revised Ordinances of the City of Seattle* (Seattle: 1893), 479–99.

65. This company, as was the case of the dominant firm in San Francisco, went through a succession of corporate incarnations and name changes over the period. Founded as the Seattle Electric Company in 1886, the firm began service with two 600-lamp Edison dynamos. Over the years 1890 through 1892, the firm gained an infusion of Villiard capital from the East and changed its name to the Seattle General Electric Company in 1891. With this help, the firm bought out its largest competitor, the Home Electric Light Company, in 1892 and again changed its name, becoming the Union Electric Company. Over the course of 1899 and 1900, the Stone and Webster partnership of Boston, a major holder of bonds in the Union Company, consolidated all of the streetcar and electric utility firms remaining in the city into the Seattle Electric Company.

66. *Seattle Mail and Herald*, February 13, 1904.

67. An 1895 editorial in the *Seattle Times*, for example, criticized the street lighting as follows: "Away from the principal business streets, Seattle is a miserably lighted town. The incandescent lights serve to mark where the corners are when the night is not foggy, but as for serving any other imaginable purpose they might as well not be there at all." Editorial in the *Seattle Times*, February 19, 1895, cited in Wesley Arden Dick, "The Genesis of Seattle City Light" (master's thesis, University of Washington, 1965), 34.

68. As of 1890, Seattle had a population of only about 43,000, compared to about 448,000 in Boston and about 299,000 in San Francisco.

69. *Seattle Daily Bulletin*, February 5, 1902, cited by Dick, "Genesis of Seattle City Light," 57.

70. According to the manager of the Snoqualmie company, Charles Baker, the strict franchise terms were put in place as part of a conspiracy to force Snoqualmie to sell out to the incumbent firm or otherwise come to terms. Baker and his father claimed that the incumbent firm obtained the cooperation of city officials in the plot through bribery, and that city aldermen had sought to shake down his firm as well. An account of the allegations can be found in Dick, "Genesis of Seattle City Light," 38–40.

71. *County of King, State of Washington vs. Jacob Furth and Samuel L. Shuffleton* (1903), in Dick, "Genesis of Seattle City Light," 75.

72. J. D. Ross, *Annual Report of the Lighting Department, Seattle, Washington, for the Year 1911, with a Review of the Work Since the Inception of the Seattle Municipal Light and Power Plant*, 20, 43.

73. Reflecting the different emphases of the municipal system and the private firms, the number of consumers and mileage of distribution line put in place by City Light were greater than for the private firms but the amount of power actually generated was considerably less. According to Wesley Dick, "exact figures are not known, but City Light furnished somewhere between twenty to thirty-three per cent of the market by 1910." See Dick, "Genesis of Seattle City Light," 89.

74. Writing in 1910, for example, the supervisor of the city's Lighting and Water Department, H. B. Youngs, gave the municipal system primary credit for ensuring that cuts in costs in the production of electricity were passed onto consumers. "Viewing the plant . . . not as an institution intended to pile up surplus revenue, but merely as an agency to fix and maintain a just and reasonable rate for electrical services, it has fulfilled its mission in the most satisfactory manner. There has been no attempt to crowd out the other companies, but only to fix a rate which would of necessity in the competitive market have to be met by all competitors." See H. B. Youngs, "Public Ownership in Seattle," *Twentieth Century Magazine* (November 1910), cited in Dick, "Genesis of Seattle City Light," 94. Writing in 1912, J. D. Ross gave the credit for both cuts in price and improvements in street lighting to the municipal plant:

> In and previous to 1902, consumers of electric current for residence lighting were paying 20 cents per K.W.H. The agitation for a municipal plant was followed by an immediate reduction in this price to 12 cents per K.W.H. . . . When the Municipal Light and Power Plant began making contracts for residence lighting in September of 1905, the

rate was fixed at 8 1/2 cents for the first 20 K.W.H., 7 ½ cents for the second K.W.H. . . . This was immediately followed by a reduction in the private lighting company's rates to 10 cents per K.W.H. for the first 20 K.W.H., 9 cents per K.W. H. for the second 20 K.W.H. . . . On July 11, 1911, the Municipal Light and Power Plant reduced its rates to 7 cents for the first 60 K.W.H. and 4 cents for all over 60 K.W.H. In November of the same year, the private companies reduced their rates, making them the same as the Municipal Light and Power Plant's rates. . . .

In addition to having caused the reduction in the cost of street light, the money for street lighting instead of being paid out to a private corporation, is now paid into the light fund, which has enabled the City of Seattle to make of itself what its daily papers proudly proclaim— "The Best Lighted City in America."

See Ross, *Annual Report of the Lighting Department, Seattle, Washington,* 24–25.

75. Historian Wesley Dick describes how the connection was made in the *Star*: "The main focus of the attack on Gill was his 'open-town' policy, with its graft and corruption. . . . The *Star* had long considered that the ills of Seattle city government were caused by an alliance among the Republican machine, the public service corporations, and the 'underworld.' This 'plunderbund' governed Seattle in its own interest—the public interest be damned. This inter-relationship was illustrated in a cartoon in the *Star* depicting Gill in the clutches of the Seattle Electric Company . . . on the one hand, and the vice syndicate on the other." Dick, "Genesis of Seattle City Light," 100.

76. In good city-boosting language, Ross set forth this view in the Seattle Lighting Department's 1911 annual report: "We feel that one of the principal uses of the City Plant is to furnish an abundance of power at the lowest rates in order that we may bring many new industries, both large and small, to Seattle, with pay rolls to employ more men and establish the city as a manufacturing center. . . . What we need and all should work for, is to build up the New York, the Pittsburg, and the Niagara of the Northwest within the boundaries of one city—SEATTLE." See Ross, *Annual Report of the Lighting Department, Seattle, Washington,* 14. In a 1927 letter, Ross expressed similar hopes: "Low industrial rates bring factories to Seattle to realize the benefits of the wonderful water power of the State of Washington. Cheap power is the key to future industrial supremacy and will make the Puget Sound Basin one of the World's busiest workshops." See letter from J. D. Ross to F. L. Earp, July 30, 1927, in William O'Dell Sparks, "J. D. Ross and Seattle City Light, 1917–1932" (master's thesis, University of Washington, 1964), 4.

77. Total horsepower at the command of Seattle's municipal utility in 1911 amounted to about 14,000, as compared to 90,000 in the hands of the city's private firms. By 1928, however, Seattle had almost caught up, with 180,000 horsepower as compared to about 230,000 in the hands of the private firms. In practice, the sorts of systems actually put in place by the private and government-owned systems also resembled one another in certain respects. By the end of the 1920s, the private system had installed water power plants with a total capacity of about 185,000 horsepower and steam plants with a capacity of about 45,000 horsepower. The City Light system, by contrast, was supplied by hydroplants with a capacity of about 130,000 horsepower and steam plants with a capacity of about 50,000 horsepower. See *Annual Report of the Lighting Department, Seattle, Wash-*

ington, 1–31; Norwood W. Brockett, *Facts about the Puget Sound Power and Light Company* (Seattle: Puget Sound Power and Light Company, 1927); and *City of Seattle, Department of Lighting Annual Report, 1928*, 17.

78. In the context of a campaign by City Light to gain federal approval for use of power sites on the Skagit River, Ross framed the issue in a 1918 letter to Seattle mayor Ole Hanson as follows: "the concern that loses the Skagit will be relegated to oblivion sooner or later. . . . If the Company controls, it will be a matter of dividends; if the City controls it means an industrial development that gives Seattle first place as an industrial city and the electrification of all of its homes at the lowest rates anywhere in America." See letter from J. D. Ross to Mayor Ole Hanson, April 6, 1918, in Sparks, "J. D. Ross and Seattle City Light," 20–21.

79. L. E. Karrer and M. T. Crawford, "Joint Pole History" (1944), PSP+L General Correspondence, in the archives at the University of Washington. See also Miner Hamilton Baker, "The Proposed City Light Merger: A Study of Public Opinion" (master's thesis, University of Washington, 1938), 17.

80. The commission defined its role as follows: "The regulatory police power of the state must be exercised in a reasonable and rational manner. The Commission must protect the public against unreasonable and excessive rates, discriminatory, unfair, and illegal practices and inferior service, but on the other hand, must assure to all such companies a reasonable return upon the fair value of their property devoted to the public use." *First Annual Report of the Public Service Commission of Washington to the Governor* (Olympia: 1912), 6–7. The commission's perspective can be seen further in a quote from United States Supreme Court justice Moody on the appropriate role of regulation: "The regulation of public service corporations, which perform their duties under conditions of necessary monopoly, will occur with greater and greater frequency as time goes on. It is a delicate and dangerous function and ought to be exercised with a keen sense of justice on the part of the regulating body, met by a frank disclosure on the part of the company to be regulated. . . . Our social system rests largely upon the sanctity of private property and that state or community which seeks to invade it will soon discover the error in the disaster which follows." Opinion of Justice Moody in *Knoxville vs. Knoxville Water Co.*, 212 U.S. 18, cited in longer form in *First Annual Report of the Public Service Commission of Washington to the Governor*, 7. The commission report also quoted with approval the following criticism of the inadequacy of municipal utility oversight of the needs and interests of privately owned service providers: "Local control as commonly practiced consists of nothing more or less than spasmodic attacks upon rates and services of public utilities regardless of the physical conditions of their plants, their financial needs or possibilities." *Third Annual Report of Public Service Commission of Wisconsin*, 18, cited in *First Annual Report of the Public Service Commission of Washington to the Governor*, 78.

81. Homer T. Bone, before the joint committee of the Washington State Legislature, quoted in *Seattle Union Record*, January 24, 1923, cited in Sparks, "J. D. Ross and Seattle City Light," 84. In an alarming editorial, the *Spokane Spokesman Review* sounded a similar theme: "Seattle . . . would possess the key to the industrial development of the

State of Washington. It could discriminate in favor of the industries within its borders and against the industries of other cities and towns." See Norwood Brockett, before the joint committee of the Washington State Legislature, quoted in *Seattle Union Record*, February 1, 1923, cited in Sparks, "J. D. Ross and Seattle City Light," 84.

82. See Norwood Brockett, before the joint committee of the Washington State Legislature, quoted in *Seattle Union Record*, February 1, 1923, cited in Sparks, "J. D. Ross and Seattle City Light," 84. In a statement quoted in the *Seattle Union Record*, the Manufacturers' Association of Washington came out against the plan on the grounds of the pernicious political influence of government-owned utilities: "Public operation develops political machines! . . . efficiency of public management is questionable." Statement quoted in *Seattle Union Record*, October 10, 1924, cited in Sparks, "J. D. Ross and Seattle City Light," 90.

83. Ross himself described what happened thus: "upon thorough study at that time, acquisition by condemnation was abandoned. Long drawn out, costly court proceedings, prospects of exceedingly high severance damages, going concern value and replacement value, and the necessity for raising the full amount in cash were reasons compelling the abandonment. With the depression came the first real opportunity to eliminate the costly duplication." J. D. Ross, *City of Seattle, Department of Lighting Annual Report, Year Ending December 31, 1936.*

84. For an assessment of these considerations by a company official, see memo from F. P. Loomis to Frank McLaughlin, October 18, 1934, PSP+L correspondence files at the University of Washington.

85. City Light's 1935 annual report, for example, made the case as follows: "The double expense of all duplication of electric system in Seattle . . . to be ultra conservative may be placed at $2,500,000 annually. . . . The Superintendent proposes to eliminate this waste by merging the private company into City Light and thereby making it possible soon to cut the light rates of the people of Seattle in half." See Ross, *City of Seattle Department of Lighting Annual Report* (1935), 71.

86. In a Civic Affairs League pamphlet, engineer Willis T. Batcheller made this case: "Due to the present taxation burden of the private company's holdings and revenues and more particularly to the coming of Grand Coulee power which will be obtainable at very low rates in the Puget Sound region, the Seattle distribution system of the power company will be obtainable by the city if desired in a very few years, for a small fraction of the price now proposed . . . The excessive investment of both the city and the power company in their present systems prevents them from competing with power to be produced by the Federal government and delivered in the Puget Sound region, as well as in Portland and Los Angeles." See Willis T. Batcheller, "Dangers in the Ross Plan," in Civic Affairs League pamphlet (February 1935).

87. William O'Dell Sparks describes what happened: "Because the recall battle had been fought by the League as a struggle between the 'Power Trust' and municipal ownership the recall victory tended to have a powerful effect on Seattle politics. Many of the men elected to public office in Seattle in the next half decade . . . were all firm supporters of municipal ownership who had gained their initial political experience as leaders of

the Citizen's Municipal Utilities Protective League. And when the conservatives triumphed in city politics during the mid-thirties they carefully avoided any direct attack against Ross or the lighting department. The recall victory had the effect of providing the security from political restraint which the superintendent had always desired for his department." See Sparks, "J. D. Ross and Seattle City Light," 180–81.

88. Both company and city officials were well aware of the potency of these sentiments. In communications promoting the buyout, City Light found it necessary to specifically disclaim any desire for Seattle to interfere in the affairs of outlying communities. City Light's annual report for 1934 made the point as follows: "The objective of the proposal is that the people of Seattle operate a monopoly of their light and power business in their city . . . but in no event to extend Seattle's field of retail distribution beyond King County. In the first announcement of the plan, it was announced that the City of Seattle would . . . split the system into various units which would be acquired by the local communities served. . . . Later, Superintendent Ross . . . urged the banking syndicate to agree that districts outside of Seattle may issue their own revenue bonds . . . thus eliminating the necessity of Seattle's underwriting more than its own part, and doing away with the objection that Seattle might be considered as wanting to exert undue influences on other communities." See Ross, *City of Seattle, Department of Lighting Annual Report* (1934), 64–65. In internal company documents, Puget Sound Power and Light officials also expressed the belief that any plan for city takeover of their entire system would be unlikely to be approved because of fears of dominance by Seattle. An internal company memorandum summarized this reading of public opinion: "the Ross proposal to purchase our property is not taken seriously. Insofar as it confirms the ambition of City of Seattle politicians to dominate the power industry in Western Washington, we find that our citizens are generally opposed to this proposition." Memorandum from Mr. Frank Walsh to Mr. Frank McLaughlin, October 11, 1934, in PSP+L archives at manuscript section, University of Washington Archives.

89. Letter from Seattle Real Estate Board to J. D. Ross, in Civic Affairs League pamphlet, "Shall We Buy Another White Elephant?" February 1935, in City Light Pamphlet File at the Seattle Public Library.

90. A University of Washington master's thesis written during the late 1930s assessed the situation as follows: "Partly because of the city's experience with the street railway purchase, partly because of a feeling that competition should be maintained, partly for other reasons, the merger was decidedly unpopular with Seattle citizens." See Baker, "The Proposed City Light Merger, 30. Indeed, according to Baker, a pro-merger publication issued by the Citizen's Cheap Power League in 1936 reported that its own polling data found the people of Seattle lined up against a municipal acquisition of Puget facilities by a six to one margin.

91. Over the years 1903 through 1930, for example, the annual output of electricity produced by the Detroit Edison Company increased from 11 million kilowatt-hours to over 2,300 million. Reflecting both price cuts and increased industrial use, average revenue declined over the same period from 4.9 cents per kilowatt-hour produced to about 2.1 cents. Except for a dip at the beginning, these trends even continued through the

Depression. By 1940, the annual output of electricity by the Detroit company had increased to over 3,600 million kilowatt-hours and average revenues declined to 1.6 cents per kilowatt-hour. These figures were compiled from Raymond Miller, *Kilowatts at Work* (Detroit: Wayne State University Press, 1957), 421, 427. Michigan enacted legislation providing for state regulation of public utilities in 1909. As the legislation contained home rule provisions, Detroit Edison (voluntarily, according to company historian Miller) continued to report its rates to city as well as state authorities. Beginning in 1922, however, the state unambiguously took control.

In Philadelphia, the situation was similar. Output of the Philadelphia Electric Company increased from 125,633,000 kilowatt-hours in 1910 before the imposition of regulation to 910,330,000 kWh in 1920 and 3,091,233,000 kWh in 1930. As the firm's service area expanded and electricity came to be increasingly used in the home, the number of customers served by the company soared from 33,000 to 631,000 over the same period. To spur increased demand, the company found it in its interest at times to cut its rates of its own volition. In 1906, for example, the company established a uniform ten cents per kilowatt-hour maximum rate on its overhead system, a reduction of about one-third in many areas of the city. At the same time as the Philadelphia company was cutting rates, its profits were increasing. In 1908 the company declared its first extra dividend of a dollar a share. See Wainwright, *Philadelphia Electric Company*, 90, 389.

In New York, too, electric companies continued to find it to be in their interests to invest in new equipment and (at times) cut prices under regulation. In 1925, for example, an article in the trade journal *Electrical World* reported that thirty-one electric utility companies in New York serving four million people had made rate reductions cutting household electric bills by about $3,270,000 for the year. The article attributed the firms' ability to make these rate cuts to better production methods, including improved generator technique, the replacement of obsolete high-cost plants with larger and more efficient ones, increased interconnection of steam and hydro facilities, and greater use of high-power transmission lines. See "New York State Rate Cuts," *Electrical World* 86 (December 19, 1925): 1273.

As historian Ronald Tobey points out, private electric utility initiative in marketing electricity also had its limits during the first decades of the twentieth century. Even during the 1920s, for example, sales of electrical appliances such as washing machines and refrigerators were mostly confined to the wealthy and upper middle class. According to Tobey, "most utility managers simply did not believe through the 1920s that the home heavy appliance market would be sufficiently profitable for them to divert massive capital to it." Instead, utility firms "focused their marketing efforts . . . on increasing consumption by the few upper-income households who could pay for full electric service." See Ronald Tobey, *Technology as Freedom: The New Deal and the Electrical Modernization of the American Home* (Berkeley: University of California Press, 1996), 12. This caveat notwithstanding, electric utility firms' aggressiveness in marketing their product and expanding output stands in sharp contrast to that of their private waterworks counterparts.

In the United States as a whole, the annual output of electricity generated by privately owned electric utilities increased almost twentyfold, from fewer than 6 billion kilowatt-hours in 1907 to almost 110 billion kilowatt-hours twenty years later. As a result of price cuts, average revenues per kilowatt-hour of electricity used by small consumers declined from five and a half cents to three and two-tenths cents over the years 1917 through 1942. For large consumers, the decline was from one and eight-tenths cents per kilowatt-hour to one cent. See Gould, *Output and Productivity*, 30–33.

92. For a discussion of government ownership movements in the electric utility industry during the 1920s that emphasizes this theme, see Jay Brigham, *Empowering the West: Electrical Politics before FDR* (Lawrence: University Press of Kansas, 1998).

93. Power Committee and Power Survey Research Staff, Twentieth Century Fund, *Electric Power and Government Policy*, 499.

94. Power Committee and Power Survey Research Staff, Twentieth Century Fund, *Electric Power and Government Policy*, 732–35.

95. More broadly, according to historian Thomas Hughes: "war did not so much stimulate the invention and development of new technologies as clear away the political, economic, and other nontechnological factors that prevented or retarded the utilization of existing technologies. The imperatives of war did not reverse the direction of technologies nor did they cause mutations; rather they broke a technological crust that had restrained adjustments in course and velocity." Hughes, *Networks of Power*, 286.

96. Hughes, *Networks of Power*, 297. Murray himself defined the advantages of the plan as follows in a 1921 presentation before the National Electric Light Association: "it is very plain that through the strategic location of large power stations, both hydro-electric and steam-electric, taking every advantage of economic coal and water, electric power can be generated and transmitted for distribution to a vast system of interconnected groups and in so doing, great economy can be effected in labor and material through the handling of power in large bulk, with consequent reduction in unit cost of production." See William S. Murray, "Superpower and the Customer," in *National Electric Light Association, Proceedings*, vol. 79 (1923), 651.

97. Gifford Pinchot, *Giant Power Survey* (1925), iv–v, as cited by Hughes, *Networks of Power*, 298.

98. Power Committee and Power Survey Research Staff, Twentieth Century Fund, *Electric Power and Government Policy*, 471–72.

99. At least in Boston and San Francisco, the imposition of state regulation did not make *any* immediate difference in electric utility pricing policies. Over the longer term, the effectiveness of state regulation is difficult to determine from the historical record, because it is hard to determine what utility firms would have done in its absence. It might be argued, for example, that knowledge on the part of utility managements that they might need to justify their rate-setting decisions to regulatory commissions, ongoing reporting requirements, and the possibility of commission intervention all have functioned to restrain monopolistic pricing policies on the part of electric utility firms in the absence of significant formal activity by regulatory commissions. Comparing prices in regulated versus nonregulated states is an obvious means to address the question of whether regulation has actually made a difference, but determining a fair basis of com-

parison can be difficult because of the wide variety of factors that affect the cost of electricity. A 1948 report by the Twentieth Century Fund argued on the basis of price trends in a group of regulated and nonregulated states, and comparisons of neighboring states, that state commissions did exert effective pressure on rate structures. In a famous 1962 article in the *Journal of Law and Economics,* economist George Stigler came to the opposite conclusion. On the basis of a regression analyses of rates and certain cost factors, Stigler argued that neither electricity charges to consumers nor rates of return to utility firms significantly differed in states with regulation as compared to those without during the period 1907–1936. See George Stigler, "What Can Regulators Regulate? The Case of Electricity," *Journal of Law and Economics* 5 (1962). Whatever the validity of Stigler's conclusion that regulation had no discernible effect on prices (a point that continues to be debated), that several factors have greatly limited the effectiveness of state regulation, particularly during its first decades of existence, is not seriously disputed.

100. Regulatory critic William Mosher characterized the effects of this limitation during the 1920s: "When one considers that the cost of initiating and carrying through a complaint which is contested by the companies may be anywhere from $20,000 to $150,000 or more, it becomes clear that few individuals and even few municipalities can afford this expense no matter how sincere their desire for an investigation. In view of the financial burden thus entailed, it is not surprising that people in many states are coming to believe that the public interest is not adequately safeguarded under public service commission regulation." See William Mosher et. al., *Electrical Utilities: The Crisis in Public Control* (New York: Harper & Brothers, 1929), 19–20.

101. The Fourteenth Amendment to the Constitution, forbidding the deprivation of property without due process of law, constitutes the fundamental legal basis for judicial intervention into regulatory matters. In its famous 1898 decision, *Smyth v. Ames,* the Supreme Court ruled that the Fourteenth Amendment prohibited regulatory agencies from setting a rate lower than that which would bring a fair return on the value of the property used. Rather than put forth a definite valuation formula, the Court suggested a number of factors that it believed relevant to the determination of fair value without stating what particular weight they should be given in any individual case. These included "original cost of construction, the amount and market value of its bonds and stocks, the present as compared with the original cost of construction, the probable earning capacity of the property under particular rates prescribed by statute, and the sum required to meet operating expenses." See 169 U.S. 546–47 L. Ed. 849. After 1898, courts sometimes used *Smyth v. Ames* as a basis to overturn regulatory decisions on the grounds that a factor of particular importance in a given case was not sufficiently taken into account. In general, courts emphasized the reproduction cost of the utility property (no matter how obsolescent) as the most important factor to be used in valuation. The threat of judicial intervention into the details of regulatory decision making only receded with the Hope Natural Gas case of 1944. In that case, the Supreme Court ruled that courts would accept the presumed validity of regulatory decisions so long as basic due process protections were afforded.

102. A Twentieth Century Fund report on the electrical utility industry summarized the opportunities for abuse as follows: "Subsidiary management and construction companies provided opportunities (which certain holding companies were not loath to take advantage of) to drain considerable sums from operating companies into the pockets of a few people who controlled the holding companies. Contracts with operating companies were usually secret, monopolistic, and outside the control of state commissions. The holding company, therefore, provided a means whereby the benefits of large-scale management could be diverted from stockholders and consumers to those in control. Furthermore, it enabled relatively few people to obtain control of vast properties." See Twentieth Century Fund, *Electric Power and Government Policy*, 34.

103. Interestingly, some members of the business community expressed concerns from quite early on that customer ownership campaigns might backfire as a public relations tool if unsound securities were marketed. At a 1923 meeting of the National Electric Light Association, for example, magazine editor B. C. Forbes warned that "nothing would more fatally hurt this whole important, vital, socially fundamental movement than a few bad, a few unsafe, a few unsound issues widely distributed in local communities." See B. C. Forbes, "America as a Nation of Investors," in *National Electric Light Association*, 226.

104. For a biting and entertaining contemporary exposé of utility industry propaganda drawn from documents compiled by the Federal Trade Commission, see Ernest Gruening, *The Public Pays: A Study of Power Propaganda* (New York: Vanguard Press, 1931).

105. Power Committee and Power Survey Research Staff, Twentieth Century Fund, *Electric Power and Government Policy*, 43.

106. The postwar history of the electric utility industry in the United States is exceedingly well documented. A quite good overview of the politics of utilities' promotional activities during the 1950s and 1960s can be found in Richard F. Hirsh, *Technology and Transformation in the American Electric Utility Industry* (Cambridge: Cambridge University Press, 1989), 47–56. See particularly the advertisement reproduced on pages 54 and 55 showing Betty Furness, Ronald Reagan, and Fran Allison touting the "All-Electric Home" and showing the "Live Better Electrically" slogan.

Notes to Chapter 4

1. *Factbook: Cable Statistics, 1993* (Washington, D.C.: Warren Publishing, 1993), F-4.

2. Richard B. Kielbowicz, *News in the Mail: The Press, Post Office, and Public Information, 1700–1860* (New York: Greenwood, 1989), 141–42.

3. Kielbowicz, *News in the Mail*, 34.

4. Ithiel de Sola Pool, *Technologies of Freedom* (Cambridge: Harvard University Press, 1983), 79.

5. U.S. Congress, Office of Technology Assessment, *Rural America at the Crossroads: Networking for the Future*, OTA–TCT–471 (Washington, D.C.: G.P.O., 1991), 65–97.

6. An 1832 report, for example, put the case against local rates for newspapers as follows: "A monopoly of influence in the large cities whose political atmosphere is not

always most congenial to a spirit of independence, will be the consequence. That freedom, that manliness of spirit, which has always characterized the great body of the common people of our country, and which constitutes the safeguard of our liberties, will gradually decline." See "Postage on Newspapers," May 19, 1832, in *American State Papers: Post Office*, volume on post office affairs, class VII, 346–48, as quoted in Kielbowicz, *News in the Mail*, 61. For insightful discussion of the controversies associated with distribution of abolitionist literature through the mails, see Richard R. John, *Spreading the News: The American Postal System from Franklin to Morse* (Cambridge: Harvard University Press, 1995), 257–83.

7. As Ithiel de Sola Pool has pointed out: "Despite the ritual praise given to free speech in civic rhetoric, the libertarian tenet of the First Amendment has never in the real world of politics had national consensus behind it, and certainly not at the beginning. In various opinion polls, only a minority of respondents support free speech for those whose views are anathema." There are always those, at times including the majority on the Supreme Court, who cannot conceive that the intent of the amendment is to deny to the government the power to prevent speech that seems patently vicious, harmful, or dangerous. See Pool, *Technologies of Freedom*, 56.

8. Pool, *Technologies of Freedom*, 259.

9. The decision was *Burstyn v. Wilson*, 343 U.S. 495 (1952). Even under this ruling, the court held that the rules for motion pictures could be different than for other forms of expression. Thus, while prohibition of prior restraint has long been a fundamental principle of First Amendment jurisprudence with respect to print, the court, in a narrow 5–4 decision, in 1961 upheld a Chicago law requiring pre-release review of motion pictures. The rationale for accepting the legitimacy of prior review was that "movies have so much greater power for evil by obscenity than the printed word." See Pool, *Technologies of Freedom*, 260.

10. As of 1880, Western Union owned 77 percent of the mileage of telegraph line in the United States and conveyed 92 percent of the messages. See Daniel J. Czitrom, *Media and the American Mind: From Morse to McLuhan* (Chapel Hill: University of North Carolina Press, 1982), 23.

11. For a classic late-nineteenth-century attack on privately owned telegraphs encompassing these themes, see Frank Parsons, *The Telegraph Monopoly* (Philadelphia: C .F. Taylor, 1899).

12. One critic made the case as follows: "The Western Union and a number of leading newspapers have formed a sort of double-star monopoly for mutual advantage and protection against competition. The understanding between the telegraph company and the press associations secures to the latter low rates and the power of excluding new papers from the field, and to the former a strong influence upon press dispatches, the support of the papers in such associations, and the exclusive right to transmit and sell market quotations." Parsons, *Telegraph Monopoly*, 85. See also Czitrom, *Media and the American Mind*, 25–26.

13. *Associated Press et al. v. United States*, 326 U.S. 20 (1945).

14. *Associated Press et. al. v. United States*, 48.

15. Hugh G. J. Aitken, *Syntony and Spark—The Origins of Radio* (Princeton: Princeton University Press, 1985), 21–26.

16. Aitken, *Syntony and Spark,* 202.

17. During the winter and spring of 1922, the number of stations licensed by the Commerce Department to broadcast on commercial wavelengths increased from eight to more than two hundred. By February of 1923, there were 576 stations licensed to broadcast. See William Peck Banning, *Commercial Broadcasting Pioneer: The WEAF Experiment, 1922–1926* (Cambridge: Harvard University Press, 1946), 131–37.

18. Susan J. Douglas, *Inventing American Broadcasting: 1899–1922* (Baltimore: Johns Hopkins University Press, 1987), 223.

19. For brief discussions of the major provisions of the act, see Czitrom, *Media and the American Mind,* 68 and Hampson Gary, "Regulation of Broadcasting in the United States," *Annals of the American Academy of Political and Social Science* 177 (January 1935): 16.

20. Hoover described the purposes of the conferences as follows: "It is . . . the purpose of this conference to enable listeners, broadcasters, manufacturers, marine and other services to agree among themselves as to the manner in which radio traffic rules may be determined. . . this may be called an experiment in industrial self-government." See Herbert Hoover, "Opening Address," in *Recommendations for Regulation of Radio Adopted by the Third National Radio Conference* (Washington, D.C.: G.P.O., 1924), 2. For a broader discussion of Hoover's "associative vision," see Ellis W. Hawley, *The Great War and the Search for a Modern Order: A History of the American People and Their Institutions, 1917–1933,* 2d ed. (New York: St. Martin's, 1992), 83–96.

21. Hoover, "Opening Address," 2.

22. Under a 1923 court ruling, the Secretary of Commerce could exercise discretion in the assignment of wavelengths to broadcasters but had no authority to deny a license to otherwise qualified applicants. Even this limited authority vanished in 1926 with a federal district court ruling in April and an opinion by the United States attorney general in July that Hoover did not have authority under the 1912 act to enforce wavelength allocations or agreements to time share. See Frank J. Kahn, ed., *Documents of American Broadcasting,* 3d ed. (Englewood Cliffs, N. J.: Prentice-Hall, 1978), 22 and William J. Donovan to Herbert Hoover, July 8, 1926, cited in Kahn's work, 23–26.

23. AT&T press release, February 11, 1922, as excerpted in Banning, *Commercial Broadcasting Pioneer,* 68.

24. An internal telephone company analysis from April of 1922 articulated the issue thus: "If there continues to be an insistent demand for broadcasting we feel rather sure that ultimately there will not be any particular advantage accruing to anyone by virtue of the fact that he owns a broadcasting station, but that facilities for broadcasting will be provided through some common agency and the public will be interested in the subject matter which is broadcasted and not whether the particular party broadcasting owns and operates his own equipment." Operation B, preliminary bulletin, "Radio Telephone Broadcasting," as excerpted in Banning, *Commercial Broadcasting Pioneer,* 75.

25. In a public announcement issued on February 11, 1922, the telephone company envisioned its role in broadcasting as follows: "The American Telephone and Telegraph

Company will provide not programs of its own, but provide the channels through which anyone with whom it makes a contract can send out their own programs. Just as the company leases its long distance wire facilities for the use of newspapers, banks and other concerns, so it will lease its radio telephone facilities and will not provide the matter which is sent out from this station." See AT&T press release, February 11, 1922, as excerpted in Banning, *Commercial Broadcasting Pioneer*, 68.

26. Banning, *Commercial Broadcasting Pioneer*, 85.

27. Banning, *Commercial Broadcasting Pioneer*, 154.

28. A 1924 public statement by the management of station WHN brought these themes together:

> Broadcasting to them [AT&T] is a commercial proposition and, if carried out as they plan, a monopoly would be established in radio broadcasting. We plan to combat this action because radio is an important blessing to the public and it would be entirely wrong to let one company control the religious and educational entertainment of the nation.
> Radio must remain free and an open field for all.
> If the American Telephone & Telegraph company wins this fight, it will mean that ultimately it will affect receiving sets and people will not be allowed to build their own sets. It would mean that this company would not only control actual broadcasting, but would also control receiving, as it would force listeners to rent sets, as is the case of the telephone.

Statement by WHN official, as quoted in *Minneapolis Tribune*, March 2, 1924, as excerpted in Banning, *Commercial Broadcasting Pioneer*, 204.

29. Susan Smuylan, *Selling Radio: The Commercialization of American Broadcasting, 1920–1934* (Washington, D.C.: Smithsonian Institution Press, 1994), 68–69. A 1922 editorial in the *Radio Dealer* criticized AT&T's "toll broadcasting" idea: "when it comes to monopolizing the air for mercenary advertising purposes, a real man sized vocal rebellion can be expected. . . . These wise would-be radio advertising monopolists are on the wrong end of a wonderful idea." *Radio Dealer* 1, no. 1, (1922): 30, as excerpted in Banning, *Commercial Broadcasting Pioneer*, 69. A 1926 committee report at the Fourth National Radio Conference expressed fears that advertising might ultimately harm the broadcasting and radio industry:

> It was the consensus of opinion that both direct and mixed advertising were objectionable to the listening public. In fact, indirect advertising could be made detrimental to the interests of both the public and the broadcasting station.
> Advertising to achieve its best results must create the good will of those to whom it is addressed. Hence the first requisite in the successful operation of any broadcasting station in which the excellence of programs depends largely upon the support of the advertiser is the presentation of the material transmitted in such a manner that it may appeal to the majority of the listening public.

"Committee No. 2: Advertising and Publicity," in *Proceedings of the Fourth National Radio Conference and Recommendations for Regulation of Radio* (Washington, D.C.: G.P.O., 1925), 18.

30. The events leading to the founding of the station represented a literal coming together of amateur activities and corporate hopes to profit by means of developing new markets for radio equipment. For his own pleasure, radio hobbyist and Westinghouse engineer Frank Conrad had been playing phonograph records over the air even before the United States entered World War I in 1917. After the war, he resumed his broadcasts and in May of 1920, Pittsburgh newspapers began to publicize them. By September, Hornes Department Store was running advertisements describing Conrad's radio concerts and offering for sale equipment that could receive this novel form of entertainment. The advertisements inspired Westinghouse vice president Harry P. Davis to establish station KDKA as a means to promote the sale of radio equipment now that wartime demand had slackened off. To receive the broadcasts, Westinghouse marketed its first civilian receiver, the Aeriola Jr. in 1921. See Steven Lubar, *InfoCulture: The Smithsonian Book of Information Age Inventions* (Boston: Houghton Mifflin, 1993), 214.

31. *The Radio Act of 1927*, Public Law 632, 69th Cong., (February 23, 1927), in Frank J. Kahn, *Documents of American Broadcasting* (Englewood Cliffs, N. J.: Prentice-Hall, 1978), 32–48.

32. Douglas, *Inventing American Broadcasting*, 305. See also Smulyan, *Selling Radio*, 12.

33. Waldemar Kaempffert, "The Social Destiny of Radio," *Forum* 71 (June 1924): 771–72, quoted in Douglas, *Inventing American Broadcasting*, 306.

34. Jacob Murray Edelman, "The Licensing of Radio Services in the United States: A Study in Administrative Formulation of Policy" (abstract of thesis, University of Illinois, 1948), 4. See also Smulyan, *Selling Radio*, 144.

35. Lubar, *InfoCulture*, 227.

36. Erik Barnouw, *The Golden Web: A History of Broadcasting in the United States, Volume II—1933 to 1953* (New York: Oxford University Press, 1968): 16–17.

37. Of the fifty-two full-time clear channel stations in the United States in 1938, fifty were NBC or CBS affiliates. See Federal Communications Commission, *Report on Chain Broadcasting*, commission order no. 37, docket no. 5060 (May 1941), 31.

38. James Baughman, *The Republic of Mass Culture: Journalism, Filmmaking, and Broadcasting in America Since 1941* (Baltimore: Johns Hopkins University Press, 1992), 143.

39. Hoover, "Opening Address," 4.

40. Senate Resolution 129 (January 12, 1932), as excerpted in Federal Communications Commission, *Public Service Responsibility of Broadcast Licensees* (March 7, 1946), 41–42. See also Smulyan, *Selling Radio*, 212.

41. "In the Matter of the Application of Great Lakes Broadcasting Co.," FRC docket no. 4900, *Third Annual Report of the Federal Radio Commission* (1929), in Kahn, *Documents of American Broadcasting*, 59–60.

42. "Application of Great Lakes Broadcasting," 59–60.

43. For a cogent statement of this point of view written during the mid-1930s, see Herman S. Hettinger, "Broadcasting in the United States," *Annals of the American Academy of Political and Social Science* 177 (January 1935): 11.

44. Announcement of Federal Radio Commission, August 23, 1928, as excerpted in Federal Communications Commission, *Public Service Responsibility of Broadcast Licensees*,

41. See also Second *Annual Report of the Federal Radio Commission* (1928) in Kahn, *Documents of American Broadcasting*, 53.

45. The informational problems were severe. According to Barnouw, the FCC

had to exercise its life-or-death authority in a near vacuum.

Thin stands of evidence were available. One consisted of complaints, which sometimes assumed unwarranted importance. . . . An innocuous schedule could mean prompt renewal. A provocative one could bring delays. . . .

Another strand was provided by questionnaires. . . . The station had to report programming time devoted to various categories, such as "entertainment," "educational," "religious," "agricultural," "fraternal." . . .

The questionnaires—even with truthful answers—produced deceptions and obfuscations. . . . An "entertainment" item could be a thing of genius or trash. Formsmanship apparently required items under "educational," "religious," "agricultural," "fraternal," which were considered license insurance but could also be works of substance or trash.

See Erik Barnouw, *The Golden Web: A History of Broadcasting in the United States*, vol. 2 (New York: Oxford University Press, 1968), 30.

46. Justice White's opinion in the *Red Lion* case decided in 1969 articulates this logic as follows: "As far as the First Amendment is concerned those who are licensed stand no better than those to whom licenses are refused. A license permits broadcasting, but the licensee has no constitutional right to be the one who holds the license or to monopolize a radio frequency to the exclusion of his fellow citizens. There is nothing in the First Amendment which prevents the Government from requiring a licensee to share his frequency with others and to conduct himself as a proxy or fiduciary with obligations to present those views and voices which are representative of his community and which would otherwise, by necessity, be barred from the airwaves." See *Red Lion Broadcasting Co., Inc., et al. v. Federal Communications Commission et al.*, 395 U.S. 367 (June 9, 1969), as excerpted in Kahn, *Documents of American Broadcasting*, 395.

47. The FCC justified the decision as follows:

The United States has rejected government ownership of broadcasting stations, believing that the power inherent in control over broadcasting is too great and too dangerous to the maintenance of free institutions to permit its exercise by one body, even though elected by or responsible to the whole people. But in avoiding the concentration of power over radio broadcasting in the hands of government, we must not fall into an even more dangerous pitfall: the concentration of that power in the hands of self-perpetuating management groups.

Under any system of broadcasting, someone must decide what a station will put on the air and what it will not. Decentralization of this power is the best protection against its abuse. We cannot permit the protection which decentralization affords to be destroyed by the gravitation of control over two major networks into one set of hands.

See Federal Communications Commission, *Report on Chain Broadcasting*, 72.

48. Baughman, *Republic of Mass Culture*, 67.

49. Lubar, *InfoCulture*, 237.

50. This account is taken from Mary Alice Mayer Phillips, *CATV: A History of Com-*

munity Antenna Television (Evanston: Northwestern University Press, 1972), 7–10. According to other accounts, the first commercial cable television system was not built in Mahoney City but in the nearby town of Lansford. See, for example, Ralph Lee Smith, *The Wired Nation* (New York: Harper & Row, 1972), 3–4.

51. *Factbook: Cable Statistics, 1993,* F-2.

52. *Factbook: Cable Statistics, 1993,* F-2–F-4.

53. No apologist for broadcast television in its treatment of minority concerns, Jessie Jackson expressed this point of view in 1976 congressional testimony: "Shall we make the present networks who are using our airwaves more accountable—or should we, the public, pay for a new system? We sustain the former position on this issue. . . . Our opposition to pay cable grows out of the fact that a larger listening audience including millions of poor families would be cut off from good TV programming by this system of taxation since they could not afford to pay." Statement of Rev. Jesse Jackson, National President, Operation PUSH, U.S. House, *Cable Television Regulation Oversight: Hearings before the Subcommittee on Communications of the Committee on Interstate and Foreign Commerce,* 94th Cong., (1976), serial no. 94–138, pt. 2: 730–31.

54. A 1958 report framed the issue as follows: "A CATV system cannot cater to local preferences in programming, cannot serve local merchants, cannot provide a local news and weather service, cannot promote local civic and charitable enterprises, and cannot furnish a forum for discussion of local problems. . . . Whereas the network programming of the distant stations repeated is normally popular everywhere, the transportation of the local programming carried by those stations into different communities —and often into different States—results in a parody on local service." See U.S. FCC, *The Television Inquiry: The Problem of Television Service for Smaller Communities,* prepared for the Senate Committee on Interstate and Foreign Commerce by Kenneth A. Cox (Washington, D.C.: G.P.O., 1959), as excerpted in Phillips, *CATV,* 53–54.

55. "Carter Mountain Transmission Corp.," 32 *FCC,* 459 (1962). For a brief discussion of the FCC decision and related court rulings, see Phillips, *CATV,* 57–59.

56. Phillips, *CATV,* 87.

57. Morton I. Hamburg, *All about Cable: Legal and Business Aspects of Pay Television* (New York: Law Journal Seminars Press, 1981), 5-4 to 5-9.

58. With cable television, the Sloan Commission report maintained, "A whole new range of possibilities suddenly appears. The analogy is not to conventional television, but the printing press. . . . Like the press it can be directed toward a wide variety of uses. . . . Along another dimension, the press can direct itself to a wide variety of audiences. . . . The television of abundance has the same characteristic." Report of the Sloan Commission on Cable Television, *On the Cable* (New York: McGraw-Hill, 1971), 42–44.

59. Deirdre Boyle, *Return of Guerrilla Television: A TVTV Retrospective,* Video Feature Program Notes (New York: International Center for Photography, 1986), as cited by Ralph Engleman, "The Origins of Public Access Cable Television: 1966–1972," *Journalism Monographs* (October 1990): 31.

60. Pool, *Technologies of Freedom,* 172.

61. One survey of cable television systems found that of franchises granted prior to

1964, about two-thirds contained no provisions regarding quality of service. More than eight out of ten contained no provisions about minimum channels to be furnished to consumers. More than half contained no provisions permitting the municipality to regulate consumer charges. Fewer than one out of ten franchises required the franchisee to offer service to all homes in a franchised area. See Martin H. Seiden, *Cable Television U.S.A.: An Analysis of Government Policy* (New York: Praeger, 1972), 68–77.

62. Seiden, *Cable Television U.S.A.*, 68–77.

63. Contemporary evidence as to the exact date that Holert began service is lacking. It is stated that service by Holert did begin in 1949, however, in a letter from Slade Gordon to Seattle Board of Public Works, "Re: CATV Application—Seattle Cablevision Inc.," November 25, 1966.

64. Seattle City Council, *CATV Advisory Committee Report* (December 1, 1972), 2.

65. "Council Faces T.V. Cable Tangle," *Seattle Times*, August 13, 1974.

66. City of Seattle, Ordinance 105427, *An Ordinance Relating to Cable Communications; Establishing the Office of Cable Communications and Providing for the Granting and Renewal of Franchises and the Terms and Conditions Thereof* (March 1976).

67. Frank Greif, *Report and Recommendations, Cable Communications Franchise for the Central Franchise District* (April 1982), 55–56.

68. Larry Wright, Seattle City Council memorandum in *Central District Cable TV Franchise—Staff Recommendation; Summary Chart . . .* (September 20, 1982).

69. Personal interview by the author with Seattle Cable Television administrator Debra Lewis and "Public Access Programming Is a TV Secret Kept Too Well," *Seattle Times*, December 9, 1983.

70. "Parents Protest Change: Viacom Hearings May Reopen," *Seattle Times*, August 11, 1982.

71. City of Pittsburgh, Cable Communications System, *Request for Proposals* (October 11 1979).

72. QUBE promotional material, quoted in Everett M. Rogers, *Communication Technology: The New Media in Society* (New York: Free Press, 1986), 62.

73. Rogers, *Communication Technology*, 62–64.

74. *Pittsburgh Post Gazette*, February 11, 1980. See also Herb Stein, "The Big Turn On," *Pittsburgh Magazine*, April 1980.

75. Harvey Adams, who headed the city's local NAACP affiliate, for example, held a five-year, fifty thousand dollar per annum retainer from Warner with provision for renewal in the event the company won the franchise. See Tom O'Boyle, "Pay TV: Adams Rewarded for Warner Cable Contract," *Pittsburgh Post Gazette*, May 26, 1981.

76. Jon Schmitz and Barbara Bolsopple, "Cable TV Rate Hikes Face Static in City Council," *Pittsburgh Press*, January 5, 1983. See also Albert Neri, "Warner TV: Millions in Red, Backs Rate Rise," *Pittsburgh Post Gazette*, March 22, 1983.

77. Jon Schmitz, "City's Cable Exec Says Rate Hike Reasonable," *Pittsburgh Press*, May 3, 1983.

78. Albert Neri, "City OKs Cable TV Rate Hikes," *Pittsburgh Post Gazette*, June 21, 1983.

79. William Russell Campbell, "Cable Television: Franchising and Refranchising in Three Texas Cities" (master's thesis, University of Texas, 1981), 70–87.

80. Campbell, "Cable Television," 70–87.

81. Todd Mason, "Warner Amex in Dallas: The Trials of City Franchises," *Business Week,* July 22, 1985, 127.

82. Robert Welch, as quoted in Cable Television Information Center, *Cable Reports* (October 1984), 2.

83. *Report of the Mayor's Cable Television Review Commission* (Boston: October 1979), 37.

84. Kevin H. White, Mayor, *Issuing Authority Report* (Boston: February 1981), ii–iii.

85. City of Boston, Final Cable Television License Granted to Cablevision of Boston, (December 15, 1982).

86. City of Boston, Office of Cable Communications, *1985 Performance Evaluation Report: Cablevision of Boston* (April 4, 1986), 12.

87. City of Boston, Final Cable Television License Granted to Cablevision of Boston, sec. 6.4.

88. City of Boston, Office of Cable Communications, *1985 Performance Evaluation,* 14.

89. Charles Dolan, quoted in *Boston Globe,* September 13, 1985.

90. Mayor Flynn, quoted in *Boston Globe,* December 6, 1984.

91. For insight into the perspectives of Boston cable office officials, I am indebted to personal interviews with Thomas P. Cohan, director, and Peter J. Epstein, counsel, conducted during the spring of 1986.

92. "Cablevision Gives Low-Income Discount as Part of New Boston Franchise Agreement," *Broadcasting,* September 26, 1988, 73.

93. As of 1988, according to economist Mark Zupin, "of the 3,516 refranchising decisions made by cities to date, only seven cities have not renewed an incumbent operator." See Mark Zupin, "Cable Franchise Renewals: Do Incumbent Firms Behave Opportunistically?" *Rand Journal of Economics* (winter 1989): 477.

94. Mark Zupin, "The Efficacy of Franchise Bidding Schemes in the Case of Cable Television: Some Systematic Evidence," *Journal of Law and Economics* (October 1989): 421–22.

95. *Home Box Office, Inc. v. FCC,* 185 U.S.App. DC 142; 566 F. 2nd 9 (1997).

96. *F.C.C. v. Midwest Video,* 440 U.S. 689 (1979). This decision is often cited as *Midwest Video II.*

97. *Associated Press et al. v. United States,* 326 U.S. 20 (1945).

98. *Red Lion Broadcasting Co. v. FCC,* 395 U.S. 367, 387, 392 (1969).

99. *Red Lion v. FCC,* 389.

100. *Red Lion v. FCC,* 389.

101. *Miami Herald Publishing Co. v. Tornillo,* 418 U.S. 241, 254 (1973).

102. For a book-length statement of this position, see George H. Shapiro, Philip B. Kurland, and James P. Mercurio, *"Cablespeech": The Case for First Amendment Protection* (New York: Law & Business, Inc., 1983).

103. *City of Los Angeles v. Preferred Communications, Inc.,* 476 U.S. 494, 495 (1986).

104. *City of Los Angeles v. Preferred Communications, Inc.,* 476 U.S. 488, 106 S. Ct. 2034,

90 L. Ed. 2d 480 (1986) as discussed in Charles D. Ferris, Frank W. Lloyd, and Thomas J. Casey, *Cable Television Law* (New York: Matthew Bender, 1993), 13–40.

105. Charles D. Ferris, Frank W. Lloyd, and Thomas J. Casey, *Cable Television Law* (New York: Matthew Bender, 1994), 13–54.

106. 678 F. Supp. 734 (E.D. Ill. 1988), aff'd, 879 F. 2d 1540 (7th Cir. 1989), as discussed in Ferris, Lloyd, and Casey, *Cable Television Law* (1993), 13–151.

107. Ferris, Lloyd, and Casey, *Cable Television Law* (1994), 13–57.

108. *Group W Cable, Inc. v. City of Santa Cruz* , 669 F. Supp. 954 (N.D. Cal. 1987), as discussed in Ferris, Lloyd, and Casey, *Cable Television Law* (1993), 13–148.

109. Ferris, Lloyd, and Casey, *Cable Television Law* (1993), 13–51. The case referred to is *Cox Cable Communications v. United States,* Civ. A. 86–79–1 MAC (DF), 1991.

110. Mark Robichaux, "Captive Audience," *Wall Street Journal*, September 24, 1992.

111. Statement of Thomas E. Wheeler, President, National Cable Television Association, U.S. Senate, *Hearings before the Subcommittee on Communications, Committee on Commerce, Science, and Transportation, "Cable Communications Act of 1983,"* 98–26 (February 1983): 132.

112. S. Rpt. 98–67 on S. 66, *Cable Telecommunications Act of 1983*, April 27, 1983 (Washington, D.C.: G.P.O. 1983), 5.

113. Statement of Thomas E. Wheeler, 126.

114. Statement of Mountain States Legal Foundation, U.S. Senate, *Hearings before the Subcommittee on Communications, Committee on Commerce, Science, and Transportation, "Cable Communications Act of 1983,* 210.

115. S. Rpt. 98–67, 2–3.

116. *Cable Communications Policy Act of 1984,* sec. 623, 47 U.S.C. 543.

117. Paul Kagan Associates, Inc., *The Cable TV Financial Databook* (June 1993), 7–8, as reprinted in National Cable Television Association, *Cable Television Developments* (April 1994), 6-A.

118. National Cable Television Association, *Cable Television Developments*, 8-A.

119. National Cable Television Association, *Cable Television Developments*, 1-A.

120. National Cable Television Association, *Cable Television Developments*, 11-A.

121. William Dutton, Jay G. Blumler, Kenneth L. Kraemer, "Continuity and Change in Conceptions of the Wired City," in *Wired Cities: Shaping the Future of Communications* (Boston: G. K. Hall, 1987), 4–5.

Notes to Chapter 5

1. Anon., "Boston to the Rescue!!" 1845 broadside in the archives of the Massachusetts Historical Society, Boston, Massachusetts.

2. William Kahrl, *Water and Power: The Conflict over Los Angeles' Water Supply in the Owens Valley* (Berkeley: University of California Press, 1982), 173.

3. Kahrl, *Water and Power,* 173.

4. Jack Hirshleifer, James De Haven, and Jerome W. Milliman, *Water Supply: Economics, Technology, and Policy* (Chicago: University of Chicago Press, 1960), 347. Writing

during the 1980s, Kenneth Frederick makes a similar point in more tempered language: "'Traditionally, water resource development has focused on managing supplies to meet off-stream demands. Withdrawals have been projected to grow roughly in step with population and economic growth, and projected levels of water use have acquired the status of requirements, of virtual necessities to be provided regardless of cost. . . . The traditional, structural approach to preventing and solving water problems may have approximated an efficient strategy when the direct costs of providing reliable supplies were low and streamflows were sufficient to meet all demands. . . . Unfortunately, such conditions no longer characterize the water situation in most of the nation. The total costs of increasing off-stream supplies are generally high and likely to exceed the value of many water uses." See Kenneth D. Frederick, "Overview," in Kenneth D. Frederick and Dianna C. Gibbons, eds., *Scarce Water and Institutional Change* (Washington, D.C.: Resources for the Future, 1986), 2.

5. Kahrl, *Water and Power,* 442–43.

6. An essay by Garrett De Bell in *The Environmental Handbook*, prepared for the First National Environmental Teach-In held in 1970, for example, put the case in terms that would have been inconceivable twenty or thirty years before: "All power pollutes. Each of the major forms of power generation does its own kind of harm to the environment. Fossil fuels—coal and oil— produce smoke and sulfur dioxide. . . . Hydroelectric power requires dams that cover up land, spoil wild rivers, increase water loss by evaporation, and eventually produce valleys full of silt. Nuclear power plants produce thermal and radioactive pollution and introduce the probability of disaster. . . . These effects can no longer be ignored, but must be directly confronted. *The perpetually accelerating expansion of power output is not necessary.*" Garrett De Bell, "Energy," in Garrett De Bell, ed., *The Environmental Handbook* (New York: Ballantine, 1970), 66.

7. Richard F. Hirsh, *Technology and Transformation in the American Electric Utility Industry* (Cambridge: Cambridge University Press, 1989), 4.

8. Overall during the 1960s and 1970s, larger generating units (greater than 600 MW) were substantially less reliable than their smaller counterparts, greatly raising costs of operation. According to historian Richard Hirsh: "Data collected between 1960 and 1972 indicated that fossil-fueled units in the United States had a forced outage rate . . . as much as five times greater for units larger than 600 MW than for units in the 100 MW range. Later data showed the same effect: between 1972 and 1976, units larger than 800 MW had been forced out of service more than 16% of the time. More modestly sized machines, those between 200 and 300 MW, had forced outage rates less than 6%. . . . Consolidated Edison's experience with its 1,000 megawatt Big-Allis turbo generator unit was particularly notorious. Installed in 1965, the unit cost 30% less per kilowatt of capacity than the more common 400 Megawatt units of the day. Over the years 1968 through 1971, however, the unit was repeatedly forced out of service because of a whole series of operating glitches. Resulting costs to the utility from having to purchase power and to rely on expensive peaking units far exceeded any of the original savings." See Hirsh, *Technology and Transformation,* 96. Discussions of reliability problems in newer and

larger generating units can also be found in the Federal Power Commission, *The 1970 National Power Survey*, part 1 (Washington, D.C.: G.P.O, 1971), 1–5–10, 1–5–11, 1–16–9.

9. Hirsh, *Technology and Transformation*, 111.

10. Richard H. K. Vietor, *Energy Policy in America since 1945: A Study of Business-Government Relations* (Cambridge: Cambridge University Press, 1984), 193.

11. As a result of these price increases, the average price per barrel of the oil burned by electric utilities went from $2.45 in 1970 to $12.38 in 1975 and $25.91 in 1980. Still abundant domestically, coal also increased in price during the 1970s but at a far less rapid rate. Average price per ton of coal burned by electric utilities increased from $7.08 to $30.04 over the course of the same period. See *Moody's Public Utility Manual, 1992*, vol. 1 (New York: Moody's Investors Service, 1992), 34.

12. According to Charles Komanoff, capacity factors for nuclear plants in the United States of 400 to 800 megawatts was 66 percent through 1980, while for plants of over 800 megawatts the capacity factor was 54 percent. See Charles Komanoff, *Power Plant Cost Escalation: Nuclear and Coal Capital Costs, Regulation, and Economics* (New York: Van Nostrand Reinhold, 1981), 249.

13. James Morone and Edward Woodhouse, *The Demise of Nuclear Energy? Lessons for Democratic Control of Technology* (New Haven: Yale University Press, 1989), 80.

14. Joseph Morone and Edward Woodhouse describe the problem as follows: "The shift to prevention expanded the realm of debate almost infinitely. Now it became necessary to envision all the possible events and sequences of events, consequences, and consequences of consequences that could plausibly lead to a meltdown. These range from operator error to tornadoes and floods, acts of terrorism, power failures, material failures, component failures, emergency system failures, maintenance errors, construction errors—the list is virtually endless. And the seemingly endless nature of the list was precisely the problem. The reliance on prevention created a regulatory, political, and analytical morass; it put nuclear decision makers in the position of having to demonstrate that they had anticipated everything that could go wrong in a reactor." See Morone and Woodhouse, *Demise of Nuclear Energy?* 88–89.

15. When the Long Island Lighting Company announced plans to build a nuclear power plant at Shoreham in 1965, for example, the company estimated that the project would cost sixty-five to seventy-five million dollars. Never actually operated because of opposition by local and state political leaders, more than $5.5 billion had been spent on the facility as of 1990. Although the Shoreham experience was unique and particularly horrific in some ways, cost increases experienced in building other nuclear power plants during the period were of a similar order of magnitude. For a detailed account, see David P. McCaffrey, *The Politics of Nuclear Power: A History of the Shoreham Nuclear Power Plant* (Dordrecht: Kluwer Academic Publishers, 1991).

16. While the years 1970 through 1980 saw the gross national product of the United States increasing at an average rate of just less than 3 percent per year, consumption of all forms of energy remained virtually flat. In this context, electricity did continue to increase its market share as a proportion of total delivered energy, but resulting growth in con-

sumption was less than half that of previous decades. See *Moody's Public Utility Manual,* 1992, A21–A23. For discussions of these trends, written during the early 1980s, see the U.S. Department of Energy's Report of the Electricity Policy Project, *The Future of Electric Power in America: Economic Supply for Economic Growth* (Washington, D.C.: 1983), 3–17 and Scott Fenn, *America's Electric Utilities: Under Siege and in Transition* (New York: Praeger, 1984), 9. For a more recent discussion of overstated industry demand forecasts and actual trends, see the testimony of Peter D. Blair, Program Manager, Energy and Materials, Office of Technology Assessment, U.S. House, *National Energy Strategy (Part 1): Hearings before the Subcommittee on Energy and Power of the Committee on Energy and Commerce,* 102d Cong., 1st sess. (1991), serial no. 102–29: 462.

17. During the late 1980s in New England, for example, the Conservation Law Foundation began to work with large privately owned utilities to develop energy efficiency programs. According to a senior attorney for the CLF, Armand Cohen, the effort, "in which the utilities are funding CLF's key energy experts to work and negotiate with company staffs, evolved as a sensible alternative to endless litigation over how much energy efficiency is available to meet New England's electric needs and avert unnecessary environmental damage." See the testimony of Armand Cohen, Senior Attorney for the Conservation Law Foundation, U.S. Senate, *National Energy Policy Act of 1989: Hearings before the Committee on Energy and Natural Resources,* 101st Cong., 1st sess. (1989), pt. 2: 389.

18. In California, for example, regulations adopted during the late 1980s permitted utilities to recover through rate increases 15 percent of the savings on average electric bills realized through demand management initiatives. In other states, regulators began to permit utilities to incorporate subsidies for demand reduction into the rate base or to treat the expenses for such programs as operating costs. See Paul Klebnikov, "Demand Siders," *Forbes* (October 26, 1992): 134.

19. Alex Radin, executive director of the American Public Power Association for more than three decades after World War II, described some aspects of this coming together in a 1991 article:

> The emergence of environmental concerns . . . brought some public power groups in closer contact, and alliance, with private power companies because of a perceived commonalty of interests. . . . In the seventies and eighties . . . the establishment of joint action agencies by local public power systems . . . permitted publicly owned utilities to build facilities jointly, or to own generation and/or transmission facilities, with private power companies.
>
> At first, many private power companies opposed creation of these agencies, fearing that they would take away their wholesale customers and provide a source of low cost wholesale power, which would facilitate the creation of new municipal utilities. However as private power companies began to experience difficulty in financing large, new facilities, many of them welcomed the creation of joint-action agencies as a way of infusing capital and bailing them out of financial problems.

Other examples of cooperation cited by Radin included membership in industry-wide organizations such as the Electric Power Research Institute, established in 1971, and the development of common positions concerning clean air legislation. See Alex Radin, "Is Public Power Still Relevant?" *Public Utilities Fortnightly* (March 1, 1991): 116–17.

20. For running accounts, see articles in the *Cleveland Plain Dealer* from August 21, 1991, September 8, 1991, November 6 and November 7, 1991, December 11, 1991, April 28, 1993, and April 30, 1993. Similar fights took place elsewhere in Ohio during these years. In northwestern Ohio, for example, the small city of Clyde actually did begin operation of its own electric utility in 1990 after a twenty-five year franchise held by Toledo Edison expired. Here, too, the city's largest business and electricity consumer, Whirlpool Appliance, strongly supported the move.

21. *Electric Power and Government Policy* (New York: Twentieth Century Fund, 1948), 691.

22. Stephen G. Breyer and Paul W. Macavoy, *Energy Regulation by the Federal Power Commission* (Washington, D.C.: Brookings Institution, 1974), 108.

23. Edward Kahn, *Electric Utility Planning and Regulation* (Washington, D.C.: American Council for an Energy-Efficient Economy, 1988), 201.

24. For an account of such a case involving the Houston Lighting and Power Company written from the perspective of utility executives, see Don D. Jordan, "The Hidden Threat," *Public Utilities Fortnightly* (March 15, 1991): 28–29. Houston Lighting and Power's experience was also discussed by Sherwood H. Smith, Jr., chairman of the Electric Reliability Coalition, in testimony for the House Energy and Power Subcommittee hearing on the Public Utility Holding Company Act and Transmission Access, U.S. House, *National Energy Strategy (Part 4): Hearings before the Subcommittee on Energy and Power of the Committee on Energy and Commerce,* 102d Cong., 1st sess., H.R. 1301, H.R. 1543, and H.R. 2224 (May 1, 1991, May 2, 1991, and June 26, 1991), serial no. 102–60: 172.

25. Arthur H. Rosenfeld and David Hafemeister, "Energy-Efficient Buildings," *Scientific American* (April 1988): 84.

26. Testimony of Armand Cohen on behalf of the Conservation Law Foundation of New England, U.S. Senate, *National Energy Policy Act of 1989: Hearings before the Committee on Energy and Natural Resources,* 101st Cong., 1st sess., serial no. 101–25, pt. 2: 393–95.

27. David Stiff, "Some Utilities' Plans to Cut Energy Use Cost More and Save Less than Projected," *Wall Street Journal,* May 27, 1993.

28. Douglas A. Houston, "A Losing Proposition for Consumers," *Public Utilities Fortnightly* (May 1, 1993): 19.

29. Statement of The Alliance for Fair Competition on Demand Side Management Provisions, U.S. House, *National Energy Strategy (Part 5)* and *National Energy Strategy (Part 1): Hearings before the Subcommittee on Energy and Power of the Committee on Energy and Commerce,* 102d Cong., 1st sess., H.R. 776 (1991), serial no. 102–171: 434–35.

30. Robert A. Dahl, "Atomic Energy and the Democratic Process," *Annals of the American Academy of Political and Social Science* 290 (November 1953): 1–2.

31. Amory Lovins made the case during the mid-1970s as follows: "discouraging nuclear violence and coercion requires some abrogation of civil liberties; guarding long-lived wastes against geological or social contingencies implies some form of hierarchical

social rigidity or homogeneity to insulate the technological priesthood from social turbulence; and making political decisions about nuclear hazards that are compulsory, remote from social experience, disputed, unknown, or unknowable may tempt governments to bypass democratic decision in favor of elitist technocracy." See Amory B. Lovins, *Soft Energy Paths: Toward a Durable Peace* (New York: Harper, 1977), 56. In a famous essay first published in 1972 in the journal *Science*, physicist and nuclear power advocate Alvin Weinberg framed the issue in more positive terms: "We nuclear people have made a Faustian bargain with society. On the one hand, we offer—in the catalytic nuclear burner —an inexhaustible source of energy. . . . But the price that we demand for this magical energy source is both a vigilance and a longevity of our social institutions that we are quite unaccustomed to." See Alvin M. Weinberg, "Social Institutions and Nuclear Energy," in *Nuclear Reactions: Science and Trans-Science* (New York: American Institute of Physics, 1992): 234.

32. Gary Coates, ed., *Resettling America: Energy, Ecology, and Community* (Andover: Brick House Publishing, 1981). The picture of the windmill can be found on page 273.

33. Steven Lubar, *InfoCulture, The Smithsonian Book of Information Age Inventions* (Boston: Houghton-Mifflin, 1993), 138.

34. Lubar, *InfoCulture*, 313.

35. Wilson Dizard, *Old Media, New Media: Mass Communications in the Information Age* (New York: Longman, 1994), 112. See also Herb Brody, "Information Highway: The Home Front," *Technology Review* (August/September 1993): 35.

36. Richard Zoglin, "Cable Gets Dished," *Time* (October 23, 1994). See also Dawn Stover, "Little Dish TV," *Popular Science* (January 1995): 60–64, 84.

37. Brody, "Information Highway," 34.

38. Charles D. Ferris, Frank W. Lloyd, and Howard J. A. Symons, *Cable Television Law Special Supplement: Cable Television Consumer Protection and Competition Act of 1992* (New York: Matthew Bender, 1982), 1.

39. *Cable Television Consumer Protection and Competition Act of 1992*, 106 Stat. 1460, 1494–97.

40. Kevin Many, "Time Warner Shows Off TV of Future," *USA Today*, December 15, 1994.

41. Ed McCracken, chairman of Silicon Graphics, as quoted in John Markoff, "I Wonder What's on the PC Tonight," *New York Times*, May 8, 1994.

42. George Gilder, *Life after Television*, rev. ed. (New York: W.W. Norton, 1994), 46.

43. Gilder, *Life after Television*, 61–62.

44. Howard Rheingold, *The Virtual Community: Homesteading on the Electronic Frontier* (Reading: Addison-Wesley, 1993), 4–5.

45. Rheingold, *The Virtual Community*, 14–15.

46. Don R. Le Duc, *Beyond Broadcasting: Patterns in Policy and Law* (New York: Longman, 1987), 189.

47. Edward Tenner, "Learning from the Net," *Wilson Quarterly* (summer 1994): 21.

References

Archives and Document Collections

Baker Library, Harvard Business School.

Bancroft Library, University of California at Berkeley.

Boston City Council Offices.

Carnegie Library, Pennsylvania Room, Pittsburgh.

Massachusetts Community Antenna Television Commission.

Massachusetts Historical Society, Boston.

Massachusetts Legislative Library, Boston.

San Francisco Public Library, History and Archives Section.

Seattle Board of Public Works.

Seattle City Clerks Office.

Seattle Public Library, City Light Pamphlet Collection.

Suzillo Library, University of Washington, Manuscripts and Archives Section and
    Pacific Northwest Collection.

Government Documents and Series

For Boston

Brimmer, Martin. *Testimony before the Massachusetts Legislature, Joint Special Committee on
    the Petition of the City of Boston for Leave to Introduce Pure Water into the City from
    Long Pond.* Boston: 1845.

City of Boston. *Records of Boston, XVI.*

Cochituate Water Board. *Report of the Cochituate Water Board . . . Relating to the Available
    Quantity and Purity of the Mystic Water . . . 1874.*

——. *Reports of the Cochituate Water Board to the City Council of Boston.* 1850–1877.

Commonwealth of Massachusetts. *An Act to Incorporate the Boston Hydraulic Company.* April 16, 1836.

Eddy, R. H. *Report on the Introduction of Soft Water into the City of Boston.* Boston: John H. Eastburn, 1836.

Hinckley, Allan. *Testimony before the Massachusetts Legislature, Joint Special Committee on the Petition of the City of Boston for Leave to Introduce Pure Water into the City from Long Pond.* Boston: 1845.

Inaugural Addresses of the Mayors of Boston. Vol. 1. Boston: Rockwell & Churchill, 1894.

Jervis, John B, and Walter Johnson. *Report to the Committee of the City Council, Having Charge of the Subject of Supplying the City of Boston with Pure Water.* Boston: November 18, 1845.

Lamp Department, City of Boston. *Annual Report of the Lamp Department for the Year 1891.*

Massachusetts Board of Gas and Electric Light Commissioners. *Annual Reports.* 1888–1911.

———. *A Statement of Its Jurisdiction and Work since Its Establishment in 1885.* Boston: May 1907.

———. *Boston—Edison Street Lighting Arbitration.* 1918.

Office of Cable Communications, City of Boston. *1985 Performance Evaluation Report, Cablevision of Boston.* April 1986.

Standing Committee on the Introduction of Pure and Soft Water into the City. *Report.* Boston: January 29, 1838.

For San Francisco

Cahill, E. G. *Plan Nine: Ownership and Operation of Entire San Francisco Electric Service.* San Francisco Public Utilities Commission, 1941.

California Railroad Commission Decisions, 1914.

Charter of the City and County of San Francisco. Ratified May 26, 1898.

City of San Francisco. *Municipal Reports.* 1870–1912.

San Francisco Board of Supervisors. *Arguments Favoring Bond Propositions.* 1933.

———. *Reports on the Water Supply of San Francisco, California, 1900–08 Inclusive.* 1908.

For Seattle

City of Seattle. *Annual Mayor's Message, with Reports of City Departments.* 1883–1912.

———. *Annual Reports of the Lighting Department.* 1911–1940.

Pratt, John W. *Revised Ordinances of the City of Seattle.* 1893.

Ross, J. D. *Annual Report of the Lighting Department . . . for the Year 1911, with a Review of the Work since the Inception of the Seattle Municipal Light and Power Plant.* Seattle: 1912.

Federal Government Documents

Electricity Policy Project. *The Future of Electric Power in America: Economic Supply for Economic Growth.* Washington, D.C.: U.S. Department of Energy, 1983.

United States Bureau of the Census. *Central Electric Light and Power Stations.* Washington, D.C.: 1902, 1927, and 1937.

United States Congress, Office of Technology Assessment. *Rural America at the Crossroads: Networking for the Future, OTA–TCT–471.* Washington, D.C.: G.P.O., 1991.

As appropriate, other government documents, such as court decisions, congressional hearings, Federal Communications Commission rules, etc., are cited in the notes.

Local Newspapers

Boston Globe, 1984–1987.

Pittsburgh Post Gazette, 1980–1986.

Pittsburgh Press, 1980–1986.

San Francisco Chronicle, 1910–1940.

Seattle Argus, 1894–1910.

Seattle Post Intelligencer, 1890–1910.

Seattle Star, 1899–1910.

Seattle Times, 1890–1910.

Published Books and Articles

Aitken, Hugh. *Syntony and Spark: The Origins of Radio.* Princeton: Princeton University Press, 1985.

American Water Works Association. *Water Works Practice.* Baltimore: Williams & Wilkins, 1925.

———. *Water Works Practices.* Baltimore: Williams & Wilkins, 1926.

Anderson, Douglas. *Regulatory Politics and Electric Utilities.* Boston: Auburn House, 1981.

Armstrong, Ellis L., ed. *History of Public Works in the United States: 1776–1976.* Chicago: American Public Works Association, 1976.

Ashley, Percy. "The Water, Gas, and Electric Light Supply of London." *Annals of the American Academy of Political and Social Science* (January 1906).

Babbitt, Harold E., and James S. Doland. *Water Supply Engineering.* New York: McGraw Hill, 1939.

Bailyn, Bernard. *The Origins of American Politics.* New York: Vintage, 1968.

Baker, Moses. *Manual of American Water Works, 1897.* New York: Engineering News, 1897.

Banning, William P. *Commerical Broadcasting Pioneer: The WEAF Experiment, 1922–1926.* Cambridge: Harvard University Press, 1946.

Barnes, Irston. *Public Utility Control in Massachusetts.* New Haven: Yale University Press, 1930.

Barnouw, Erik. *The Golden Web: A History of Broadcasting in the United States.* Vol. 2, *1933 to 1953.* New York: Oxford University Press, 1968.

Barzel, Yoram. "Measurement Cost and the Organization of Markets." *Journal of Law and Economics* 25 (April 1982).

Baughman, James. *The Republic of Mass Culture: Journalism, Filmmaking, and Broadcasting in America since 1941.* Baltimore: Johns Hopkins University Press, 1992.

Bean, Walton. *Boss Ruef's San Francisco.* Berkeley: University of California Press, 1952.

Blackford, Mansel. *The Politics of Business in California, 1890–1920.* Columbus: Ohio State University Press, 1977.

Blake, John B. "Lemuel Shattuck and the Boston Water Supply." *Bulletin of the History of Medicine* 29, no. 6 (November-December 1955).

Blake, Nelson. *Water for the Cities.* Syracuse: Syracuse University Press, 1956.

Breyer, Stephen G., and Paul W. Macavoy. *Energy Regulation by the Federal Power Commission.* Washington, D.C.: Brookings Institution, 1974.

Brigham, Jay. *Empowering the West: Electrical Politics before FDR.* Lawrence: University Press of Kansas, 1998.

Brody, Herb. "Information Highway: The Home Front." *Technology Review* (August-September, 1993).

Bruchey, Stuart. *Enterprise: The Dynamic Economy of a Free People.* Cambridge: Harvard University Press, 1990.

"Cablevision Gives Low-Income Discount as Part of New Boston Franchise Agreement." *Broadcasting* (September 26, 1988).

Chandler, Alfred D., Jr. *The Visible Hand: The Managerial Revolution in American Business.* Cambridge: Harvard University Press, 1977.

Coase, Ronald H. "The Nature of the Firm." *Economica* (November 4, 1937).

Coates, Gary, ed. *Resettling America: Energy, Ecology, and Community.* Andover: Brick House Publishing, 1981.

Coleman, Charles M. *P.G. & E. of California.* New York: McGraw Hill, 1952.

Committee No. 2: Advertising and Publicity. "Report." *Proceedings of the Fourth National Radio Conference and Recommendations for Regulation of Radio.* Washington, D.C.: G.P.O., 1925.

Cook, Ann, Marilyn Gittell, and Herb Mack, eds. *Views of Urban America.* New York: Praeger, 1973.

Cronon, William. *Nature's Metropolis: Chicago and the Great West*. New York: W. W. Norton, 1991.

Crosby, Everett. "Fire Prevention." *Annals of the American Academy of Political and Social Science* 24, no. 2 (September 1905).

Czitrom, Daniel J. *Media and the American Mind: From Morse to McLuhan*. Chapel Hill: University of North Carolina Press, 1982.

Dahl, Robert. "Atomic Energy and the Democratic Process." *Annals of the American Academy of Political and Social Science* 290 (November 1953).

De Bell, Garrett. "Energy." In *The Environmental Handbook*, edited by Garrett De Bell. New York: Ballantine, 1970.

Demsetz, Harold. "Why Regulate Utilities?" *Journal of Law and Economics*, 57 (April 1968).

Dizard, Wilson. *Old Media, New Media: Mass Communications in the Information Age*. New York: Longman, 1994.

Douglas, Susan J. *Inventing American Broadcasting: 1899–1922*. Baltimore: Johns Hopkins University Press, 1987.

Dutton, William, Jay G. Blumler, and Kenneth L. Kraemer. "Continuity and Change in Conceptions of the Wired City." In *Wired Cities: Shaping the Future of Communications*, edited by William Dutton, Jay G. Blumler, and Kenneth L. Kraemer. Boston: G. K. Hall, 1987.

Eldon, L. L. *The Boston Edison System*. Boston: Edison Electric Illuminating Co., 1909.

Englement, Ralph. "The Origins of Public Access Cable Television: 1966–1972." *Journalism Monographs* (October 1990).

Factbook: Cable Systems, 1993. Washington, D.C.: Warren Publishing, 1993.

Fenn, Scott. *America's Electric Utilities: Under Siege and in Transition*. New York: Praeger, 1984.

Ferris, Charles D., Frank W. Lloyd, and Thomas J. Casey. *Cable Television Law*. New York: Matthew Bender, 1993.

Fogelson, Robert. *The Fragmented Metropolis: Los Angeles, 1850–1930*. Cambridge: Harvard University Press, 1967.

Forbes, B. C. "America as a Nation of Investors." *National Electric Light Association, Proceedings, 46th Convention*. Vol. 79. 1923.

Frederick, Kenneth D. "Overview." In *Scarce Water and Institutional Change*, edited by Kenneth D. Frederick and Dianna C. Gibbons. Washington, D.C.: Resources for the Future, 1986.

Gary, Hampson. "Regulation of Broadcasting in the United States." *Annals of the American Academy of Political and Social Science* 177 (January 1935).

Gilder, George. *Life after Television*. Rev. ed. New York: W. W. Norton, 1994.

Goldman, Joanne Abel. *Building New York's Sewers: Developing Mechanisms of Urban Management*. West Lafayette: Purdue University Press, 1997.

Gould, Jacob Martin. *Output and Productivity in the Electric and Gas Utilities: 1899–1949*. New York: National Bureau of Economic Research, 1946.

Gruening, Ernest. *The Public Pays: A Study of Power Propaganda*. New York: Vanguard Press, 1931.

Hamburg, Morton I. *All about Cable: Legal and Business Aspects of Pay Television*. New York: Law Journal Seminars Press, 1981.

Hanke, Steve H., and Stephen J. K. Walters. "Privatizing Waterworks." *Proceedings of the Academy of Political Science* 36, no. 3 (1986).

Hawley, Ellis W. *The Great War and the Search for a Modern Order: A History of the American People and Their Institutions, 1917–1933*. New York: St. Martin's Press, 1992.

Hettinger, Herman S. "Broadcasting in the United States." *Annals of the American Academy of Political and Social Science* 177 (January 1935).

Hillhouse, A. M. *Municipal Bonds: A Century of Experience*. New York: Prentice Hall, 1936.

Hirsh, Richard F. *Technology and Transformation in the American Electric Utility Industry*. Cambridge: Cambridge University Press, 1989.

Hirshleifer, Jack, James De Haven, and Jerome W. Milliman. *Water Supply: Economics, Technology, and Policy*. Chicago: University of Chicago Press, 1960.

Holusha, John. "Some Corporations Plead for the Firm Hand of Uncle Sam." *New York Times*, February 24, 1991.

Hoover, Herbert. "Opening Address." In *Recommendations for Regulation of Radio Adopted by the Third National Radio Conference*. Washington, D.C.: G.P.O., 1924.

Houston, Douglas A. "A Losing Proposition for Consumers." *Public Utilities Fortnightly* (May 1, 1993).

Hughes, Thomas P. "The Evolution of Large Technological Systems." In *The Social Construction of Technological Systems*, edited by Wiebe E. Bijker, Thomas P. Hughes, and Trevor Pinch. Cambridge: MIT Press, 1989.

Issel, William, and Robert W. Cherny. *San Francisco 1865–1932: Politics, Power, and Urban Development*. Berkeley: University of California Press, 1986.

John, Richard. *Spreading the News: The American Postal System from Franklin to Morse*. Cambridge: Harvard University Press, 1995.

Jordan, Don D. "The Hidden Threat." *Public Utilities Fortnightly* (March 15, 1991).

Jordan, T. Eugene. "Cedar River System." *Seattle Idea* (1895).

Kahn, Edward. *Electric Utility Planning and Regulation*. Washington, D.C.: American Council for an Energy-Efficient Economy, 1988.

Kahn, Frank J., ed. *Documents of American Broadcasting*. 3d ed. Englewood Cliffs, N.J.: Prentice-Hall, 1978.

Kahrl, William. *Water and Power: The Conflict over Los Angeles' Water Supply in the Owens Valley.* Berkeley: University of California Press, 1982.

Kelman, Steven. "Why Public Ideas Matter." In *The Power of Public Ideas*, edited by Robert B. Reich. Cambridge: Harvard University Press, 1988.

Kielbowicz, Richard B. *News in the Mail: The Press, Post Office, and Public Information, 1700–1860.* New York: Greenwood Press, 1989.

Klebnikov, Paul. "Demand Siders." *Forbes*, October 26, 1992.

Klein, Benjamin, Robert Crawford, and Armen Alchian. "Vertical Integration, Appropriable Rents, and the Competitive Contracting Process." *Journal of Law and Economics* 21 (1978).

Kolesar, Robert J. "The Politics of Development: Worcester, Massachusetts in the Late Nineteenth Century." *Journal of Urban History* 16, no. 1 (November 1989).

Komanoff, Charles. *Power Plant Cost Escalation: Nuclear and Coal Capital Costs, Regulation, and Economics.* New York: Van Nostrand Reinhold, 1981.

Lampl, Elizabeth Jo, and Kimberly Prothro Williams. *Chevy Chase: A Home Suburb for the Nation's Capital.* Crownsville: Maryland Historical Trust Press, 1998.

Le Duc, Don R. *Beyond Broadcasting: Patterns in Policy and Law.* New York: Longman, 1987.

Leury, Louis. "Address." *Transactions of the Commonwealth Club of California* 28, no. 7 (December 1923).

Lovins, Amory B. *Soft Energy Paths: Toward a Durable Peace.* New York: Harper Colophon Edition, 1977.

Lubar, Steven. *InfoCulture: The Smithsonian Book of Information Age Inventions.* Boston: Houghton Mifflin, 1993.

Manson, Marsden. "Struggle for Water in Great Cities." *Journal of Association of Engineering Societies* 38, no. 3 (March 1907).

Mason, Todd. "Warner Amex in Dallas: The Trials of City Franchises." *Business Week*, (July 22, 1985).

McCaffrey, David P. *The Politics of Nuclear Power: A History of the Shoreham Nuclear Power Plant.* Dordrecht: Kluwer Academic Publishers, 1991.

McDonald, Forrest. *Let There Be Light: The Electric Utility Industry in Wisconsin, 1881–1955.* Madison: American History Research Center, 1957.

McDonald, Terrence J. *The Parameters of Urban Fiscal Policy: Socioeconomic Change and Political Culture in San Francisco, 1860–1906.* Berkeley: University of California Press, 1986.

Miller, Raymond. *Kilowatts at Work: A History of the Detroit Edison Company.* Detroit: Wayne State University Press, 1957.

Monkkonen, Eric. *America Becomes Urban: The Development of U.S. Cities and Towns, 1780–1980.* Berkeley: University of California Press, 1988.

Morgan, Edmund. *Inventing the People: The Rise of Popular Sovereignty in England and America*. New York: W. W. Norton, 1988.

Morgan, Murray. *Skid Road: An Informal Portrait of Seattle*. New York: Viking Press, 1951.

Morone, James, and Edward Woodhouse. *The Demise of Nuclear Energy: Lessons for Democratic Control of Technology*. New Haven: Yale University Press, 1989.

Mosher, William, et. al. *Electrical Utilities: The Crisis in Public Control*. New York: Harper & Brothers, 1929.

Murray, William S. "Superpower and the Customer." *National Electric Light Association Proceedings, 46th Convention*. Vol. 79 (1923).

Nesbit, Robert C. *He Built Seattle: A Biography of Judge Thomas Burke*. Seattle: University of Washington, 1961.

Nesson, Fern. *Great Waters*. Hanover: University Press of New England, 1983.

"New York State Rate Cuts." *Electrical World* 86 (December 19, 1925).

"New York's Water Supply—Present and Future Capacity." *Scientific American* (March 24, 1900).

North, Douglass C. *Institutions, Institutional Change, and Economic Performance*. Cambridge: Cambridge University Press, 1990.

Nye, David E. *Electrifying America: Social Meanings of a New Technology*. Cambridge: MIT Press, 1990.

Office of Technology Assessment. *Rural America at the Crossroads: Networking for the Future*. Washington, D.C.: G.P.O., 1991.

Owen, David. *The Government of Victorian London, 1855–1889: The Metropolitan Board of Works, the Vestries, and the City Corporation*. Cambridge: Harvard University Press, 1982.

"Pacific Gas and Electric Rates to Be Reduced." *Electrical World* (January 6, 1923).

Parsons, Frank. *The Telegraph Monopoly*. Philadelphia: C. F. Taylor, 1899.

Passer, Harold C. *The Electrical Manufacturers*. Cambridge: Harvard University Press, 1953.

Phelan, James D. "Address." *Transactions of the Commonwealth Club of California* 28, no. 7 (December 1923).

Philips, Mary Alice. *CATV: A History of Community Antenna Television*. Evanston: Northwestern University Press, 1972.

Platt, Harold. *City Building in the New South: The Growth of Public Services in Houston, Texas, 1830–1910*. Philadelphia: Temple University Press, 1983.

———. *The Electric City: Energy and the Growth of the Chicago Area, 1880–1930*. Chicago: University of Chicago Press, 1991.

Pool, Ithiel de Sola. *Technologies of Freedom*. Cambridge: Harvard University Press, 1983.

Posner, Richard A. "Theories of Economic Regulation." *Bell Journal of Economics* (autumn 1974).

Radin, Alex. "Is Public Power Still Relevant?" *Public Utilities Fortnightly* (March 1, 1991).

Ramsey, James B. "Selling the New York City Subways: Wild-Eyed Radicalism or the Only Feasible Solution?" *Proceedings of the Academy of Political Science* 36, no. 3 (1986).

Rex, Frederic. "Chicago: The Relation of the Municipality to the Water Supply." *Annals of the American Academy of Political and Social Science* 30, no. 3 (November 1907).

Rheingold, Howard. *The Virtual Community: Homesteading on the Electronic Frontier*. New York: Addison-Wesley, 1993.

Rice, Jean, ed. *Cable TV Renewals and Refranchising*. Washington, D.C.: Communications Press, 1983.

Rip, Arie, Thomas J. Misa, and Johan Schot, eds. *Managing Technology in Society*. New York: St. Martin's Press, 1995.

Rogers, Everett M. *Communication Technology: The New Media in Society*. New York: Free Press, 1986.

Rose, Mark H. *Cities of Light and Heat: Domesticating Gas and Electricity in Urban America*. University Park: Pennsylvania State University Press, 1995.

Rosen, Christine. *The Limits of Power*. New York: Cambridge University Press, 1986.

Rosenfeld, Arthur H., and David Hafemeister. "Energy-Efficient Buildings." *Scientific American*, April 1988.

Rosenkranz, Barbara. *Public Health and the State*. Cambridge: Harvard University Press, 1972.

Sale, Roger. *Seattle: Past to Present*. Seattle: University of Washington Press, 1976.

Sappington, David E. M., and Joseph E. Stiglitz. "Privatization, Information, and Incentives." *Journal of Policy Analysis and Management* 6 (1987).

Schap, David. *Municipal Ownership in the Electric Utility Industry*. New York: Praeger, 1986.

Scheiber, Harry N. "Federalism and the American Economic Order." *Law & Society Review* 10, no. 1 (fall 1975).

Seiden, Martin H. *Cable Television U.S.A.: An Analysis of Government Policy*. New York: Praeger, 1972.

Shapiro, George H., Philip B. Kurland, and James P. Mercurio. *Cable Speech: The Case for First Amendment Protection*. New York: Law and Business, 1983.

Siems, V. Bernard, and D. Benton Biser. "Fire Protection Requirements in Distribution System Design." *Journal of the American Water Works Association* 11 (January 24, 1924).

Sinsheimer, Paul A. "Public Utility Regulation in California." *Outlook* (September 6, 1916).

———. "Ten Rules for Service." *Annals of Political and Social Science* 53 (1914).

"Six Months Gain in Business Offsets Rate Decrease." *Electrical World* (August 4, 1923).

Sloan Commission on Cable Television. *On the Cable.* New York: McGraw-Hill, 1971.

Smith, Michael L. *Pacific Visions: California Scientists and the Environment, 1850–1915.* New Haven: Yale University Press, 1987.

Smith, Ralph Lee. *The Wired Nation: Cable TV, the Electronic Communications Highway.* New York: Harper & Row, 1972.

Smuylan, Susan. *Selling Radio: The Commercialization of American Broadcasting, 1920–1934.* Washington, D.C.: Smithsonian Institution Press, 1994.

Stein, Herb. "The Big Turn On." *Pittsburgh Magazine,* April, 1980.

Stigler, George. "What Can Regulators Regulate? The Case of Electricity." *Journal of Law and Economics* 5 (1962).

Stover, Dawn. "Little Dish TV." *Popular Science,* January 1995.

Sutcliffe, Anthony. *Towards the Planned City: Germany, the United States, and France, 1780–1914.* New York: St. Martin's Press, 1981.

Tarr, Joel A. *The Search for the Ultimate Sink.* Akron: University of Akron Press, 1996.

Taylor, Ray W. *Hetch Hetchy.* San Francisco: Ricardo J. Orozco, 1924.

Tenner, Edward. "Learning from the Net." *Wilson Quarterly* (summer 1994).

Tobey, Ronald C. *Technology as Freedom: The New Deal and the Electrical Modernization of the American Home.* Berkeley: University of California Press, 1996.

Twentieth Century Fund. *Electric Power and Government Policy.* New York: Twentieth Century Fund, 1948.

Vietor, Richard H. K. *Energy Policy in America Since 1945: A Study of Business-Government Relations.* (Cambridge: Cambridge University Press, 1984.

Wainright, Nicholas B. *History of the Philadelphia Electric Company.* Philadelphia: Philadelphia Electric Company, 1961.

Weber, Adna Ferrin. *The Growth of Cities in the Nineteenth Century: A Study in Statistics.* New York: Macmillan, 1899.

Weinberg, Alvin M. "Social Institutions and Nuclear Energy." In *Nuclear Reactions: Science and Trans-Science.* New York: American Institute of Physics, 1992.

Weisbrod, Burton A. "Rewarding Performance that Is Hard to Measure: The Private Nonprofit Sector." *Science,* no. 244 (May 5, 1989).

White, Leonard. "The Origin of Utility Commissions in Massachusetts." *Journal of Political Economy* (March 1921).

Williamson, Oliver E. *The Economic Institutions of Capitalism.* New York: Free Press, 1985.

Wilson, James Q. *The Politics of Regulation.* New York: Basic Books, 1980.

Winner, Langdon. "Do Artifacts Have Politics?" In *Technology and Politics,* edited by Michael E. Kraft and Norman J. Vig. Durham: Duke University Press, 1988.

Zoglin, Richard, "Cable Gets Dished." *Time,* October 23, 1994.

Zupin, Mark. "Cable Television Renewals: Do Incumbent Firms Behave Opportunistically?" *Rand Journal of Economics* (winter 1989).

——. "The Efficacy of Franchise Bidding Schemes in the Case of Cable Television: Some Systematic Evidence." *Journal of Law and Economics* (October 1989).

Unpublished Dissertations and Other Papers

Anderson, Letty. "The Diffusion of Technology in the Nineteenth Century American City: Municipal Water Supply Investments." Ph.D. diss., Northwestern University, 1980.

Baker, Miner Hamilton. "The Proposed City Light Merger: A Study of Public Opinion." Master's thesis, University of Washington, 1938.

Campbell, William Russell. "Cable Television: Franchising and Refranchising in Three Texas Cities." Master's thesis, University of Texas, 1981.

Dick, Wesley Arden. "The Genesis of Seattle City Light." Masters Thesis, University of Washington, 1965.

Edelman, Jacob Murray. "The Licensing of Radio Services in the United States: A Study in Administrative Formulation of Policy." Ph.D diss., University of Illinois, 1948.

Heys, Marguret Louise. "The Seattle Municipal Water Systems." Master's thesis, University of Washington, 1907.

Hichborn, Franklin. "Why the Corporations Win before the State Railroad Commission." 1926. On deposit in the Bancroft Library, University of California at Berkeley.

Karrer, L. E., and M. T. Crawford. "Joint Pole History." 1944. In *Puget Sound Power and Light Co. General Correspondence,* on deposit in the Suzillo Library, University of Washington, Manuscripts and Archives Section.

Knowles, Barton Harvey. "The Early History of San Francisco's Water Supply, 1776–1858." Master's thesis, University of California at Berkeley, 1948.

Sicilia, David. "Selling Power: Marketing and Monopoly at Boston Edison, 1888–1926." Paper presented at the annual meeting of the Organization of American Historians, 1986.

Sparks, William O'Dell,. "J. D. Ross and Seattle City Light: 1917–1932." Master's thesis, University of Washington, 1964.

Index

Skagit River (Wash.), 121, 242n78
Sloan Commission, 158–59
Smyth v. Ames, 247n101
Snoqualmie Falls Power Company (Seattle), 115–16, 118
Sparks, William O'Dell, 243n87
Spring Hill Water Company (Seattle), 64–65
Spring Valley Water Company (San Francisco), 51–61, 69
Standard Electric Company (Calif.), 97
State chartered corporations, 25
State government regulation: of cable television, 184–85; of electric utilities, 84–87, 99–102, 107–9, 122, 130, 134, 184, 194, 246n99; of waterworks, 53, 76
Staudenmaier, John, 202
Stigler, George, 247n99
Stone and Webster (partnership firm), 114, 116, 119, 121
Streetcars, 113
Street lighting, 2, 78, 80–83, 232n7; in Boston, 85–90, 93, 233n13; in San Francisco, 93, 98; in Seattle, 112–13, 117
Street railways, 94
Suburban Electric Light Company, 87–88
Sullivan (San Francisco fire chief), 226n96
Summit Communications, 165
Sutcliffe, Anthony, 229n127
Sutro (San Francisco mayor), 55

Tarr, Joel, 6–7
TCI (Tele-Communications, Inc.), 166, 168–70, 179, 203
Technological impacts: on cable television, 138, 155–57, 187, 201–4, 206; on computer communications, 206–8; on electric utilities, 79–80, 90, 96, 109, 193; on radio and television broadcasting, 144, 154; on waterworks, 43–45, 72, 190
Technology: and economies of scale limitations, 79–80; history of, 4–7
Telegraph networks, 6, 142–43
Telephone networks, 2, 6, 140
TelePrompTer, 161–65
Television broadcasting, 150, 153–55, 157, 182. *See also* Cable television
"Television of abundance," 158–59
Tennessee Valley Authority, 133, 135
Three Rivers (Pittsburgh), 166–67
Tobey, Ronald, 5, 245n91
Toll broadcasting, 147, 149
Tornillo, Miami Herald v., 182
Transaction cost analysis, 9, 12, 14; applied to cable television, 138, 177; applied to elec-

tric utilities, 77, 81–82, 196, 198–99; applied to waterworks, 26–27, 29–31, 36–37, 49, 71–72
Transaction-specific assets, 10
Transportation systems, 24
Treadwell, Daniel, 34
True Whigs, 16
Two-way communications networks, 206–8

U.S. Bureau of Reclamation, 131, 134, 191
U.S. Department of the Interior, 58
U.S. Postal Service, 139
U.S. Secretary of Commerce, 146–47
Uhl, Adolph, 238n56
Union Electric Company (Seattle), 112
Union Water Company (Seattle), 64–65
United States, Associated Press v., 181
Urbanization: and population growth, 22–23, 33, 48–49, 51, 64, 68, 110, 113, 117, 240n68; and waterworks development, 22–25, 27–29, 66. *See also* Economic development
Utopian visions: in novels, 214n21; of utilities, 15, 110, 136. *See also* Economic development

Vahnu Incorporated, 164
VCRs (video cassette recorders), 187–88
Vertical integration, 10, 197, 201, 203, 214n18
Viacom, 161–63, 165
Villard, Henry, 111–12
Voltage systems, 78–80, 88

Warner Amex Cable Communications, 166–70, 172–73, 184, 206
Washington, DC, 212n11, 229n127
Washington Power and Transmission Company, 116
Washington Water Power, 116
Water closets, hopper, 44
Water Commission (NY), 6
Water conservation measures, 42–44, 72
Water consumption, 42–44, 46, 53–54, 67, 191–92, 231n130
Water filtration technology, 31–32, 192
Water meters, 43, 71
Watershed lands, 192
Waterworks, 18–19, 22–73, 190–93; in Baltimore, 70, 231n130; in Boston, 32–48, 69, 191; comparisons with other networked systems, 2–4, 77, 81–83, 90, 137–39, 179–80; and fire protection, 2, 27–31, 36, 44–46, 53, 55, 57–58, 63–65, 67, 70, 72–73; historical setting in development of, 3; in Houston, 70–71; in Los Angeles, 70–71, 191–92;

Waterworks *(continued),*
in New York, 6, 70; performance measurement of, 30, 51; in Philadelphia, 22; and public health, 2, 27–28, 31, 36, 65–66; public role of, 29, 35, 51–52; in San Francisco, 48–62, 69, 130, 191; in Seattle, 62–69; transaction cost analysis applied to, 29–31, 36–37, 49; and urbanization, 24–25, 27–29, 66; utopian visions of, 15
Weinberg, Alvin, 262n31
Welch, Robert, 170
Wells (Boston mayor), 32
Western Union, 142
Westinghouse Corporation, 79–80, 115, 147–48, 150, 165
Wheeler, Thomas, 185

White (Boston mayor), 171–72
Wild rivers, 192
Williams, Benezette, 229n116
Williamson, Oliver, 10, 26
Wilson, Burstyn v., 249n9
Wilson (Seattle waterworks superintendent), 68
Winner, Langdon, 5
Wireless Telegraph and Signal Company, 144
Woodhouse, Edward, 259n14

Yesler, Henry, 62–63
Youngs, H. B., 240n74
Yuba Electric Power Company, 96

Zupin, Mark, 256n93